MW01054896

Political Control of America's Courts

Recent Titles in Contemporary Debates

POLITICAL CONTROL OF AMERICA'S COURTS

Examining the Facts

Helena Silverstein

Contemporary Debates

An Imprint of ABC-CLIO, LLC

Santa Barbara, California • Denver, Colorado

Copyright © 2023 by ABC-CLIO, LLC

Library of Congress Cataloging-in-Publication Data

Names: Silverstein, Helena, author.
Title: Political control of America's courts: examining the facts / Helena Silverstein.
Description: Santa Barbara : ABC-CLIO, 2023. | Series: Contemporary debates | Includes bibliographical references and index.
Identifiers: LCCN 2022032813 (print) | LCCN 2022032814 (ebook) | ISBN 9781440878053 (hardback) | ISBN 9781440878060 (ebook)
Subjects: LCSH: Courts—Political aspects—United States. | Political questions and judicial power—United States. | Judicial process—United States.
Classification: LCC KF5130 .S55 2022 (print) | LCC KF5130 (ebook) | DDC 347.73/12—dc23/eng/20220924
LC record available at https://lccn.loc.gov/2022032813
LC ebook record available at https://lccn.loc.gov/2022032814

ISBN: 978-1-4408-7805-3 (print)
       978-1-4408-7806-0 (ebook)

27 26 25 24 23   1 2 3 4 5

This book is also available as an eBook.

ABC-CLIO
An Imprint of ABC-CLIO, LLC

ABC-CLIO, LLC
147 Castilian Drive
Santa Barbara, California 93117
www.abc-clio.com

This book is printed on acid-free paper ∞

Manufactured in the United States of America

Contents

Acknowledgments

My work on this book benefited from the exceptional research assistance provided by Kelly Mwaamba, Lafayette College, class of 2022. Kelly's methodical research, sharp insights, and outstanding analytical skills proved enormously helpful. I am indebted to her and grateful to Lafayette College for supporting students and faculty through its undergraduate research assistantship program.

How to Use This Book

Political Control of America's Courts: Examining the Facts is part of ABC-CLIO's Contemporary Debates reference series. Each title in this series, which is intended for use by high school and undergraduate students as well as members of the general public, examines the veracity of controversial claims or beliefs surrounding a major political/cultural issue in the United States. The purpose of this series is to give readers a clear and unbiased understanding of current issues by informing them about falsehoods, half-truths, and misconceptions—and confirming the factual validity of other assertions—that have gained traction in America's political and cultural discourse. Ultimately, this series has been crafted to give readers the tools for a fuller understanding of controversial issues, policies, and laws that occupy center stage in American life and politics.

Each volume in this series identifies 30 to 40 questions swirling about the larger topic under discussion. These questions are examined in individualized entries, which are in turn arranged in broad subject chapters that cover certain aspects of the issue being examined: for example, history of concern about the issue, potential economic or social impact, or findings of latest scholarly research.

Each chapter features 3 to 10 individual entries. Each entry begins by stating an important and/or well-known **Question** about the issue being studied—for example, "Are nominations and confirmations to the federal bench based on factors beyond merit?" "Did President Trump's judicial appointments fundamentally re-make the federal judiciary for decades to come?" "Do judges' political attitudes and ideologies influence their legal decisions?" "Is public faith and confidence in the Supreme Court in decline?"

The entry then provides a concise and objective one- or two-paragraph **Answer** to the featured question, followed by a more comprehensive, detailed explanation of **The Facts**. This latter portion of each entry uses quantifiable, evidence-based information from respected sources to fully address each question and provide readers with the information they need to be informed citizens. Importantly, entries also acknowledge instances in which conflicting data exists or data is incomplete. Finally, each entry concludes with a **Further Reading** section, providing users with information on other important and/or influential resources.

The ultimate purpose of every book in the Contemporary Debates series is to reject "false equivalence," in which demonstrably false beliefs or statements are given the same exposure and credence as the facts; to puncture myths that diminish our understanding of important policies and positions; to provide needed context for misleading statements and claims; and to confirm the factual accuracy of other assertions. In other words, volumes in this series are being crafted to clear the air surrounding some of the most contentious and misunderstood issues of our time—not just add another layer of obfuscation and uncertainty to the debate.

1

❖❖❖

Nominations, Confirmations, and Departures of Federal Judges

Federal court judges, including those who serve on the District Courts, the Circuit Courts of Appeal, and the U.S. Supreme Court, are nominated by the president and must be confirmed by the Senate. Methods for selecting judges to serve on state courts vary considerably by state and even within states depending on the nature of the vacancy and the court. Although most states use elections as part of the process to determine who occupies the bench, several have selection processes that parallel the nomination and confirmation process at the federal level. Others give governors the authority to appoint judges from a slate of candidates submitted by a bipartisan nominating commission.

The judicial branch of federal and state governments is, in theory, supposed to function in an apolitical fashion. Independence from the other branches of government is part of a structural design aimed at insulating the judiciary from direct political influence. But when the structural design of the judiciary includes the appointment of jurists by elected executives and legislators, questions inevitably arise about the extent to which political factors shape not only the selection of judges but also the decisions judicial bodies produce. The questions taken up in this chapter focus on the federal bench and explore, in particular, the influence of politics on the selection, rejection, and tenure of judges.

Q1. ARE NOMINATIONS AND CONFIRMATIONS TO THE FEDERAL BENCH BASED ON FACTORS BEYOND MERIT?

Answer: Yes, though merit is among the many factors that influence the federal judicial selection process.

The Facts: According to Article III of the Constitution, federal judicial power "shall be vested in one supreme Court, and in such inferior Courts as the Congress may from time to time ordain and establish." Since 1789, under Article III authority, Congress has established multiple "inferior" courts that have come to comprise the federal judiciary. They include federal trial courts, known as the U.S. District Courts, and an intermediate tier of appellate courts, called the Circuit Courts of Appeal. The federal judges who staff these Article III tribunals are sometimes known as Article III judges.

The Constitution is silent on the qualifications of those who will serve on the federal judiciary. While Article II of the Constitution gives the president the authority to appoint Article III judges to the federal bench with the "advice and consent" of the Senate, no minimum credentials—not even a law degree—restrict the selection. Still, the legal and professional qualifications of candidates for the federal bench matter to both the president charged with making nominations and members of the Senate tasked with deciding whether to confirm nominees. In addition, norms shape the selection process and merit-based considerations. Thus, for example, legal education is not a formal prerequisite for becoming a federal judge, but it is effectively required as a matter of custom and practice.

Vetting of the professional qualifications of prospective judges is performed by the White House, the Justice Department, the Senate Judiciary Committee, the American Bar Association, various interest groups, and media organizations. Merit-based considerations for picking federal judges include legal education, experience, competence, judicial temperament, and integrity. These are among the factors reviewed by the American Bar Association (ABA), which has long played an important role in evaluating the merit of judicial candidates. As detailed in Q2, the ABA, the leading professional organization of lawyers in the United States, evaluates and rates nominees to the federal bench as "Well Qualified," "Qualified," or "Not Qualified." The assigned ratings, especially in instances when a candidate is judged to be not qualified, can influence the prospects for nomination and confirmation.

While there is little doubt that merit matters in the selection of federal judges, it is not the sole or even determining factor. According to one study, choosing the most qualified judges is "the motivation least likely to drive presidential considerations" (Watson and Stookey 1995, 64). In general, research indicates that merit is almost always a necessary rather than a sufficient condition for appointment and confirmation, providing a floor or baseline for judicial selection. Candidates lacking in legal experience, knowledge of the law, or demonstrated analytical competence are unlikely to make it onto the federal courts. As political scientist Lawrence Baum puts it, legal competence and adherence to ethical standards "can be considered screening criteria for potential nominees. These criteria may eliminate some people from consideration, but enough candidates survive the screening process to give presidents a wide range of choices for a nomination" (Baum 2001, 43).

Since there is no shortage of meritorious candidates, what factors other than merit determine who is chosen from among the wide array of qualified contenders? Political science research and legal scholarship point to a variety of political considerations that influence who serves on the federal bench. At the heart of these political considerations is the observation that a political party that gains control of all three branches of the federal government wields tremendous power; conversely, a loss of control of one of the branches, including the judiciary, can obstruct a political party's agenda. Political scientist Keith Whittington explains that the federal courts "have been a political prize to be won and a lagging indicator of political success. Through that political influence, the effective constitutional rules of the political system itself are ultimately responsive to political currents" (Whittington 2018, 522).

It should not be surprising, then, that "[t]raditionally, scholars have found, the overwhelming majority of all federal judicial nominees come from the same party as the nominating President" (Rutkus 2016, 12). A political party that controls the presidency or the Senate or both can seek to gain control over the federal courts by nominating and confirming judges to the bench who have exhibited compatible ideological positions and judicial philosophies. A president's choice to fill a judicial vacancy is influenced by a candidate's prior record, which can be discerned through such things as judicial opinions, academic writings and speeches, work experience, and party affiliation. Members of the Senate are similarly influenced, and when the party that controls the Senate and the presidency are the same, that party is in a much better position to fill the federal bench with judges who share the party's policy preferences and judicial philosophies.

When the Senate and presidency are controlled by different political parties, nominations are often influenced by how much resistance the president expects to receive from the opposition party. In addition, nominations and confirmations to the federal bench are shaped by electoral considerations and, in particular, an interest in appealing to and mobilizing electoral constituencies. In some instances, presidents use judicial nominations to mobilize blocs of voters based on policy and ideology, declaring that they will only appoint judges who hold particular judicial philosophies or positions that will advance certain policy goals.

Shortly after winning the 2016 presidential election, for example, Donald Trump was asked if he would seek to fill an open seat on the Supreme Court with an eye toward ultimately reversing *Roe v. Wade*, the 1973 decision that legalized abortion. He responded with an answer directed toward pro-life evangelicals, a core constituency of his Republican party: "So, look, here's what's going to happen—I'm going to—I'm pro-life. The judges will be pro-life" (Tackett 2019).

In other instances, presidents appeal to voting constituencies through "'representative' factors, such as religion, race, ethnicity, and gender or, alternatively, taking into account the nominee's home state or the geographical balance on a court" (Banks and O'Brien 2008, 131). President Ronald Reagan, for example, nominated Sandra Day O'Connor to serve on the U.S. Supreme Court in 1981 after committing during his 1980 presidential campaign to appointing the first woman to serve on the high Court. Joe Biden made a similar campaign pronouncement in February 2020 when he promised that, if elected, he would nominate an African American woman to serve on the Supreme Court. On January 27, 2022, during an appearance at which Supreme Court Justice Stephen Breyer formally announced his retirement from the bench, President Biden reaffirmed that promise, saying the "person I will nominate will be someone with extraordinary qualifications, character, experience and integrity. And that person will be the first Black woman ever nominated to the United States Supreme Court. It's long overdue, in my view" (Watson 2022). A month later, Biden nominated federal appeals court judge Ketanji Brown Jackson, and on April 7, 2022, the Senate confirmed Jackson as the 116th Supreme Court justice, making her the first Black woman to be elevated to the high Court.

Research shows additional political considerations in the selection of judges to the federal bench. The age of those appointed is a factor, especially for appointments to the Supreme Court. Because positions on the federal bench come with lifetime tenure, when presidents select those who are relatively younger, the impact of those appointments can be felt years or even decades after the president leaves office. The relationship of the candidate to the president or to members of the Senate has also been a notable variable in identifying and choosing judges. Research shows that appointments to the federal bench have been used at times to reward party loyalists. When

President Dwight D. Eisenhower named Earl Warren to serve as chief justice, for example, he did so in part because Warren staunchly supported Eisenhower for the 1952 Republican nomination (Baum 2001, 47).

Personal friendships have assuredly influenced a considerable number of nominations to the Supreme Court as well. "In Taft's choice of Horace H. Lurton, in Wilson's of Louis D. Brandeis, in Truman's of Harold H. Burton, and in Kennedy's of Byron R. White, to cite some obvious illustrations, personal friendship figured prominently," wrote political scientist Henry J. Abraham (Abraham 1993, 63). Occasionally, however, the temptation for a president to nominate a known friend or associate can backfire. When President George W. Bush selected his former personal attorney and close associate Harriet Miers to fill a vacancy on the high Court in 2005, the nomination ran into strong opposition from both Republicans, who distrusted her views on abortion, and Democrats, who emphasized that she had no judicial experience. Miers withdrew her name from consideration after two days of widespread criticism, and Bush ultimately filled the opening with Samuel Alito.

It is a common refrain from presidents and members of the Senate that while they are seeking the best qualified candidates to fill the bench, their counterparts on the other side of the aisle are motivated by politics. Evidence demonstrates, however, that merit *and* politics matter to both political parties in selecting and opposing candidates to serve on the federal bench. In turn, as discussed in Q2 and Q3, interest groups have come to play an important role in nomination and confirmation processes.

FURTHER READING

Abraham, Henry J. 1992. *Justices and Presidents: A Political History of Appointments to the Supreme Court.* 3rd Edition. New York: Oxford University Press.

Abraham, Henry J. 1993. *The Judicial Process.* 6th Edition. New York: Oxford University Press.

Banks, Christopher P., and David M. O'Brien. 2008. *Courts and Judicial Policymaking.* Upper Saddle River, New Jersey: Prentice Hall.

Baum, Lawrence. 2001. *The Supreme Court.* 7th Edition. Washington, DC: CQ Press.

Collins, Paul M., Jr., and Lori A. Ringhand. 2013. *Supreme Court Confirmation Hearings and Constitutional Change.* New York: Cambridge University Press.

Epstein, Lee, and Jeffrey A. Segal. 2005. *Advice and Consent: The Politics of Judicial Appointments.* New York: Oxford University Press.

Goldman, Sheldon, Elliot Slotnick, and Sara Schiavoni. 2013. "Obama's First Term Judiciary: Picking Judges in the Minefield of Obstructionism." *Judicature*, 97, no. 1: 7–47.

McMillion, Barry J. 2018. *Supreme Court Appointment Process: President's Selection of a Nominee* (CRS Report No. R44235). Congressional Research Service. https://fas.org/sgp/crs/misc/R44235.pdf

McMillion, Barry J., and Denis Steven Rutkus. 2018. *Supreme Court Nominations, 1789 to 2017: Actions by the Senate, the Judiciary Committee, and the President* (CRS Report No. RL33225). Congressional Research Service. https://fas.org/sgp/crs/misc/RL33225.pdf

O'Brien, David. 2014. *Storm Center: The Supreme Court in American Politics*. 10th Edition. New York: W.W. Norton.

Rutkus, Denis Steven. 2016. *The Appointment Process for U.S. Circuit and District Court Nominations: An Overview* (CRS Report No. R43762). Congressional Research Service. https://fas.org/sgp/crs/misc/R43762.pdf

Tackett, Michael. 2019. "Trump Fulfills His Promises on Abortion, and to Evangelicals." *New York Times*, May 16, 2019.

Watson, George L., and John A. Stookey. 1995. *Shaping America: The Politics of Supreme Court Appointments*. New York: Longman.

Watson, Kathryn. 2022. "Biden Says He'll Name a Black Woman as Supreme Court Pick by End of February." *CBS News*, January 28, 2022. https://www.cbsnews.com/live-updates/biden-supreme-court-black-woman-pick-february

Whittington, Keith E. 2006. "Presidents, Senates, and Failed Supreme Court Nominations." *Supreme Court Review*, 2006: 401–438.

Whittington, Keith E. 2018. "Partisanship, Norms, and Federal Judicial Appointments." *Georgetown Journal of Law & Public Policy*, 16: 521–535.

Q2. DO OUTSIDE ORGANIZATIONS INFLUENCE WHOM THE PRESIDENT NOMINATES TO THE FEDERAL BENCH?

Answer: Since the 1950s, yes. As noted in Q1, the American Bar Association (ABA) has had a longstanding role in rating the legal qualifications of candidates under consideration for the federal bench. Beginning with the Eisenhower administration, most presidents have sought input from the ABA in vetting potential nominees. More recently, the Federalist Society has become a key organization shaping Republican perspectives on candidates for judgeships.

The Facts: During Donald Trump's presidency, critics of his federal judicial appointments took aim at what they described as his outsourcing of the nomination process to the conservative Federalist Society (Sherman, Freking, and Daly 2020). Defenders of Trump's nominations, while often taking issue with the charge that his selection process had been outsourced, generally have not denied the sizable influence of the Federalist Society. For example, law professor Steven Calabrisi, co-founder of the Federalist Society and co-chair of its board of directors, acknowledged that the organization "has become a clearinghouse of sorts for candidates" (Wheeler 2017). At a Federalist Society gala in 2017, White House Counsel Donald McGahn, who played a leading role in identifying and vetting prospective nominees for Trump, "joked that it was 'completely false' that the White House had 'outsourced' picking federal judges. . . . There was no need, he said: 'I've been a member of the Federalist Society since law school—still am. So frankly, it seems like it's been in-sourced'" (Fredrickson and Segall 2020). At the following year's Federalist Society gala, Orrin Hatch, former Republican Senator from Utah, offered this retort to the outsourcing claim: "Some have accused President Trump of outsourcing his judicial selection process to the Federalist Society. I say, 'Damn right!'" (Fredrickson and Segall 2020).

Whether or not it is accurate to characterize Trump's nominations as "outsourcing," there is no disagreement that since the 1980s the nonprofit Federalist Society has taken on an increasingly important role in identifying and influencing the selection of conservative candidates for the federal bench. There is also no disagreement that the ABA—a professional organization of lawyers with some 400,000 members—has played a substantial role in the process since the 1950s, though recent Republican administrations have diminished that role. The ABA and the Federalist Society plainly exemplify that federal judicial nominations are shaped not only by the president, the executive branch, the Senate, and other government officials, but also by outside organizations.

As noted in Q1, the Constitution provides little guidance on the process of nominating federal judges beyond specifying that the president shall, "by and with the Advice and Consent of the Senate," appoint Supreme Court judges and all other officers of the United States (Article II, section 2). Though the president has the sole authority to name candidates to fill vacant seats on the federal bench, other government officials assist in the process of compiling lists of prospective judges, evaluating possible nominees, and whittling down the pool of candidates. Within the executive branch, presidents often rely on guidance from the White House counsel, various White House aides, the attorney general, and other Department of

Justice officials. The Federal Bureau of Investigation conducts background checks covering financial matters, conflicts of interest, and potentially disqualifying personal actions (e.g., prior history of drug use). Presidents seek guidance from government officials outside the executive branch, including members of Congress and governors, party leaders, and, occasionally, members of the Supreme Court.

But presidents also look for nomination guidance from those situated outside governing institutions. The ABA, a non-partisan interest group and trade organization founded in 1878, has been one the most influential outside organizations involved in the judicial selection process. The "nation's largest and most prestigious lawyer's association" (Sen 2014), the ABA was tapped by Republican President Dwight D. Eisenhower in 1952 to participate in vetting judicial candidates. As legal scholar Laura E. Little explains, the Eisenhower Administration turned to the ABA after the attorney general "concluded that the administration needed an independent review body to examine the qualifications of potential judicial nominees so that the administration could more ably resist pressure to repay political debts by appointing individuals of questionable talents and abilities to the federal bench. . . . The ABA's role quickly became institutionalized as an adjunct to the executive's constitutional role of nominating federal judges" (Little 2001, 39–40).

Following Eisenhower's lead, most subsequent presidents also utilized the ABA, in particular by sending confidential lists of judicial prospects to the organization's Standing Committee on the Federal Judiciary for pre-vetting of their legal qualifications. The Standing Committee on the Federal Judiciary is composed of 15 lawyers, and its goal, as described by the ABA, is "to support and encourage the selection of the best-qualified persons for the federal judiciary" (ABA 2022a). While the ABA is an advocacy organization and, as such, takes positions and lobbies on a variety of policy issues, it maintains that the Standing Committee's review of judicial candidates is impartially dedicated to professional qualifications. Using a peer-review process "structured to achieve impartial evaluations of the integrity, professional competence and judicial temperament of nominees for the federal judiciary," the Committee states that it "restricts its evaluation to issues bearing on professional qualifications and does not consider a nominee's philosophy or ideology" (ABA 2022a).

Though the process of review is slightly different for nominations to the Supreme Court as compared to the lower courts, the Standing Committee conducts extensive interviews, considers candidates' years of legal experience, and examines their legal writings "for quality, clarity, knowledge of the law, and analytical ability" (ABA 2022b). Based on this review, the Standing Committee rates potential and actual nominees as "Well Qualified," "Qualified," or "Not Qualified." The ABA shares the nominee's ratings, though not the confidential report that provides the basis of the ratings, with the White House. For candidates formally nominated by the president, the ABA shares the ratings with the Senate Judiciary Committee and makes the ratings publicly available. Public reports of the ratings indicate if the Standing Committee assessment was unanimous or split.

Because ABA ratings are only advisory in nature, a "Not Qualified" rating is not necessarily disqualifying. In many cases, presidents have proceeded with appointments even after receiving a negative rating of the candidate. For instance, four of Clinton's nominees to the federal District Courts were deemed "Not Qualified" by the ABA, as were three of Carter's, three of Johnson's, seven of Kennedy's, and eight of Eisenhower's (McMillion 2017). Similarly, Ford, Johnson, Kennedy, and Eisenhower each nominated a candidate to the Circuit Courts despite pre-vetting that generated a "Not Qualified" rating (McMillion 2017).

Still, for some administrations, a "Not Qualified" assessment has doomed a prospective candidate's chances of nomination (or confirmation). For example, after 14 of roughly 185 potential Obama nominees received negative ABA ratings, the administration declined to proceed with those nominations (Savage 2011).

Thus, the ABA's evaluation has proven influential in the selection of candidates to the bench. However, whereas some presidents have broadened the ABA's involvement, others have diminished it (Smelcer, Steigerwalt, and Vining 2012, 827). George W. Bush and Donald Trump are among those to have reduced the influence of the ABA, choosing not to seek the organization's input prior to nomination. Though the ABA still evaluates and issues ratings on announced nominations, which has the potential to influence the confirmation process, in the case of the 10 Trump nominees to the federal bench deemed "Not Qualified" by the ABA, eight received confirmation from the GOP-controlled Senate (Alder 2020).

Other presidents have taken different paths with respect to the ABA's input. Presidents Clinton and Obama both sought ABA evaluations after identifying potential nominees. The Reagan and George H. W. Bush administrations submitted names of nominees to the ABA after their selection but prior to formal nomination. "President Carter, in his quest to increase the representativeness of the federal bench, created the Circuit Judge Nominating Commission and pushed the ABA to relax its standards as to the minimum number of years of legal experience a nominee needed to be deemed Qualified" (Smelcer, Steigerwalt, and Vining 2012, 827).

The decision made by George W. Bush's administration to forgo the ABA's pre-vetting of candidates is illuminating. A 2001 letter to the ABA's president from then White House Counsel Alberto Gonzales explained that while the Bush administration continued to welcome the ABA's suggestions and evaluations, it also welcomed suggestions and evaluations from other interested parties and judged it to be neither "appropriate or fair" for the ABA to "alone—out of the literally dozens of groups and many individuals who have a strong interest in the composition of the federal courts"—to receive advance and confidential notice of the identities of possible nominees (Gonzales 2001). "It would be particularly inappropriate," Gonzales continued, "to grant a preferential, quasi-official role to a group, such as the ABA, that takes public positions on divisive political, legal, and social issues that come before the courts. . . . [C]onsiderations of sound constitutional government suggest that the President not grant a preferential, quasi-official role in the judicial selection process to a politically active group" (Gonzales 2001).

Tellingly, Gonzales quoted Senator Orrin Hatch in his letter—the same Senator Hatch who, as noted earlier, in 2018 praised Trump's alleged outsourcing of judicial selection to the Federalist Society. "As [Senate Judiciary] Chairman Hatch explained [in 1997], '[p]ermitting a political interest group to be elevated to an officially sanctioned role in the confirmation process not only debases that process, but, in my view, ultimately detracts from the moral authority of the courts themselves'" (Gonzales 2001).

The waxing and waning of the ABA's influence are owed in part to criticisms leveled against the organization's ratings, which heightened in the aftermath of the failed nomination of Robert Bork to the Supreme Court in 1987. "Republican displeasure was resounding and unanimous—particularly in reaction to the ABA Committee's failure to recommend unanimously Robert Bork as 'well qualified' for the Supreme Court (four Committee members apparently found Bork unqualified for lack of a judicial temperament)" (Little 2001, 44). Some critics say the ABA's review process is biased against conservatives, and there is some empirical support for this finding (Lindgren 2001; Lott 2001; Smelcer, Steigerwalt, and Vining 2012). Other critics say that the ABA's process is biased against minorities and women, and there is some empirical support for this finding as well (Haire 2001; Sen 2014).

Even in the face of criticisms from different ends of the political spectrum, the ABA continues to have significant influence. But the emergence and growth of the Federalist Society has been an important factor in the ABA's diminished role in the decision making of Republican presidents.

Founded in 1982 by law school students, the Federalist Society for Law and Public Policy Studies describes itself as "a group of conservatives and libertarians" interested in and "dedicated to reforming the current legal order" (Federalist Society 2021). In particular, the Federalist Society claims that it is dedicated to the principle that "the state exists to preserve freedom, that the separation of governmental powers is central to our Constitution, and that it is emphatically the province and duty of the judiciary to say what the law is, not what it should be" (Federalist Society 2021). To achieve its goals, "the Society has created a conservative and libertarian intellectual network that extends to all levels of the legal community" (Federalist Society 2021).

As of January 2021, membership in the Federalist Society had risen to some 65,000 legal professionals and 10,000 students (Federalist Society 2021). Neither a traditional interest group nor a think tank, the Federalist Society does not "fit comfortably into any of the social science boxes that students of American politics traditionally use to study the impact of civic groups on law and politics" (Hollis-Brusky 2015, 9). It does not, for example, "lobby Congress, support judicial or political candidates, or officially participate in litigation as *amici curiae* (though individual members do)" (Hollis-Brusky 2015, 9).

Nevertheless, the non-profit organization has succeeded in developing an extensive and influential network of legal professionals with a shared set of conservative and libertarian values and a shared interest in implementing those values in their professional activities. "Ties to the society constitute a marker of a commitment to the textualist and originalist approaches to legal interpretation that it favors as well as conservative views on legal issues" (Baum and Devins 2018).

It did not take long after its establishment for the Federalist Society to become influential in the selection of judges to the federal bench. As law professors Lawrence Baum and Neal Devins explain, during Reagan's second term of office, Attorney General Edwin Meese "sought aggressively to advance conservative goals in the judiciary. By hiring staffers on the basis of ideological commitment, Meese sought to groom young conservative lawyers who would later become federal court judges" (Baum and Devins 2018).

The nascent Federalist Society "was an important component of this strategy; it enabled Meese and others in the administration to identify promising candidates for significant government posts. Meese hired the society's founders as special assistants and tapped Stephen Markman, who headed the Washington chapter of the Federalist Society, to become the assistant attorney general in charge of judicial selection" (Baum and

Devins 2018). The administration of George H. W. Bush followed a similar strategy of leaning heavily on Federalist Society officials in identifying
judges for open seats. Combined, the Reagan and the first Bush administrations nominated several Federalist Society members to the appellate
courts, including Robert Bork and Antonin Scalia, two of the organization's original faculty advisers, and Clarence Thomas.

It was the George W. Bush administration that significantly decreased the
role of the ABA and simultaneously elevated the influence of the Federalist Society, which had by 2001 "grown in size and prominence. For the first
time, the conservative legal movement dominated Department of Justice
and judicial appointments" (Baum and Devins 2017). Two of Bush's Supreme
Court nominees—John Roberts and Samuel Alito—had ties to the organization, and Federalist Society members comprised roughly half of Bush's
appointments to the federal appellate courts. In addition, two Federalist
Society members who were later appointed by Trump to the Supreme Court
served in the Bush administration: Brett Kavanaugh was in charge of judicial selection and Neil Gorsuch served in Bush's Justice Department before
being appointed to the federal court of appeals (Baum and Devins 2017).

In some respects, the Trump administration followed Bush's lead in
turning to the Federalist Society. The Trump administration, for example,
relied on Leonard Leo, on leave from his role as executive vice president
of the organization, to help compile and narrow nominees to vacancies on
the federal bench and help steer the Supreme Court confirmation process
for Gorsuch and Kavanaugh (Montgomery 2019).

But Trump went even further than previous Republican presidents to
enlarge the impact of the Federalist Society. During his first presidential
campaign, Trump released a list of potential nominees to the Supreme
Court "curated by the Federalist Society" (McCarthy 2020), and said,
"[w]e're going to have great judges, conservative, all picked by the Federalist Society" (Regnery 2016). Following through on the pledge to rely on the
Federalist Society, by January 2019—two years into his administration—
25 of his 30 appellate court judge appointments had ties to the organization (Montgomery 2019).

Other outside organizations have influenced judicial appointments as
well. For example, Trump received advice from the Heritage Foundation,
a conservative think tank, in gathering potential nominees. In addition,
a broad array of organized special-interest groups seek to shape not just
the nomination but also the confirmation of judges to the bench (see
Q3). But the American Bar Association and the Federalist Society have
played especially pivotal roles, and likely will continue to do so. As law
professor and Federalist Society co-chair Steven Calabresi summarizes,

"the Federalist Society has come to play over the last 30 years for Republican presidents something of the role the American Bar Association has traditionally played for Democratic presidents. . . . The last two Republican presidents have disregarded ABA ratings, and I think they are relying on the Federalist Society to come up with qualified nominees" (Wheeler 2017).

FURTHER READING

ABA. 2022a. "Standing Committee on the Federal Judiciary." American Bar Association. https://www.americanbar.org/groups/committees/federal_judiciary

ABA. 2022b. "Supreme Court Evaluation Process: Evaluations of Nominees to the Supreme Court of the United States." American Bar Association. https://www.americanbar.org/groups/committees/federal_judiciary/ratings/supreme-court-evaluation-process

Alder, Madison. 2020. "Trump, GOP Defy Precedent with Lame Duck Judicial Appointees." *Bloomberg Law*, November 18, 2020.

Baum, Lawrence, and Neal Devins. 2017. "Federalist Court: How the Federalist Society Became the De Facto Selector of Republican Supreme Court Justices." *Slate*, January 31, 2017.

Baum, Lawrence, and Neal Devins. 2018. "The Federalist Society Majority." *Slate*, July 6, 2018.

Federalist Society. 2021. "Our Background." https://fedsoc.org/our-background

Fredrickson, Caroline, and Eric J. Segall. 2020. "Trump Judges or Federalist Society Judges? Try Both." *New York Times*, May 20, 2020.

Goldman, Sheldon. 1997. *Picking Federal Judges: Lower Court Selection from Roosevelt through Reagan*. New Haven, CT: Yale University Press.

Gonzales, Alberto. 2001. "Letter to the ABA From AL Gonzales." March 22, 2001. https://georgewbush-whitehouse.archives.gov/news/releases/2001/03/20010322-5.html

Haire, Susan Brodie. 2001. "Rating the Ratings of the American Bar Association Standing Committee on Federal Judiciary." *Justice System Journal*, 1, no. 1: 1–17.

Hollis-Brusky, Amanda. 2015. *Ideas with Consequences: The Federalist Society and the Conservative Counterrevolution*. New York: Oxford University Press.

Lindgren, James. 2001. "Examining the American Bar Association's Ratings of Nominees to the U.S. Courts of Appeals for Political Bias, 1989–2000." *Journal of Law & Politics*, 17, no. 1: 1–40.

Little, Laura E. 2001. "The ABA's Role in Prescreening Federal Judicial Candidates: Are We Ready to Give Up on the Lawyers?" *William & Mary Bill of Rights Journal*, 10, no. 1: 37–73.

Lott, John R., Jr. 2001. "The American Bar Association, Judicial Ratings, and Political Bias." *Journal of Law & Politics*, 17, no. 1: 41–62.

McCarthy, Tom. 2020. "Why Has Trump Appointed So Many Judges— And How Did He Do It?" *The Guardian*, April 28, 2020.

McMillion, Barry J. 2017. *U.S. Circuit and District Court Nominees Who Received a Rating of "Not Qualified" from the American Bar Association: Background and Historical Analysis* (CRS Insight IN10814). Congressional Research Service. https://fas.org/sgp/crs/misc/IN10814.pdf

Montgomery, David. 2019. "Conquerors of the Courts." *Washington Post Magazine*, January 2, 2019.

Regnery, Alfred. 2016. "The Sleeper Issue: Judicial Appointments." *National Review*, September 9, 2016.

Rutkus, Denis Steven. 2016. *The Appointment Process for U.S. Circuit and District Court Nominations: An Overview* (CRS Report No. R43762). Congressional Research Service. https://fas.org/sgp/crs/misc/R43762.pdf

Savage, Charlie. 2011. "Ratings Shrink President's List for Judgeships." *New York Times*, November 22, 2011.

Sen, Maya. 2014. "How Judicial Qualification Ratings May Disadvantage Minority and Female Candidates." *Journal of Law and Courts*, 2, no. 1: 33–66.

Sherman, Mark, Kevin Freking, and Matthew Daly. 2020. "Trump's Impact on Courts Likely to Last Long Beyond His Term." *Associated Press*, December 26, 2020. https://apnews.com/article/joe-biden-donald-trump-mitch-mcconnell-elections-judiciary-d5807340e86d05fbc78ed50fb43c1c46

Smelcer, Navarro, Amy Steigerwalt, and Richard L. Vining, Jr. 2012. "Bias and the Bar: Evaluating the ABA Ratings of Federal Judicial Nominees." *Political Research Quarterly*, 65, no. 4: 827–840.

Wheeler, Lydia. 2017. "Meeting the Powerful Group Behind Trump's Judicial Nominations." *The Hill*. November 16, 2017.

Q3. DO INTEREST GROUPS INFLUENCE THE SUPREME COURT CONFIRMATION PROCESS?

Answer: Yes, especially over the past 50 years. As discussed in Q2, organizations such as the American Bar Association and the Federalist Society have played significant roles in the nomination process. In addition, numerous special-interest groups line up in support of—or in opposition to—nominations after presidents announce their selections. Though many factors affect whether the Senate confirms or rejects a nominee, research shows a significant relationship between interest-group activity and confirmation outcomes. Interest groups also use the confirmation process to advance other political goals, such as voter mobilization and fundraising.

The Facts: Interest groups (also called advocacy groups) are formal organizations that seek to advance their goals by, among other things, working to shape policy, law, and elections. While often associated with their efforts to lobby and influence lawmakers, interest groups also seek to influence courts. Given the U.S. Supreme Court's role in shaping outcomes on a host of policy areas, such as health care, the environment, economic regulation, civil rights, abortion, and voting rights, interest groups "have incentives to promote the confirmation or defeat of Supreme Court nominees" (Vining 2011, 791). Beyond directly influencing Senate confirmation, incentives exist for interest groups to mobilize to indirectly support their goals. For example, Supreme Court confirmation hearings—especially contentious ones—can provide a vehicle for interest groups to mobilize for purposes such as getting out the vote and fundraising.

Consider President Trump's nomination of Amy Coney Barrett to the Supreme Court, formally announced on September 26, 2020, eight days after the death of Justice Ruth Bader Ginsburg. "By the time [Barrett] had finished her speech accepting the nomination, less than 30 minutes later, more than a dozen groups supporting and opposing her nomination had announced, or were poised to announce, advertising and grass-roots advocacy campaigns that were expected to bombard airwaves, Facebook feeds and Senate inboxes" (Vogel, Haberman, and Peters 2020). On October 26—30 days and tens of millions of dollars later—the Senate confirmed Barrett by a vote of 52 to 48.

According to one account of interest-group spending on Barrett's behalf, a "constellation of conservative groups" supported the nomination "on a larger scale than for either of Trump's two previous Supreme Court nominees. . . . The major organizations in this ecosystem on the right, including Judicial Crisis Network, Heritage Action for America, Club for Growth and others, spent nearly $30 million in total to support Barrett's nomination" (Berenson 2020). Judicial Crisis Network, a conservative advocacy group formed in 2005 to promote Bush's nominations to the bench, spent "at least $6.3 million in five weeks on national television spots supporting the Republican effort to confirm President Donald Trump's nominee a week before the election. The group spent an additional $2.9 million on

digital ads, direct mail and text messages supporting Barrett as of Oct. 26"
(Biesecker and Slodysko 2020).

The Barrett nomination and confirmation were unusual in many
respects. The vacancy came quite late in the president's term of office, and
the confirmation was pushed through far more rapidly than other confirmations in the modern era. The appointment also came during an excep-
tionally polarized presidential election and in the midst of a pandemic.
However, the GOP-controlled Senate pressed forward with confirmation,
determined to fill the open Supreme Court seat before a potential Democratic victory in the 2020 presidential election.

Though an unusual confirmation case to be sure, advertising campaigns
sponsored by interest groups for or against a Supreme Court nominee are
not new. Neither are other forms of interest-group involvement in the confirmation process. Summarizing prior existing research on interest-group
involvement, political scientist Richard L. Vining, Jr. notes that groups,
in efforts to confirm or defeat Supreme Court nominees, sometimes testify at confirmation hearings, lobby members of the Senate, or campaign to
achieve their preferred outcomes. In addition to the direct goal of winning
or blocking confirmation, interest groups may use confirmation processes for
their own "organizational maintenance"—that is, to enhance their institutional health, well-being, and longevity. "Few political contests provide such
clearly defined alternative outcomes as Supreme Court nominations. During the confirmation process, pressure groups can demonstrate that they are
active, recruit new members, and raise funds" (Vining 2011, 791).

That said, incentives for advocacy groups to become involved in Supreme
Court confirmation processes have not always been high, and their participation has been variable. Although examples of interest-group involvement
in Supreme Court selection date back to the 1800s, that involvement was
intermittent until the 1960s. Since 1969, however—and especially beginning in 1987—involvement has not only expanded, but also has changed in
terms of the types of groups involved (Cameron et al. 2020).

Early instances of interest-group involvement in Supreme Court nominations trace back at least to the 1881 nomination of Stanley Matthews
and the 1916 confirmation of Louis Brandeis. In the case of Matthews, a
national farming organization known as the Grange led a push to derail
his nomination out of concern that he would vote to overturn federal
railroad regulations. Matthews, who initially had been nominated during
the last weeks of the presidency of Rutherford B. Hayes, was eventually
confirmed—but only after being renominated by James Garfield, who succeeded Hayes in the White House. In the contentious though ultimately
successful Brandeis confirmation, "individuals connected to railroad commissions, newspapers, manufacturers, and unions participated actively,

although typically as individuals rather than formal representatives of organizations per se" (Cameron et al. 2020, 303–304).

In 1930, the nomination of John J. Parker by President Herbert Hoover was torpedoed by opposition from both the American Federation of Labor (AFL) and the National Association for the Advancement of Colored People (NAACP) (Cameron et al. 2020, 304). Interest groups also played a role in two failed Nixon administration appointments, those of Clement Haynsworth Jr. in 1969 and G. Harrold Carswell in 1970 (O'Connor, Yannus, and Patterson 2006). Other than these instances, however—and the ABA's growing involvement in rating judicial nominees beginning in the 1950s (see Q2)—interest-group activity pertaining to selections for the Supreme Court and the federal bench was scant prior to the 1970s.

A 2020 study by a group of political scientists offers an extensive account of interest-group involvement in 52 Supreme Court nominations from 1930 through 2017 based on analysis of press coverage in the *New York Times* and *Los Angeles Times*. The study found that levels of mobilization were light prior to 1969. For the 29 nominations from Charles Evans Hughes to Warren Burger (1930–1969), a mean level of 3.1 groups was mobilized. That number was low in part because nearly half of those nominations spurred no interest-group mobilization at all (Cameron et al. 2020, 307).

Nixon's failed nomination of Haynsworth in 1969, however, "marked a shift, with higher levels of mobilization subsequent to his controversial nomination. From 1969 to 1986, the year in which William Rehnquist was promoted to chief justice and Antonin Scalia was appointed, the mean number of groups that mobilized was 9.8" (Cameron et al. 2020, 307). An even bigger shift took place with the controversial confirmation fight over President Reagan's Supreme Court nominee Robert Bork in 1987. Bork's nomination, which ultimately fell short of confirmation, galvanized involvement from more than 80 groups supporting or opposing the nominee. Following the Bork controversy, "levels of mobilization have fluctuated, with the nominations of Clarence Thomas, John Roberts, and Samuel Alito triggering a large number of groups. The mean number of groups in the 1987 to 2017 period was 32.4 (28.3 if Bork is excluded)" (Cameron et al. 2020, 307).

This study also demonstrates other characteristics of interest-group advocacy beyond levels of mobilization. First, the research finds that although advocacy groups have typically mobilized against candidates, supportive mobilization became more common following the Bork nomination, and especially in recent years. Moreover, and with respect to nominations beginning with George W. Bush's selection of John Roberts in 2005, "the ratio of supportive to opposing mobilization has virtually equalized in the past few nominations. This equalization may reflect a growing sophistication of the president in organizing what are virtually political campaigns on behalf of a Supreme Court nominee" (Cameron et al. 2020, 308).

Second, the research shows the types of advocacy groups involved in the confirmation process. From 1930 through 2017, labor, civil rights, and abortion groups have been the most active, though labor group mobilization has declined in the 21st century and civil rights organizations were especially active from the 1960s to the 1980s (Cameron et al. 2020, 310–311). With respect to the ideology of the groups involved, the study found that while there has been a rise in participation of both liberal and conservative groups over time, "in the last period conservative mobilization has often outpaced liberal mobilization (which has trended downward in recent years), a pattern consistent with the increased emphasis in the conservative legal movement on the importance of judicial selection" (Cameron et al. 2020, 313). Furthermore, data shows that compared to corporate, business, and occupational interest groups, there has been a "striking increase in mobilization by identity and public interest/citizen groups; in the 1987–2017 period, these classes of groups combined accounted for about 90% of all mobilization" (Cameron et al. 2020, 313). This change may have contributed to the prominence of social issues and "culture war" debates in confirmation hearings.

Finding an increase in the activities and political orientation of interest groups, however, does not indicate whether advocacy has an effect on the outcome of the confirmation process. Furthermore, determining the direct impact of interest groups on Senate voting can be challenging, especially because multiple factors may influence voting behavior. In addition, as legal scholar Martin Shapiro cautions, "any claim to scientific generalization about Supreme Court appointments is highly dubious. The total number of these events is very small, and the total number within any reasonably fixed historical and political context is tiny. Moreover, the sequencing of Presidential nominations to the Court is often a major determinant of outcome and, for that reason, each nomination is unique" (Shapiro 1990, 935). Still, several research studies have concluded that interest-group advocacy is among the variables that directly affect whether high Court nominees are confirmed.

One 1992 study by political scientists Jeffrey A. Segal, Charles M. Cameron, and Albert D. Cover found that "strong interest group mobilization against a nominee can hurt a candidate, while interest group mobilization for a nominee can have substantively slight but statistically significant positive effects" (Segal, Cameron, and Cover 1992, 112). The research examines Senate roll-call voting on nominations from John Harlan in 1955 to Anthony Kennedy in 1988, looking at multiple factors that potentially influence outcome, including "the ideological distance between the senator's constituents and the nominee, . . . the perceived qualifications of the nominee, and . . . the interaction between the two" (Segal, Cameron, and Cover 1992, 113).

The evidence the researchers used to measure interest-group effect focused on the number of groups testifying at confirmation hearings (rather than on broader evidence of group mobilization). Based on this data, the authors of the 1992 study concluded that "the relative mobilization of interest groups around a nominee can have a profound effect on voting" (Segal, Cameron, and Cover, 1992, 114).

A 1998 study by political scientists Gregory A. Caldeira and John R. Wright also found evidence that lobbying around confirmations is influential. Based on data gathered through surveys of interest groups about the Supreme Court nominations of Robert Bork, David Souter, and Clarence Thomas, the research shows that interest-group advocacy had a statistically significant effect on senators' confirmation votes (Caldeira and Wright 1998, 501).

In addition, Caldeira and Wright offer an explanation of the mechanism for this direct effect. By "providing information to senators and their constituents about how nominees are likely to behave on the Court if confirmed; and by communicating information about constituents' preferences through grassroots lobbying campaigns, interest groups help shape senators' preferences for nominees and inform them about the appropriate importance to attach to constituency preferences" (Caldeira and Wright 1998, 499).

Another facet of information interest groups may share is informing "senators of what *they* will do if the senator votes the wrong way" (Epstein and Owens 2008, 482). Consider, for example, this characterization offered by political scientists Lee Epstein and Jeffrey A. Segal of how a liberal group claimed it would respond "if Senator Joe Biden (D-DE) had voted to confirm a conservative nominee: 'We would have had every Delaware donor of Joe Biden on an airplane, and they would've been standing in his office. . . . We could've gone that far and we would have.' By threatening to mobilize a senator's constituents, interest groups can supply additional, potentially electorally relevant information" (Epstein and Owens 2008, 482, quoting Epstein and Segal 2005, 101).

Even if other factors prove more powerful than interest groups in swaying Senate votes for or against confirmation, it is clear that there has been a notable growth of interest-group involvement in Supreme Court confirmations. Today, advocacy organizations willingly spend sizable amounts of money and seek to mobilize their supporters around confirmation battles, whether to affect the outcome, perform organizational maintenance and fundraising, or both.

FURTHER READING

Berenson, Tessa. 2020. "Senate Confirms Amy Coney Barrett to the Supreme Court Just Over a Week Before Election Day." *TIME*, October 26, 2020.

Biesecker, Michael, and Brian Slodysko. 2020. "Barrett Ads Tied to Interest Groups Funded by Unnamed Donors." *Associated Press*, October 26, 2020.

Caldeira, Gregory A., and John R. Wright. 1998. "Lobbying for Justice: Organized Interests, Supreme Court Nominations, and United States Senate." *American Journal of Political Science*, 42, no. 2: 499–523.

Cameron, Charles M., Cody Gray, Jonathan P. Kastellec, and Jee-Kwang Park. 2020. "From Textbook Pluralism to Modern Hyperpluralism: Interest Groups and Supreme Court Nominations, 1930–2017." *Journal of Law and Courts*, 8, no. 2: 301–332.

Epstein, Lee, and Ryan J. Owens. 2008. "Interest Groups." In *Encyclopedia of the Supreme Court of the United States*, Volume II, ed. David S. Tanenhaus, 481–484. Farmington Hills, MI: Macmillan.

Epstein, Lee, and Jeffrey A. Segal. 2005. *Advice and Consent: The Politics of Judicial Appointments*. New York: Oxford University Press.

Maltese, John A. 1995. *The Selling of Supreme Court Nominees*. Baltimore, MD: Johns Hopkins University Press.

O'Connor, Karen, Alixandra B. Yannus, and Linda Mancillas Patterson. 2006. "Where Have All the Interest Groups Gone? An Analysis of Interest Group Participation in Presidential Nominations to the Supreme Court of the United States." In *Interest Group Politics*, ed. Allan J. Cigler and Burdett A. Loomis, 340–365. Washington, DC: CQ Press.

Segal, Jeffrey A., Charles M. Cameron, and Albert D. Cover. 1992. "A Spatial Model of Roll Call Voting: Senators, Constituents, Presidents, and Interest Groups in Supreme Court Confirmations." *American Journal of Political Science*, 36, no. 1: 96–121.

Shapiro, Martin. 1990. "Interest Groups and Supreme Court Appointments." *Northwestern University Law Review*, 84: 935–961.

Vining, Richard L., Jr. 2011. "Grassroots Mobilization in the Digital Age: Interest Group Response to Supreme Court Nominees." *Political Research Quarterly*, 64, no. 4: 790–802.

Vogel, Kenneth P., Maggie Haberman, and Jeremy W. Peters. 2020. "Political Groups Begin Dueling Over Barrett in a Costly Clash." *New York Times*, September 27, 2020.

Q4. IS IT UNUSUAL FOR THE SENATE TO REJECT A SUPREME COURT NOMINEE?

Answer: Yes, at least since 1900, but rejections of Supreme Court nominees are more common than those of any other federal appointment.

The Facts: Between 1789, when the Supreme Court was established, and Amy Coney Barrett's nomination in October 2020, presidents have formally submitted to the Senate 164 Supreme Court nominations; 21 of these nominations have been to fill the seat of chief justice, and the remainder have been to fill associate justice vacancies. Another handful of candidates announced by a president but withdrawn before their nominations were officially submitted to the Senate do not count among these 164. In 1987, for example, President Ronald Reagan announced his intent to formally nominate Douglas Ginsburg to a vacancy on the Court, but Ginsburg withdrew his candidacy after he admitted to smoking marijuana.

Of the 164 formally submitted nominations, 127—just over 77 percent—received confirmation. Seven of these confirmed individuals ultimately declined to serve for one reason or another. These numbers standing alone, however, do not provide a complete picture of the rate of Senate rejection of Supreme Court nominees. In some ways, they understate the historical trend of positive Senate confirmations. In other ways, they understate the uniqueness of how the Senate treats its constitutional "advise and consent" power in the context of high Court nominations.

Not all of the 37 unconfirmed nominations were Senate rejections. In two instances, nominees were withdrawn by presidents for reasons unrelated to potential Senate opposition. In 2005, President George W. Bush withdrew his nomination of John Roberts to fill the seat vacated by Justice Sandra Day O'Connor. But he did so following the death of Chief Justice William Rehnquist in order to instead name Roberts to the chief justice seat on the bench. Far earlier, President George Washington withdrew his nomination of William Paterson out of concern that it might violate the Constitution, but re-nominated Paterson when that concern passed (Hogue 2010). The Senate confirmed both Roberts and Paterson after their re-nominations.

Even if these two instances are excluded from what counts as a nomination failure, we are left with 35 unconfirmed nominations—a total of 21 percent of total nominees—stemming from Senate resistance. This total includes several candidates who presidents nominated more than once: four of the 35 who were later re-nominated ultimately received Senate confirmation, whereas another four were not confirmed upon re-nomination. Among the re-nominations that the Senate later confirmed was one for Roger Taney, who was named and confirmed to the position of chief justice in 1836. (In 1835, Whig party opposition to President Andrew Jackson contributed to the indefinite postponement of his nomination of Taney to serve as associate justice.)

In 1881, the nomination of Stanley Matthews by President Rutherford B. Hayes met with Senate opposition and postponement. When new President James Garfield re-nominated Matthews just a few months later, the Senate confirmed him by a vote of 24 to 23, the narrowest margin in Court history. In addition, two other unconfirmed nominations were instances in which the Senate opposed elevating sitting associate justices to the position of chief justice. John Rutledge, nominated in 1795 by President Washington to the position of chief justice, held the position of associate justice from 1789 to 1791 and also briefly held the job of chief justice in 1795 under a recess appointment before being voted down by the Senate. Associate Justice Abe Fortas was on the Court when nominated in 1968 to the chief justice seat by President Lyndon Johnson, but a Senate filibuster led Johnson to withdraw the nomination.

With Senate opposition accounting for one in five unconfirmed nominations, how does it make sense to say that Senate rejection of Supreme Court nominees is unusual? First, a single president, John Tyler, accounts for a disproportionate number of the failed nominations. Tyler had been elected vice president in 1840 and became the 10th president shortly thereafter when President William Henry Harrison died just a month into his term. During Tyler's presidency, from 1841 to 1845, and owing largely to conflicts within his own party—he was expelled from the Whig Party 1842—only one of his nine submitted Supreme Court nominations earned confirmation. This means that a whopping eight of the 37 unconfirmed nominations occurred on Tyler's watch.

Second, the confirmation rate has been comparatively higher since the beginning of the 20th century. From 1900 to 2020, the Senate confirmed 62 out of 73 nominations, or nearly 85 percent. By contrast, prior to 1900 the Senate confirmed 65 of 91 nominations, for a confirmation rate of just over 70 percent. Another 26 were either rejected, not acted upon, postponed, or withdrawn from consideration. These counts include John Roberts and William Paterson.

Still, a few additional comparisons are worth examining in considering whether Senate rejections of high Court nominees are unusual. For one thing, the confirmation rate for Supreme Court nominees compares quite poorly to that for appointments to cabinet-level positions. Senate confirmation of cabinet nominations stood at about 99 percent in the early 2000s (Whittington 2006).

In addition, looking at the Supreme Court nominations made between 1960 and 2020, Senate opposition appears to be on the rise. Excluding the first nomination of John Roberts (discussed earlier), the confirmation rate of Court nominees during that 60-year span stands at 77 percent. Among those not confirmed were two appointments made by President Lyndon B. Johnson but withdrawn in the face of Senate resistance: sitting Associate Justice Abe Fortas, nominated for the position of chief justice; and Homer Thornberry. President Richard Nixon's selections of Clement Haynsworth and G. Harrold Carswell met with Senate rejection as well. The Senate also denied confirmation to President Ronald Reagan's nomination of Robert Bork in 1987, following combative hearings. President George W. Bush's selection of Harriet Miers did not make it to the Senate hearing stage but was withdrawn in the face of opposition by members of the president's own political party. Most recently, Merrick Garland, nominated by President Barack Obama in 2016, did not receive a confirmation hearing because Senate Republicans, who controlled the chamber, refused to act upon it for transparently partisan reasons (see Q5).

Whether we are likely to see an increase in Senate rejection of Supreme Court nominees in years to come is a related, though more challenging, question. Somewhat telling, though, is that Senate votes in favor of confirmation have narrowed over the past few decades as party polarization has grown starker. As a simple measure of this changing pattern, consider the 16 candidates confirmed to the high Court between 1975 and 2020. From 1975 to 2000, nine earned confirmation, but only two faced notable Senate opposition. William Rehnquist gained the chief justice position by a 65 to 33 margin, and the Senate confirmed Clarence Thomas after a 52 to 48 vote. The other seven received overwhelmingly favorable Senate votes. Indeed, for these seven nominees— John Paul Stevens, Sandra Day O'Connor, Antonin Scalia, Anthony Kennedy, David Souter, Ruth Bader Ginsburg, and Stephen Breyer—the worst result was a confirmation vote of 87 to 9, and four of the seven received no negative votes.

By contrast, the confirmation votes that took place between 2000 and 2020 tell a different and more consistently contested story. Seven justices earned confirmation during this 20-year stretch. The most support went to John Roberts for the job of chief justice, as he was confirmed by the Senate with a 78 to 22 vote. The remaining six nominees—Samuel Alito (58 votes in support, 42 against), Sonia Sotomayor (68–31), Elena Kagan (63–37), Neil Gorsuch (54–45), Brett Kavanaugh (50–48), and Amy Coney Barrett (52–48)—earned confirmation but with much narrower margins.

Though narrowing vote margins and party polarization might suggest a greater chance of Senate rejection, under changes to Senate rules that took effect in 2017, the filibuster no longer applies to Supreme Court confirmation votes (see Q17 and Q18). Since 1975, the filibuster rule required a 60-vote margin rather than a simple majority of the 100 members of the Senate to confirm high Court nominations. In 2017, ahead of the Senate's consideration of Trump nominee Neil Gorsuch, the Republican-controlled Senate modified its rules to allow confirmation of justices by a simple majority vote. The absence of the filibuster makes it considerably easier for the majority party that controls the Senate to push nominations through, even in the face of united minority party opposition.

FURTHER READING

Collins, Paul M., Jr., and Lori A. Ringhand. 2013. *Supreme Court Confirmation Hearings and Constitutional Change.* New York: Cambridge University Press.

Gerhardt, Michael J. 2003. *The Federal Appointments Process.* Chapel Hill, NC: Duke University Press.

Hogue, Henry B. 2010. *Supreme Court Nominations Not Confirmed, 1789–2009* (CRS Report No. RL31171). Congressional Research Service. https://fas.org/sgp/crs/misc/RL31171.pdf

Krutz, Glen S., Richard Fleisher, and Jon R. Bond. 1998. "From Abe Fortas to Zöe Baird: Why Some Presidential Nominations Fail in the Senate." *American Political Science Review,* 92, no. 4: 871–881.

Maltese, John Anthony. 1995. *The Selling of Supreme Court Nominees.* Baltimore, MD: Johns Hopkins University Press.

McCarty, Nolan, and Rose Razaghian. 1999. "Advice and Consent: Senate Responses to Executive Branch Nominations 1885–1996." *American Journal of Political Science,* 43, no. 4: 1122–1143.

"Supreme Court Nominations (1789–Present)." 2021. United States Senate. https://www.senate.gov/legislative/nominations/SupremeCourtNominations1789present.htm

Whittington, Keith E. 2006. "Presidents, Senates, and Failed Supreme Court Nominations." *Supreme Court Review,* 2006: 401–438.

Q5. WAS THE SENATE'S REFUSAL TO TAKE ACTION ON PRESIDENT OBAMA'S SUPREME COURT NOMINATION OF MERRICK GARLAND REALLY UNPRECEDENTED?

Answer: The Senate's refusal to act on the Garland nomination has no precedent since the turn of the 20th century. Moreover, even prior to the 20th century, the cases of inaction by the Senate when presented with a nominee to fill a vacancy on the high Court are not comparable. Those instances occurred only in cases of *non-elected* presidents nominating Supreme Court candidates or in cases of nominations that took place during an administration's "lame duck" session.

The Facts: Supreme Court Justice Antonin Scalia died on February 13, 2016, just over eight months ahead of the 2016 presidential election and with 11 months remaining in President Barack Obama's second term of office. Mere hours after the news of Scalia's unexpected death, Senate Majority Leader Mitch McConnell announced that the Senate would not consider *any* candidate nominated by Obama to fill the vacant seat. McConnell, a Republican from Kentucky, offered the following as his stated justification for his remarkable declaration: "The American people should have a voice in the selection of their next Supreme Court Justice. Therefore, this vacancy should not be filled until we have a new president" (Condon 2016).

McConnell would later boast about his refusal to take action on Obama's appointment to replace Scalia: "One of my proudest moments was when I looked Barack Obama in the eye and I said, 'Mr. President, you will not fill the Supreme Court vacancy'" (Elving 2018). McConnell's refusal to take action forestalled a likely shift on the Court from a narrow conservative majority to a narrow liberal majority. Justice Scalia, advocate of an originalist approach to constitutional interpretation, sat among a bloc of five conservative justices serving on the Court at the time. Though Justice Anthony Kennedy was less reliably conservative than the four other justices who formed this conservative bloc (he sometimes voted with the Court's more liberal justices on issues such as same-sex marriage and abortion), the conservatives held a majority on the Court prior to Scalia's death. If the Senate had permitted Obama—a Democrat who had already appointed two justices situated on the liberal side of the bench—to replace Scalia, the conservative hold on the Court would almost certainly have come to an end.

That did not happen, as McConnell stuck to his pledge, even after Obama nominated Merrick Garland, a candidate widely viewed as a centrist. In March 2016 when Obama announced the selection, Garland was Chief Judge of the U.S. Court of Appeals for the District of Columbia Circuit and had in total 19 years of service on the appellate court. His confirmation to the DC Circuit Court in 1997, following his nomination by President Bill Clinton, came by a vote of 76 to 23. Obama selected the relatively moderate candidate over more progressive contenders in part because Garland was "a jurist better known for his meticulous work ethic and adherence to legal principles than for an ideological bent" (Shear, Davis, and Harris 2016). Aiming to pressure the Republican-controlled Senate to reverse course from its initial refusal to act, Obama stated that "[t]o suggest that someone as qualified and respected as Merrick Garland doesn't even deserve a hearing, let alone an up-or-down vote, to join an institution as important as our Supreme Court, when two-thirds of Americans believe otherwise—that would be unprecedented" (Shear, Davis, and Harris 2016).

McConnell's action—or, rather, promise of inaction—triggered outraged claims that he was violating long-standing Senate norms about the institution's advice and consent role. The assertion that McConnell violated *norms* is not, however, equivalent to alleging that he was acting in violation of the Constitution. In fact, McConnell's pledge fit within the explicit scope of Senate authority granted by the U.S. Constitution. Article II of the Constitution stipulates, with exceptions for temporary appointments made during Senate recess, that the president "shall nominate, and by and with the Advice and Consent of the Senate, shall appoint . . . Judges of the supreme Court." Senate advice and consent are necessary for confirmation—features of the system of checks and balances established by the framers of the Constitution. And the Senate can legally and constitutionally withhold its advice and consent.

That said, there is no question that McConnell's refusal to act violated longstanding norms. Since 1955, the norms governing the selection of federal judges include at least giving Supreme Court nominees a Senate Judiciary Committee hearing. Public confirmation hearings for high Court nominees became the norm beginning with the appointment of John Harlan in 1955, and televised confirmation hearings became the norm beginning in 1981 with the appointment of Sandra Day O'Connor.

But even if it violated longstanding norms, was the Senate's lack of action on the Garland nomination truly unprecedented? As discussed in Q4, there had been other occasions in American history when the Senate postponed or did not act upon Supreme Court nominations. Garland's was not the first nomination to have received no Senate action. That fact alone, however, does not clearly answer the question.

According to a 2016 study by legal scholars Robin Bradley Kar and Jason Mazzone, the Senate's treatment of Garland was without historical precedent in important respects. Kar and Mazzone examined each of the prior vacancies on the Supreme Court. In doing so, they concluded that the only times the Senate had previously refused to consider Supreme Court nominations were under "the highly unusual circumstance where the nominating President's status as the most recently elected President has been in doubt." These cases "involved a President who either (a) attained office by succession rather than election or (b) began the nomination process after the election of his successor" (Kar and Mazzone 2016, 58, 60). Detailing these unusual cases, Kar and Mazzone differentiate appointments made by Presidents John Tyler, Millard Fillmore, and Andrew Johnson (all of whom were vice presidents who assumed the Oval Office by succession after the deaths of sitting and elected presidents), and Presidents John Quincy Adams, James Buchanan, and Rutherford B. Hayes.

In addition, these successions to the position of president occurred "prior to the passage of the Twenty-fifth Amendment, when there was still some ambiguity over whether a Vice President literally became the President or merely acted as President under the Constitution's rule of succession then in place" (Kar and Mazzone 2016, 66). According to Kar and Mazzone, Senate refusal to act on several of the nominations made by Tyler, Fillmore, and Johnson did not provide precedent for McConnell's refusal to act on the nominations of an elected president or even a vice president who ascended to the presidency after the Twenty-Fifth Amendment was ratified. Concerning the Supreme Court nominations from presidents Adams, Buchanan, and Hayes that were not acted upon, those all occurred during the "lame duck" period of their administrations—that is, *after* the election of a presidential successor, not before. "There have been 103 prior cases in which—as in the case of Obama's nomination of Garland—an elected President nominated someone to fill an actual Supreme Court vacancy and began the nomination process prior to the election of a successor" (Kar and Mazzone 2016, 60). In these instances, "the sitting President was able to both nominate *and appoint* a replacement Justice—by and with the advice and consent of the Senate, and regardless of the senatorial rules and procedures in place. Hence, in none of the 103 cases that most closely resemble the current controversy has a sitting President been unable to fill an existing Supreme Court vacancy with *some* nominee" (Kar and Mazzone 2016, 60). In these instances, the Senate has sometimes rejected a president's first nominee or pressured for the withdrawal of a candidate; but in every instance, the president was ultimately permitted to fill a vacant seat with the advice and consent of the Senate.

Viewed in this light, there is no precedent for the Senate's treatment of Obama's Supreme Court nomination of Garland. Can precedent be found in how the Senate has treated other appointments to the federal bench? Kar and Mazzone reject this argument, correctly noting the significant differences in how Supreme Court nominations are treated and noting the significant differences in the roles of Supreme Court justices as compared to lower federal court judges.

But even if Kar and Mazzone wrongly treat those nominations as categorically different and lacking in precedent, the following is clear from the historical record: there is no example since the turn of the 20th century comparable to the Senate's treatment of the Garland nomination. From 1900 to 2020, there were only two instances in which the Senate did not immediately act upon two nominees, but in both cases the circumstances were quite unlike those of the Garland nomination.

In November 1922, President Warren Harding nominated Pierce Butler to the Court during the third session of the 67th Congress. Though consideration by the full Senate did not occur during that session, Pierce's nomination, unlike Garland's candidacy, received favorable action by the Judiciary Committee. Moreover, Harding renominated Butler shortly thereafter, during the following congressional session, and Butler earned confirmation in December 1922.

President Dwight D. Eisenhower nominated John Harlan in November 1954, near the end of the 83rd Congress. The nomination met with some resistance and was not released out of the Judiciary Committee when the 83rd Congress adjourned two months later. But Eisenhower renominated Harlan in January 1955 at the outset of the 84th Congress, and Harlan easily won confirmation in March 1955 by a vote of 71 to 11.

In sum, while a few historical cases demonstrate Senate refusal to act on a president's Supreme Court nominee, the GOP-controlled Senate's refusal to consider the Garland nomination was without precedent.

FURTHER READING

Chafetz, Josh. 2016. "What the Constitution Has to Say About the Supreme Court Vacancy." *The Hill*, February 16, 2016.

Condon, Stephanie. 2016. "Mitch McConnell: Senate Should Wait for Next President to Replace Antonin Scalia." *CBS News*, February 13, 2016.

Elving, Ron. 2018. "What Happened with Merrick Garland in 2016 and Why It Matters Now." National Public Radio, June 29, 2018. https://www.npr.org/2018/06/29/624467256/what-happened-with-merrick-garland-in-2016-and-why-it-matters-now

Gerhardt, Michael, and Richard Painter. 2016. "The New Normal: Unprecedented Judicial Obstruction and a Proposal for Change." *Advance: The Journal of the ACS Issue Briefs*, 10: 29–38.

Hogue, Henry B. 2010. *Supreme Court Nominations Not Confirmed, 1789–2009* (CRS Report No. RL31171). Congressional Research Service. https://fas.org/sgp/crs/misc/RL31171.pdf

Kar, Robin Bradley, and Jason Mazzone. 2016. "The Garland Affair: What History and the Constitution Really Say About President Obama's Powers to Appoint a Replacement for Justice Scalia." *NYU Law Review*, 91: 53–114 [On-Line Features].

Shear, Michael D., Julie Hirschfeld Davis, and Gardiner Harris. 2016. "Obama Chooses Merrick Garland for Supreme Court." *New York Times*, March 16, 2016.

Tobias, Carl. 2017. "Confirming Supreme Court Justices in a Presidential Election Year." *Washington University Law Review*, 94: 1089–1108.

Q6. ARE SUPREME COURT CONFIRMATION HEARINGS A "VAPID AND HOLLOW CHARADE"?

Answer: Observers accurately note that Supreme Court nominees often evade answering substantive questions at their confirmation hearings. That evasiveness has contributed to a common assertion that confirmation hearings are empty political performances. Recent research shows that nominees are not as evasive as the common wisdom suggests. Still, scholars disagree on whether hearings amount to pointless political performances or, by contrast, provide a valuable contribution to democratic governance.

The Facts: In 1995, future Supreme Court Associate Justice Elena Kagan—then Assistant Professor of Law at the University of Chicago—described confirmation hearings as a "vapid and hollow charade, in which repetition of platitudes has replaced discussion of viewpoints and personal anecdotes have supplanted legal analysis" (Kagan 1995, 941). Kagan specifically took aim at the Supreme Court confirmation hearings that followed Robert Bork's failed nomination in 1987, including those held for Anthony

Kennedy, David Souter, Clarence Thomas, Ruth Bader Ginsburg, and Stephen Breyer. But Kagan has not been alone in offering unflattering characterizations of confirmation hearings. As political scientist Paul Collins and law professor Lori Ringhand summarize, the hearings "are routinely criticized as empty rituals (at best) or deceptive debacles (at worst)" (Collins and Ringhand 2013, 1). Similarly, political scientists Dion Farganis and Justin Wedeking note that Kagan's characterization

> enjoys nearly universal assent among scholars, pundits, senators, and just about anyone else who follows the Supreme Court confirmation process. The precise descriptions themselves may vary—from "exercise[s] in obfuscation" (Yalof 2008) to a "'kabuki' dance" (Fitzpatrick 2009), a "farce" (Benson 2010), or simply a "mess" (Carter 1988)—but the basic idea is the same: Supreme Court nominees are no longer forthcoming during their testimony, and Supreme Court confirmation hearings are no longer working properly as a result. (Farganis and Wedeking 2014, 2)

Kagan's portrayal of Supreme Court confirmation hearings has become a dominant narrative. However, there is less consensus about whether this narrative accurately captures the character and value of Supreme Court confirmation hearings. On one side of the debate sit those who emphasize routine nominee evasiveness in answering questions. On the other side of the debate are studies that find the hearings offer more substantive discussion than Kagan and others acknowledge. Some observers also conclude that hearings produce other values that contribute to democratic governance.

It is worth noting, at the outset, that the public versions of Senate Judiciary Committee confirmation hearings to which we have become accustomed are relatively recent developments. Indeed, the Constitution does not mandate confirmation hearings for Supreme Court justices, and all but three nominations prior to 1925 were handled without a hearing. In the first three confirmation hearings—for George Williams (1873), Louis Brandeis (1916), and Pierce Butler (1922)—the nominees did not testify as they do today, and only the 1916 hearing on the Brandeis nomination was public (Collins and Ringhand 2016). Though the Senate adopted a rule in 1929 to make public hearings the ordinary procedure for nominees to the bench, "most of the early hearings were just formalities" (Farganis and Wedeking 2014, 10). Not until John Harlan's appointment in 1955 did the Senate establish the practice of holding public hearings with testimony from the nominee. Even with the onset of that practice, some hearings remained formalities. For example, Byron White's testimony during his 1962 confirmation hearing lasted just 11 minutes (Cohen 2012).

Worth noting as well is that televised hearings did not begin until 1981 with President Reagan's appointment of Sandra Day O'Connor. By 1987, when Robert Bork's contentious nomination played out in the Senate, hearings were broadcast not just on C-SPAN but also on CNN and PBS. By the time Clarence Thomas was narrowly confirmed in 1991, hearings aired as well on CBS, ABC, and NBC (Farganis and Wedeking 2014, 18).

More generally, media coverage of hearings expanded dramatically during these decades, with potential consequences for how hearings might function. According to one analysis, increased media coverage "may have had an effect on how senators on the Judiciary Committee approach the questioning of nominees. They might, for example, use the hearings as a platform to appeal to their constituents, knowing that the proceedings are reaching millions of voters. They also might be less prepared to seem sympathetic to nominees who were selected by a president of the opposing party" (Farganis and Wedeking 2014, 18).

It is in this era of the publicly broadcast confirmation hearing, and especially those that followed the tumultuous and ultimately failed Bork nomination, that sharp criticisms of hearings have emerged. One of the primary critical refrains is that hearings lack substance because Bork was undone by his own statements. A number of factors contributed to the Senate's 58–42 vote against Bork, but "his long and candid answers to questions about his views on constitutional interpretation and issues such as privacy gave Democrats all the ammunition they needed to paint Bork as a radical conservative who would take the Court too far away from the mainstream" (Farganis and Wedeking 2014, 16).

One of the purported takeaways from the politically contentious episode was that future nominees should be evasive in answering substantive questions posed by senators. "The self-defeating lesson which official Washington took from the political savagery of the 1987 proceedings was that nominees were better off saying nothing publicly about their views of the law and were better off serving up empty platitudes when backed into a corner by their Judiciary Committee inquisitors" (Cohen 2012).

Covering nominations in the post-Bork era through that of Stephen Breyer in 1994, Kagan opined in 1995 that not since Bork "has any nominee candidly discussed, or felt a need to discuss, his or her views and philosophy. It is true that in recent hearings senators of all stripes have proclaimed their prerogative to explore a nominee's approach to constitutional problems. The idea of substantive inquiry is accepted today to a far greater extent than it was a decade ago. But the practice of substantive inquiry has suffered a precipitous fall since the Bork hearings, so much so that today it hardly deserves the title 'practice' at all" (Kagan 1995, 925).

Describing the avoidance techniques used by Ruth Bader Ginsburg during her 1993 confirmation hearing, Kagan noted that candidates often skirt substantive questions by saying they cannot talk about specific cases because such cases might come before the justice once seated on the Court. Yet candidates also skirt substantive questions by saying they cannot talk in generalities about legal questions without knowing details of the specific cases (1995, 925). Kagan argued that such a "pincer" move (925) leaves little room for discussion of actual substance, although she also acknowledged that both Ginsburg and Breyer did speak at times about substantive matters, including their previous writings and judicial philosophies.

Although criticism of the vacuousness of hearings has intensified with respect to post-Bork confirmations, scholars note that candidate evasiveness predates Bork. Legal scholar Grover Rees III, for example, observed that Sandra Day O'Connor "politely refused to tell the Senators anything that would help them to predict how she would vote" at her 1981 hearings (Rees 1983, 918). As O'Connor stated during the hearing, "I do not believe that as a nominee I can tell you how I might vote on a particular issue which may come before the Court, or endorse or criticize specific Suprem[e] Court decisions presenting issues which may well come before the Court again. To do so would mean that I have prejudged the matter or have morally committed myself to a certain position" (Rees 1983, 919 n. 24). According to political scientist David Yalof, O'Connor "thus offered a preview of the so-called impartiality defense that would eventually prove so difficult for the opposition to puncture. . . . Once O'Connor's strategy succeeded, no level of obfuscation might be deemed unacceptable for a nominee to the Supreme Court" (Yalof 2008, 156–157).

Some researchers also suggest that the hollow quality of hearings has continued since the turn of the 21st century. For example, during John Roberts's hearing for the position of chief justice in 2005, he repeatedly quoted Ruth Bader Ginsburg's declaration that she could provide "[n]o hints, forecast, previews" of how she would rule on cases before the Court. Roberts "repeated that guideline no less than 10 times during the first day of testimony alone" and "used it to fend off questions about almost any specific precedent, past or present" (Yalof 2008, 167).

It is undeniable that nominees now deploy a common avoidance script during hearings. Still, some recent and noteworthy studies provide evidence that modern Supreme Court confirmation testimony has not been wildly divergent from how nominees handled questions in earlier decades.

In one such study, political scientists Dion Farganis and Justin Wedeking conducted an exhaustive analysis of questions posed to nominees and the answers provided in hearings from 1955, beginning with John Marshall Harlan II, through Kagan's hearing in 2010. Evaluating almost 11,000 exchanges between senators and nominees, Farganis and Wedeking identify the types of questions posed ("facts" versus "views") and rate the responses as "forthcoming," "qualified," or "not forthcoming." Their findings indicate that the "degree to which nominees answer questions" has not really changed in the period of time they cover (Farganis and Wedeking 2014, 3). "Indeed, the entire chorus of criticism surrounding the confirmation hearing process is predicated on the belief that there was a time when the hearings were more substantive, but that in the 1980s nominees began strategically avoiding controversial queries that could sink their confirmation prospects" (Farganis and Wedeking 2014, 2). This belief, the researchers conclude, is not borne out by the evidence.

That is not, however, to say that nominees always answer questions in forthcoming ways. Farganis and Wedeking find that all the nominees in the post-Bork era engaged in sidestepping of uncomfortable questions. Nevertheless, they discover that nominees "do not actually sidestep or evade questions nearly as often as the media, scholars, and other Court watchers suggest" (Farganis and Wedeking 2014, 42).

Legal scholars Paul Collins and Lori Ringhand also used transcripts to assess the value of confirmation hearings and the prevailing critical narrative. Based on coding "every question asked and every answer given at every open public hearing of a Supreme Court nominee" from 1939 through 2010 (Collins and Ringhand 2013, 9), they find that hearings function to ratify constitutional change and the current constitutional consensus. At the center of this thesis is the argument that when constitutional choices made by a non-elected and insulated judiciary achieve public acceptance, "nominees are expected to pledge their adherence to those choices at their confirmation hearings. Over time, subsequent nominees from across the political spectrum voice their support for those changes, allowing the hearings to function as a formal mechanism through which the Court's constitutional choices are ratified as a part of our constitutional consensus—the long-term constitutional commitments embraced by the public" (Collins and Ringhand 2013, 3).

By functioning in this way, Collins and Ringhand assert, confirmation hearings serve as a vehicle for democratic accountability. Even while nominees skirt substantive discussion of "currently contested issues, such as abortion, affirmative action, and gay rights, the repeated affirmation of seminal cases, such as *Brown*, plays an important role in both validating the Court's choices in previously contested areas and defining the constitutional issues that are and are not actively in play" (Collins and Ringhand 2013, 8).

The analysis presented by Collins and Ringhand also raises questions about just how evasive nominees have been. For example, they find that Anthony Kennedy, whose confirmation hearing followed directly in the wake of Bork's failed nomination, "was every bit as forthcoming as Bork on the issues that proved problematic for Bork." Moreover, "the nominees immediately following Kennedy, a group that included individuals put forth by both Democratic and Republican presidents, embraced the positions articulated by Kennedy and rejected those espoused by Bork" (Collins and Ringhand 2013, 12–13).

Nevertheless, evasiveness remains a common characterization of confirmation hearings. *New York Times* legal reporter Adam Liptak, for example, described Amy Coney Barrett's October 2020 hearing before the Senate Judiciary Committee as one in which she offered "sure-footed accounts of Supreme Court precedents and then, almost without exception, declined to say whether the decisions were correct" (Liptak 2020). In so doing, Barrett "expertly followed" the "playbook" Kagan identified in her 1995 article: "'The safest and surest route to the prize,' she wrote, 'lay in alternating platitudinous statement and judicious silence'" (Liptak 2020).

FURTHER READING

Benson, Robert W. 2010. "The Senate Farce for Kagan's Confirmation to the Supreme Court." *Huffington Post*, June 7, 2010.

Carter, Stephen L. 1988. "Essays on the Supreme Court Appointment Process: The Confirmation Mess." *Harvard Law Review*, 101: 1185–1201.

Carter, Stephen L. 1994. *The Confirmation Mess: Cleaning Up the Federal Appointments Process*. New York: Basic Books.

Cohen, Andrew. 2012. "The Sad Legacy of Bork." *The Atlantic*, December 19, 2012.

Collins, Paul M., Jr., and Lori A. Ringhand. 2013. *Supreme Court Confirmation Hearings and Constitutional Change*. New York: Cambridge University Press.

Collins, Paul M., Jr., and Lori A. Ringhand. 2016. "The Institutionalization of Supreme Court Confirmation Hearings." *Law & Social Inquiry*, 41: 126–151.

Czarnezki, Jason J., William K. Ford, and Lori A. Ringhand. 2007. "An Empirical Analysis of the Confirmation Hearings of the Justices of the Rehnquist Natural Court." *Constitutional Commentary*, 24, no. 1: 127–198.

Epstein, Lee, and Jeffrey A. Segal. 2005. *Advice and Consent: The Politics of Judicial Appointments*. New York: Oxford University Press.

Farganis, Dion, and Justin Wedeking. 2014. *Supreme Court Confirmation Hearings in the U.S. Senate: Reconsidering the Charade*. Ann Arbor, MI: University of Michigan Press.

Fitzpatrick, Brian. 2009. "Confirmation 'Kabuki' Does No Justice." *Politico*, June 20, 2009.

Kagan, Elena. 1995. "Review: Confirmation Messes, Old and New" [review of *The Confirmation Mess* by Stephen L. Carter]. *University of Chicago Law Review*, 62, no. 2: 919–942.

Liptak, Adam. 2020. "Barrett's Testimony Is a Deft Mix of Expertise and Evasion." *New York Times*, October 13, 2020.

Rees, Grover, III. 1983. "Questions for Supreme Court Nominees at Confirmation Hearings: Excluding the Constitution." *Georgia Law Review*, 17: 913–967.

Yalof, David. 2008. "Confirmation Obfuscation: Supreme Court Confirmation Politics in a Conservative Era." *Studies in Law, Politics, and Society*, 44: 141–171.

Q7. IS THE TIMING OF JUDICIAL RETIREMENTS FROM THE SUPREME COURT INFLUENCED BY POLITICS?

Answer: To some extent. Common wisdom holds that Supreme Court justices often take politics into consideration when deciding to leave the bench. They seek to time their retirements to increase the chances that their replacements will hold similar political, ideological, and legal views. This commonly held perception often drives media coverage of the Court, leading to speculation about when justices might depart and whether presidents will be able to shape the bench. Social science research on so-called strategic retirement is not quite so definitive, however. Evidence also points to other factors influencing retirement timing, such as age, personal health, the availability of pension benefits, and the justice's sense of his or her own position and importance on the Court.

The Facts: On January 9, 2021, just a few days after two critical run-off elections in Georgia resulted in Democrats taking narrow control of the United States Senate away from Republicans, speculation mounted that the Supreme Court's oldest justice, liberal Stephen G. Breyer, would retire to give incoming President Joe Biden the opportunity to fill the seat.

As one CNN legal analyst summarized, "Breyer, who before becoming a judge was chief counsel to the Senate Judiciary Committee, knows better than most how last week's surprise Georgia election has transformed the prospects for Biden to fulfill a progressive agenda related to the judiciary" (Biskupic 2021).

In April 2021, "a new phase in an extraordinary year-long campaign was launched to pressure Breyer to rethink his loyalties and focus far more on the political party that helped secure his appointment and the court's dwindling liberal minority. A group of Democratic operatives circulated an online petition. Activists protested his events. Op-eds appeared in newspapers. A truck circled the Supreme Court building with a billboard that read: 'Breyer, retire'" (Viser et al. 2022).

When the end of the Supreme Court's 2021 session came and went without Breyer announcing an impending departure, calls for him to retire intensified. "[M]any Democrats worried he would stay on the court beyond the 2022 midterms and risk the possibility that Republicans could take control of the Senate—and with it, control of judicial confirmations" (Viser et al. 2022). On January 27, 2022, Breyer finally released a formal announcement that he would retire at the end of the 2022 term. Given the opportunity to replace Breyer while the Senate remained under the Democratic control, Biden nominated Ketanji Brown Jackson. In April 2022, the Senate confirmed her appointment by a 53–47 vote.

Breyer is far from the first Supreme Court justice to be the subject of this type of attention. Indeed, the prospects and timing of judicial departures have become a hot topic—especially in the aftermath of Justice Ruth Bader Ginsburg's death in September 2020. Ginsburg, a liberal justice who had battled multiple illnesses during her long tenure on the Court, faced pressure to retire during President Barack Obama's term of office so that a Democratic president could name her replacement. She rebuffed that pressure and remained on the Court until she died at age 87, just 46 days ahead of the 2020 presidential election. That put selection of her replacement in the hands of Republican President Donald Trump, who pushed through the confirmation of conservative jurist Amy Coney Barrett. The ascension of Barrett created a heavily conservative Court composed of six justices nominated by Republican presidents and only three nominated by a Democrat.

Does the pressure placed on justices to time their departures from the bench demonstrate that justices act politically in deciding how long to stay and when to step down? Does Ginsburg's decision to remain on the bench and risk being replaced by a Republican suggest the opposite—that she was not moved by politics? According to Artemus Ward, author of a book on the retirement of justices, "[p]olitical scientists have demonstrated again and again how Supreme Court justices exhibit political behavior in the many facets of their day-to-day work, from selecting law clerks to setting the court's agenda and deciding cases. It should not be surprising that their final move—the decision to retire—is similarly political" (Ward 2018).

While it should not be surprising, evidence confirming the political basis and strategic approach of judicial retirements is not always transparent. After all, justices typically aim to present themselves as insulated from politics and insist that their rulings and other actions reflect "legal" rather than "political" considerations.

That said, anecdotal evidence suggests that the link exists. According to political scientists Lee Epstein and Jeffery A. Segal, Chief Justice Earl Warren sought to time his retirement to allow President Lyndon B. Johnson to replace him. "The liberal Warren retired only conditionally, 'at such time as a successor is qualified,' in effect threatening to stay on the Court if the Senate refused to confirm his replacement. The Republicans, along with conservative southern Democrats, called Warren's bluff and rejected, through a filibuster, Abe Fortas's promotion to chief justice. Richard Nixon, Warren's long-time nemesis, was then elected president and Warren chose to retire, his scheme to guarantee a liberal successor a failure" (Epstein and Segal 2005, 38).

Evidence is strong, for example, that Justice Harry Blackmun took the 1992 election of Democratic candidate Bill Clinton to the presidency after 12 years of Republican control of the White House as a key consideration in his decision to retire. The day after Clinton was elected in 1992, in fact, Blackmun wrote the following in his personal notes taken during oral arguments: "What do I do now? Retire at once; Retire at 6/30/93; Retire at 6/30/94" (Nelson and Ringsmuth 2009, 486).

Eight years later, conservative Justice Sandra Day O'Connor was deeply disappointed when she thought Democratic nominee Al Gore was going to win that year's closely contested election against Republican George W. Bush. O'Connor's husband told people at an election night party that "they were planning on retiring to Arizona but that a Gore presidency meant they would have to wait another four years since she did not want a Democrat to name her successor" (Ward 2003, 1).

Chief Justice William Rehnquist acknowledged the influence of politics on retirement during a 1999 interview. In response to the interviewer's characterization of Supreme Court justices making retirement decisions based on whether the party of their choice controls the White House, Rehnquist offered this response: "That's not one hundred percent true but it certainly is true in more cases than not, I would think" (Ward 2003, 218).

Justice Breyer's retirement announcement adds to this list. A vocal defender of the view that courts should be viewed as above politics, "Breyer has been one of the justices most loudly proclaiming that political machinations could be the ruin of the institution he has served for nearly 28 years. He wrote a book about it [in 2021], worrying that stacking the court with additional members for partisan goals would besmirch the image of the people he says put politics aside when they put on the black robe" (Barnes 2022).

Nevertheless, although he has not plainly said that he stepped down to give Biden the opportunity to choose his successor, Breyer intimated that the timing of his decision was influenced in part by that consideration. In an interview in August 2021, Breyer discussed the difficulty of deciding when to retire and noted that many factors figure into the decision. Among those factors, Breyer also invoked Justice Antonin Scalia, who said, according to Breyer, "I don't want somebody appointed who will just reverse everything I've done for the last 25 years" (Liptak 2021). What's more, upon the announcement of his retirement, Breyer's brother, a federal district judge in San Francisco, reported, "I think it's clear that politics played a role . . . . He's pragmatic and politics is a factor . . . that has to be considered" (Barnes 2022).

Because anecdotal evidence is not a reliable indicator of a broader practice, however, social scientists have undertaken studies to determine whether justices act strategically in timing their departures. Empirical research on the question of the link between politics and retirement provides support for the hypothesis that political considerations play a role in the timing of justices' decisions to leave the bench. However, the findings of the research are mixed rather than definitive. Meanwhile, other research points to personal and institutional factors as being more influential.

Among the main bucket of political variables that researchers have tested to explain when Supreme Court justices retire are: "(1) justices' partisan or ideological alignment with the president and Senate; (2) presidential term and year in office; and (3) the Court's partisan or ideological balance" (Peretti and Rozzi 2011, 144). As political scientists Terri Peretti and Alan Rozzi summarize, studies by Hagle (1993), Stolzenberg and Lindgren (2010), and Zorn and Van Winkle (2000) find that the retirements are influenced by the president's term or year in office; research by Hagle (1993) and Nelson and Ringsmuth (2009) show the impact of partisan or ideological makeup of the Senate on retirements; and research by several scholars suggests that partisan or ideological alignment with the sitting president proves influential (see, e.g., Bailey and Yoon 2009, Beckstrom 2004, Stolzenberg and Lindgren 2010, and Ward 2003) (Peretti and Rozzi 2011, 144–145).

Competing findings, however, do not support the strategic model of retirement. For example, and as cataloged by Peretti and Rozzi (2011, 144–145), studies by several scholars do not find that justices take the Court's partisan or ideological balance into consideration when making retirement decisions (see Bailey and Yoon 2009; Box-Steffensmeier and Zorn 2001; Perry and Zorn 2008; Zorn and Van Winkle 2000). Studies by Nelson and Ringsmuth (2009) and Yoon (2006) do not support the claim that the president's term or year in office influences the timing of Supreme Court retirements. Furthermore, multiple studies do not show empirical support for the hypothesis that ideological or partisan congruence between the justice and the president and/or Senate is influential (see Box-Steffensmeier and Zorn 2001; Brenner 1999; Krehbiel 2007; Nelson and Ringsmuth 2009; Squire 1988; Vining, Zorn and Smelcer 2006; Yoon 2006; Zorn and Van Winkle 2000).

One study finds that the proximity of a presidential election did appear to be a consideration for justices weighing retirement. However, the influence of other external political variables, including the ideological or partisan identity of the president and Senate, are "consistently outperformed by internal ones reflecting intra-Court positioning and influence" (Peretti and Rozzi 2011, 157). While acknowledging that timing their departure "to insure an ideologically-suitable replacement may in fact be a goal of Supreme Court justices," the authors of the study assert that consideration appears "to be secondary to other objectives such as continuing to exercise power and preserving their ideological and leadership roles on the Court" (Peretti and Rozzi 2011, 159). In addition, politically strategic retirement decisions may still not succeed given intervening factors, such as the outcomes of elections and the health and longevity of the justices themselves.

It is worth noting, though, that while Peretti and Rozzi do not find substantial support for the conclusion that *external* political variables are primary factors, they do conclude that among the influencing variables is a justice's "sense of ideological mission" and "their institutional influence and leverage when writing majority opinions" (Peretti and Rozzi 2011, 157). According to this finding, "justices who are more ideologically distant from the Court median are less likely to step down, as are justices who are writing more majority opinions and thus more engaged and influential in determining the content of the Court's doctrines" (Peretti and Rozzi 2011, 155–156).

FURTHER READING

Bailey, Michael A., and Albert Yoon. 2009. "The Politics of Leaving the Court: An Exploration." Prepared for presentation at the American Political Science Association Annual Meeting, Toronto, September 2009 (unpublished manuscript).

Barnes, Robert. 2021. "With Democrats Poised to Take Over Washington, Supreme Court's Breyer Faces Renewed Calls to Retire." *Washington Post*, January 9, 2021.

Barnes, Robert. 2022. "Is Justice Breyer's Exit Politics or Pragmatism?" *Washington Post*, January 27, 2022.

Beckstrom, Darryn C. 2004. "Deciding When to Step Down: Revisiting Strategic Retirements on the U.S. Supreme Court, 1954–1994." (unpublished manuscript).

Biskupic, Joan. 2021. "Stephen Breyer Gifted the Chance for a Liberal Successor—When Will He Take It?" *CNN*, January 10, 2021.

Box-Steffensmeier, Janet M., and Christopher J. W. Zorn. 2001. "Duration Models and Proportional Hazards in Political Science." *American Journal of Political Science*, 45, no. 4: 972–988.

Brenner, Saul. 1999. "The Myth that Justices Strategically Retire." *Social Science Journal*, 36: 431–439.

Epstein, Lee, and Jeffrey A. Segal. 2005. *Advice and Consent: The Politics of Judicial Appointments*. New York: Oxford University Press.

Hagle, Timothy M. 1993. "Strategic Retirements: A Political Model of Turnover on the United States Supreme Court." *Political Behavior*, 15: 25–48.

Krehbiel, Keith. 2007. "Supreme Court Appointments as a Move-the-Median Game." *American Journal of Political Science*, 51, no. 2: 231–240.

Liptak, Adam. 2021. "Justice Breyer on Retirement and the Role of Politics at the Supreme Court." *New York Times*, August 27, 2021.

Nelson, Kjersten R., and Eve M. Ringsmuth. 2009. "Departures from the Court." *American Politics Research*, 37: 486–507.

Peretti, Terri, and Alan Rozzi. 2011. "Modern Departures from the U.S. Supreme Court: Party, Pensions, or Power." *Quinnipiac Law Review*, 30, no. 1: 131–162.

Perry, Jessica, and Christopher J. Zorn. 2008. "The Politics of Judicial Departures in the U.S. Federal Courts." April 15, 2008. https://papers.ssrn.com/sol3/papers.cfm?abstract_id=1120773 (unpublished manuscript).

Squire, Peverill. 1988. "Politics and Personal Factors in Retirement from the United States Supreme Court." *Political Behavior*, 10: 180–190.

Stolzenberg, Ross M., and James Lindgren. 2010. "Retirement and Death in Office of U.S. Supreme Court Justices." *Demography*, 47, no. 2: 269–298.

Vining, Richard L., Jr., Christopher Zorn, and Susan Navarro Smelcer. 2006. "Judicial Tenure on the U.S. Supreme Court, 1790–1868: Frustration, Resignation, and Expiration on the Bench." *Studies in American Political Development*, 20, no. 2: 198–210.

Viser, Matt, Tyler Pager, Seung Min Kim, and Robert Barnes. 2022. "Inside the Campaign to Pressure Justice Stephen Breyer to Retire." *Washington Post*, January 29, 2022.

Ward, Artemus. 2003. *Deciding to Leave: The Politics of Retirement from the United States Supreme Court*. Albany, NY: SUNY Press.

Ward, Artemus. 2018. "Justices Are Supposed to be Above Partisan Politics. They Aren't, Even in Retirement." *Los Angeles Times*, June 29, 2018.

Yoon, Albert. 2006. "Pensions, Politics, and Judicial Tenure: An Empirical Study of Federal Judges, 1869–2002." *American Law and Economics Review*, 8, no. 1: 143–180.

Zorn, Christopher J. W., and Steven R. Van Winkle. 2000. "A Competing Risks Model of Supreme Court Vacancies, 1789–1992." *Political Behavior*, 22: 145–166.

Q8. DID PRESIDENT TRUMP'S JUDICIAL APPOINTMENTS FUNDAMENTALLY RE-MAKE THE FEDERAL JUDICIARY FOR DECADES TO COME?

Answer: Yes. All presidents have influence over the composition and direction of the federal courts. But when compared to other presidents, Donald Trump's single term of office left a lasting, conservative mark on the judiciary, with three appointments to the Supreme Court, 54 to the Circuit Courts of Appeal, and 174 to the District Courts. Several factors contributed to the re-make of the judiciary, including changes to Senate rules and actions taken by Republican Senate Majority Leader Mitch McConnell, both during and prior to Trump's election in 2016.

The Facts: Presidents, in general, have substantial power to shape the federal judiciary. That power derives from a president's constitutional authority to nominate judges to the federal bench, including judges on federal district courts, appeals courts, and the Supreme Court. The president's power is amplified by the fact that federal judges have lifetime appointments. Thus, while presidents face a two-term limit restricting their time in office, judges appointed to the federal judiciary typically stay on the bench well beyond the departure of the presidents who appointed them. The younger the judges are when confirmed to the bench, the longer their influence is likely to be felt.

The president's impact on the federal judiciary can, of course, be limited by the Senate. The Constitution's stipulation that non-temporary nominations to the federal bench be confirmed by the Senate means that the president does not have unilateral power to shape the judiciary. Nominated individuals must be supported by a Senate majority to be seated. Generally speaking, when the Senate and executive branch are controlled by the same political party, a president's influence on the judiciary will likely be greater. Likewise, a president's influence on the judiciary is often weaker when the presidency and Senate are controlled by opposing political parties.

In addition, the reach of a president's influence depends on the number of vacant positions on the federal bench. Typically, vacancies occur as a result of departures from the bench (through retirement, resignation, death, or, in very rare instances, impeachment). The number of seats a president has to fill can also depend on what occurred in the previous administration. Seats unfilled by a preceding administration can compound the influence of an incoming president by providing even more judgeships to fill.

Positions can also become available when the size of the federal bench changes through acts of Congress. Article III of the Constitution authorizes Congress to determine the size of the federal bench. Hence, if Congress chooses to grow the size of the judiciary—as it did when it created 150 new federal judge positions during the presidency of Jimmy Carter—that can give a president additional leverage to shape the courts (Sherman, Freking, and Daly 2020).

These facts are applicable to all presidents and set the broad parameters and variables for an individual president's influence. In the case of Republican President Donald Trump, several variables amplified his impact on the federal courts during his term in office from January 2017 to January 2021. First, the Republican Party controlled the Senate throughout Trump's presidency. Second, and relatedly, Senate rule changes that took place first in 2013 (when Democrats controlled the Senate) and then again in 2017 (when Republicans controlled the Senate) ended the use of the filibuster in federal judicial appointments.

As detailed in Q17, since 1975 the filibuster had effectively required judicial nominations to be confirmed by a 60-vote margin rather than a simple majority of the 100-member Senate. That gave the minority party in the Senate considerable capacity to block nominations if they held at least 41 seats and stayed united. But in 2013, Senate rules changed to allow confirmation of all federal judges except Supreme Court justices by a simple majority vote rather than a supermajority. Four years later, the Senate extended that rule change to apply to Supreme Court nominations as well.

The demise of the filibuster in the context of judicial appointments now allows the majority party in the Senate to more easily confirm judicial appointments, because that party does not have to rely on support from the minority party. This important change in Senate confirmation rules facilitated rapid confirmation of Trump appointments to the federal bench.

Third, the number of vacancies available to Trump was substantially augmented as a direct result of actions taken by Republicans in the Senate during Barack Obama's presidency. Though Democrats controlled the Senate during the first six years of the Obama administration, Republicans gained control in the 2014 midterm elections. Republican Majority Leader Mitch McConnell led the 114th Congress during the final two years of Obama's second term and actively obstructed many of Obama's appointments to the federal bench.

When inaugurated in January 2017, Donald Trump inherited 88 district and 17 court of appeals vacancies left over from the Obama years, many of which were directly attributable to McConnell's prior actions (Wheeler 2018). According to a 2018 analysis by Russell Wheeler of the Brookings Institution, many of these vacancies could have been filled by Obama were it not for Republican resistance.

> The 114th Senate both confirmed far fewer judges than its recent other-party predecessors and stopped confirming them at a much earlier point. Some of the 2016 vacancies Trump inherited occurred after any confirmation clock would have stopped. Still, of the 21 circuit vacancies he's filled as of late May and others he soon will, up to seven could have had Obama appointees under pre-2015 norms. So too, up to 71 of the district vacancies he inherited and has only begun to fill could have had Obama appointees. (Wheeler 2018)

With inherited vacancies to fill, new ones that became available from 2017 through 2020, and what Wheeler described as "an accommodating, filibuster-free Senate" (Wheeler 2020), Trump's impact on the makeup of the appellate bench, including the Supreme Court, has been remarkable. Trump appointed three justices, the most since Ronald Reagan's four appointments in his two terms as president. Trump also made 54 appointments to the 13 Circuit Courts of Appeal, which amounts to 30 percent of the 179 judges who serve on those intermediate courts (Hurley 2021). By comparison, two-term presidents Barack Obama, George W. Bush, and Bill Clinton appointed, respectively, 55, 62, and 66 appeals court judges (Gramlich 2021). Trump also appointed another 174 judges to the U.S. District Courts, or roughly 25 percent of the nation's 678 district judgeships. Combined with his appointments to the Supreme Court and the Circuit Courts, 28 percent of active federal judges were Trump appointees when he left office in January 2021 (Gramlich 2021).

On this point, liberals and conservatives agree: Trump's appointments have shifted the federal bench in a decidedly conservative direction. Compare, for example, statements by Russ Feingold, president of the liberal American Constitution Society, and Mike Davis, president of the conservative Article III Project. According to Feingold, "Having such a very high number of ideologically driven young courts of appeal judges around the country not only tipped the balance on a number of these circuits but has also tipped it in a way that could last for a long time." Similarly, Davis claimed that "President Trump's biggest and most consequential accomplishment is his transformation of the federal judiciary, including the first true conservative majority on the Supreme Court in nearly a century and the appointment of a near-record number of circuit judges to the critically important federal courts of appeals" (Hurley 2021).

The sheer number of Trump appointees to the federal judiciary is telling, especially when considered in light of how they have affected the balance of particular appeals courts. One analysis noted that at the time "Trump took office, Democratic-appointed judges held majorities on nine of the 13 appeals courts. Under Trump, the 11th Circuit and two other regional appeals courts—the New York-based 2nd Circuit and the Philadelphia based 3rd Circuit—have 'flipped' to have a majority of Republican appointees" (Hurley 2021).

Because the 13 Circuit Courts of Appeal adjudicate as many as 60,000 cases each year—far surpassing the 100-plus cases handled by the Supreme Court—shifts in the ideological composition of these courts are consequential. Indeed, the "real measure of what Trump has been able to do will be revealed in countless court decisions in the years to come on abortion, guns, religious rights and a host of other culture wars issues" (Sherman, Freking, and Daly 2020).

Evidence already shows that judges appointed by Trump "are much more conservative in the areas of civil liberties/rights and labor/economic regulation than judges appointed by any previous Republican or Democrat dating back to JFK [John F. Kennedy]" (Manning, Carp, and Holmes

2020). For example, Trump appointees accounted for five of the six votes in a 6–4 decision by the full Eleventh U.S. Circuit Court of Appeals in 2020 making it more difficult for felons in Florida to regain the right to vote (Sherman, Freking, and Daly 2020).

That Trump's appointments to the appellate courts in particular are likely to have a long-lasting impact is owed, in part, to the fact that the judges he has named have been relatively young. As of January 2020, the median age of judges Trump appointed to the Circuit Courts of Appeal was 48.2. This has continued a downward trend in the age of newly installed judges from previous presidential appointments (Wheeler 2020).

The impact that Trump has had on the federal judiciary is also attributable to McConnell's efforts both during and prior to Trump's presidency. McConnell's refusal to consider Obama's appointment of Merrick Garland for a vacancy on the Supreme Court—discussed in Q5—formed a piece of a broader strategy to keep seats on the federal bench available in the event a Republican was elected president in 2016. As McConnell explained at a Federalist Society gala in 2019, "My goal . . . is to do everything we can for as long as we can to transform the federal judiciary, because everything else we do is transitory. The closest thing we will ever have an opportunity to do to have the longest impact on the country is confirming these great men and women and transforming the judiciary for as long into the future as we can" (Montgomery 2019).

FURTHER READING

Federal Judicial Center. n.d. "Caseloads: U.S. Courts of Appeals, 1892–2017." https://www.fjc.gov/history/courts/caseloads-us-courts-appeals-1892-2017

Federal Judicial Center. n.d. "Establishing a Federal Judiciary: Talking Points." https://www.fjc.gov/history/talking/establishing-federal-judiciary-talking-points

Gramlich, John. 2021. "How Trump Compares with Other Recent Presidents in Appointing Federal Judges." Pew Research Center, January 13, 2021. https://www.pewresearch.org/fact-tank/2021/01/13/how-trump-compares-with-other-recent-presidents-in-appointing-federal-judges

Hurley, Lawrence. 2021. "On Guns, Abortion and Voting Rights, Trump Leaves Lasting Mark on U.S. Judiciary." *Reuters*, January 15, 2021.

Manning, Kenneth L., Robert A. Carp, and Lisa M. Holmes. 2020. "The Decision-Making Ideology of Federal Judges Appointed by President Trump." UMass Dartmouth Working Paper.

Montgomery, David. 2019. "Conquerors of the Courts." *Washington Post Magazine*, January 2, 2019.

Sherman, Mark, Kevin Freking, and Matthew Daly. 2020. "Trump's Impact on Courts Likely to Last Long Beyond His Term." *Associated Press*, December 26, 2020. https://apnews.com/article/joe-biden-donald-trump-mitch-mcconnell-elections-judiciary-d5807340e86d05fbc78ed50fb43c1c46

Wheeler, Russell. 2018. "Senate Obstructionism Handed a Raft of Judicial Vacancies to Trump—What Has He Done with Them?" *Brookings Institution*, June 4, 2018. https://www.brookings.edu/blog/fixgov/2018/06/04/senate-obstructionism-handed-judicial-vacancies-to-trump

Wheeler, Russell. 2020. "Judicial Appointments in Trump's First Three Years: Myths and Realities." *Brookings Institution*, January 28, 2020. https://www.brookings.edu/blog/fixgov/2020/01/28/judicial-appointments-in-trumps-first-three-years-myths-and-realities

2

❖

Judicial Elections to State Courts

Electoral processes—associated, as they often are, with political campaigns, party platforms, and partisan politics—may seem unsuitable for the task of choosing judges. The judicial branch is, after all, supposed to adjudicate conflict in a manner that is free—or at least insulated—from politics and partisan pressure. Thus, a common method for selecting judges is through appointment, based on the supposition that appointment processes are less political than elections. Many states have adopted judicial selection by appointment, some using models approximating the one employed at the federal level and others giving appointment authority to the legislative branch. Several states have opted for appointment by a "merit selection" process that relies on a nominating committee to identify a slate of candidates from which a governor or the legislature can choose.

By contrast, a number of states populate their judicial benches using contested popular elections. Most of these use nonpartisan judicial elections, in which candidates are not identified by political party on the electoral ballot. Others use partisan elections. Some even use a combination of partisan and nonpartisan elections, with political parties nominating judicial candidates but party identification not included on the ballot.

Elections are also sometimes combined with judicial selection by appointment in what are known as retention elections. Unlike regular contested elections, judicial retention elections are uncontested. Used after an appointed (or sometimes regularly-elected) judge has served a set term of office, a retention election puts the judge on the ballot without an opponent and gives voters the option to keep or remove the judge from the bench.

Reliance on elections to fill judgeships on state courts has not always been common. At the time of the Founding, when the Constitution placed the selection of federal judges in the hands of the president, subject to the advice and consent of the Senate, states adopted appointment processes as well. Most gave state legislatures the power to appoint judges. Following calls for reforming judicial selection processes, popular election of some judges emerged in Georgia in 1812 and when Indiana joined the Union in 1816. Mississippi went further in 1832, opting to use elections for all state court judges.

Judicial elections became increasingly common starting in the mid-1800s and continuing through the first half of the 20th century. The push toward judicial elections grew in part out of an interest in shielding judges from politics and promoting judicial independence. Popular elections also aimed to professionalize and build public respect for state judiciaries, which had been seen as subject to political cronyism.

In the modern era, and especially since the 1980s, judicial elections have faced mounting criticism. Though they remain popular among voters, legal professionals and a growing chorus of reformers urge the adoption of merit selection processes or, at least, nonpartisan elections. Calls for reform owe, in part, to claims that judicial elections, especially partisan ones, promote politicization, interfere with judicial independence, and undermine the legitimacy of the courts. Whether these types of claims are warranted is the subject of the questions taken up in this chapter.

Q9. HAVE CONTESTED JUDICIAL ELECTIONS BECOME MORE POLITICAL OVER RECENT DECADES?

Answer: Yes. Leaving aside judicial retention elections (but see Q11), most analysts find growing politicization of regular contested elections. However, a few recent studies suggest that the changes are not as widespread as commonly thought and may be heavily concentrated in certain states.

The Facts: In the late 1980s, Roy Schotland, Georgetown law professor and campaign finance expert, famously remarked that judicial campaigns are becoming "noisier, nastier, and costlier" (Woodbury 1988). With respect to regular contested election campaigns for state courts, this trend has continued. Partisanship in regular judicial elections also appears to be on the rise, even in contests that are nominally nonpartisan. Researchers have identified a number of factors explaining the growing politicization and partisanship of judicial elections.

Prior to the 1980s, most elections of state judges had been "formally or effectively uncontested" events (Hojnacki and Baum 1992, 921). Other scholars describe earlier iterations of judicial elections as "low-key affairs, conducted with civility and dignity" (Webster 1995, 19). Moreover, contested elections were not typically issue-based, nor did they commonly generate much in the way of campaign spending or media coverage.

This state of affairs, however, showed early signs of erosion in Los Angeles in 1978, "when a group of deputy district attorneys offered to support any candidate who would run against any unopposed incumbent trial judge, producing a record number of contests and defeated judges. Similarly, throughout the 1980s, battles over tort law in Texas produced 'unprecedentedly costly, heated races' for its supreme court" (Kang and Shepherd 2011, 81). As a result, a "new style" of judicial elections marked by higher spending, campaign activity, media attention, and policy orientation started becoming more commonplace in the 1980s (Hojnacki and Baum 1992, 922).

According to most research, practices once characteristic of a small minority of elections grew far more common over the next three decades. As one analysis concluded in 2008, "costly and corrosive court campaigns have fast become the new norm" (Brandenburg and Schotland 2008, 1231). Elections of judges to the highest courts of states turned "increasingly contested, competitive, and controversial" in the 1990s, according to political scientist Chris Bonneau (Bonneau 2007a, 68). By 2008, according to one account, state supreme court elections in particular transformed into a type of new normal: "Across America, attorneys, partisans, and special interests with cases in court are pouring millions into judicial contests, mostly for high courts but increasingly into appellate and even district court contests. Broadcast television ads seek to push wedge-issue politics into the courts of law. Aggressive questionnaires from special interest groups seek to pressure judges to take stands on controversial issues" (Brandenburg and Schotland 2008, 1231).

According to professors Brandice Canes-Wrone and Tom S. Clark, this "new style" of political campaigning for judgeships

> significantly altered the political landscape in which judicial elections take place: interest groups now publicize judicial candidates' positions and decisions in "attack ads" and other sorts of advertising, the media covers these campaigns more heavily, and judges themselves are more apt to publicize their records and policy positions.

Compounding these trends is an influx of money that has enabled campaigns to use advertisements and travel to publicize candidates' views and records. In short, judicial campaigns have become more issue based and therefore more similar to legislative or executive campaigns. (Canes-Wrone and Clark 2009, 31)

Political scientist Matthew J. Streb concurs with this depiction: "Judicial elections have changed immensely, perhaps more so than elections for any other office. Once compared to playing a game of checkers by mail, many of today's judicial races are as rough and tumble as any congressional election" (Streb 2007b, 2). Among the changes Streb highlights are increasing activity of interest groups and political parties, "massive amounts of money that are flooding campaigns," and rule changes allowing judicial candidates to announce their views on legal and political issues (Streb 2007b, 2).

Summarizing the findings of multiple studies, legal scholars Michael S. Kang and Joanna M. Shepherd note that since the 1980s, "judicial elections have become increasingly politicized, more competitive, and have created new electoral pressures for judges. By 2000, 75% of nonpartisan elections were contested, up from 44% in 1990. Similarly, a staggering 95% of partisan elections were contested in 2000, up from 68% in 1990" (Kang and Shepherd 2011, 81).

Kang and Shepherd also emphasize the remarkable impact of increasing competition on incumbency of state supreme court judges. In particular, they found substantially higher rates of incumbents losing elections. "In 1980, roughly 4% of incumbents were defeated in nonpartisan elections, but in 2000, the loss rate for incumbents seeking reelection had doubled to 8%. In partisan elections, only a quarter of incumbents were defeated in 1980, but in 2000, this loss rate had also doubled to nearly 50%. By comparison, the loss rate for incumbent judges is *higher* than the average rate at which incumbents lose reelection bids for state legislatures, the U.S. Senate, and the House of Representatives" (Kang and Shepherd 2011, 82).

Dramatic changes in campaign spending are also evident in judicial elections. Bonneau analyzed campaign spending from 1990 to 2004 by all candidates in state supreme court elections, except for those in retention elections. The research showed that "[t]he average contested race in 1990 (all elections) involved $364,348 in spending, while a similar race in 2004 cost $892,755" (Bonneau 2007b, 63). Bonneau confirmed that inflation does not account for the significant upward trend.

Researchers have also found evidence that campaign fundraising in state high court elections has changed. "The breakthrough year for big-money court campaigns was 2000, when Supreme Court candidates raised a record $45.6 million—a 61 percent increase over the previous election cycle" (Brandenburg and Schotland 2008, 1237). Another study found that between 2000 and 2007, more than $168 million in campaign contributions were made in state supreme court elections, more than twice the amount contributed during the 1990s (Kang and Shepherd 2011, 71). Finally, a detailed 2010 report of state supreme court elections by the Brennan Center for Justice states that campaign fundraising "more than doubled, from $83.3 million in 1990–1999 to $206.9 million in 2000–2009. Three of the last five Supreme Court election cycles topped $45 million. All but two of the 22 states with contestable Supreme Court elections had their costliest-ever contests in the 2000–2009 decade" (Sample et al. 2010, 1).

Among the most commonly cited indications of the new style of judicial elections is the growth of television campaign ads. According to several studies, televised ads in judicial elections were not commonplace prior to the beginning of the 21st century. Since then, however, they have become "the norm in contested elections across the nation" and "now play a central role in many judicial elections" (Hall 2014, 2).

Again, the 2000 election cycle was pivotal in this development, with political parties and interest groups spending "at least $10–$16 million more on independent TV ads" over the previous election cycle (Brandenburg and Schotland 2008, 1237). And from 2000 through 2009, "an estimated $93.6 million was spent on air time for high court candidate TV ads, including an estimated $6.6 million spent in the unusually costly odd-year elections in 2007" (Sample, Hall, and Casey 2010, 53). Moreover, research by political scientist Herbert Kritzer confirms an increase in television advertising, jumping from approximately one-third of contested state supreme court elections in the 2000 elections to just under two-thirds of 2012 elections. Kritzer notes, however, that the percent of attack ads remained relatively constant, at or below 20 percent of overall television campaign spots (Kritzer 2015, 165–166).

Analysts also cite the sources of campaign funding as evidence of politicization, with business interests and lawyers footing much of the bill. By one account published in 2008, most of the contributions come from "attorneys and political interests who view campaign spending as a litigation investment. Of the $157 million raised by [supreme court] judges from 1999 to 2006, 35 percent came from businesses and business groups, another 26 percent from attorneys (plaintiff and defense), 11 percent from political parties, and seven percent from the candidates themselves" (Brandenburg and Schotland 2008, 1238). Once again, the turn of the 21st century appears pivotal. "In 2000, the U.S. Chamber of Commerce and affiliated organizations devoted about $10 million in soft money to state supreme court elections in Michigan, Mississippi, and Ohio" (Kritzer 2015, 133). The trend of campaign contributions from business groups continued. "For example, in the 2005–2006 election cycle, business groups directly contributed over $15 million to candidates, or 44% of the total and twice the amount contributed by the second-largest contributing interest group" (Kang and Shepherd 2011, 73).

Organized business interests have also become a dominant player in producing campaign ads, typically on behalf of conservative candidates seen as friendly to corporations. For example, the U.S. Chamber of Commerce's decision to increase spending in the 2000 judicial election cycle "combined with advertising by groups opposed to tort reform represented an early volley of the televised 'issue ads' that have come to be a factor in hard-fought state supreme court elections" (Kritzer 2015, 133). That trend persisted. "In 2006 alone, over $16 million was spent on TV ads in states with contested supreme court campaigns. Business groups were responsible for more than 85% of the special interest ads and 90% of the advertising spending that year" (Kang and Shepherd 2011, 73).

Those who suggest that judicial elections have undergone dramatic change offer multiple explanations for these developments. Legal scholars Lawrence Baum, David Klein, and Matthew Streb suggest that "[o]rganized interests began to realize that it was much more efficient to try to influence a group of five, seven, or nine justices than it was to persuade a much larger Congress or state legislature to support their causes" (Baum, Klein, and Streb 2017, 21). Others identify a mix of factors, such as "[c]hanges in elections generally (like the spread of television in major races, and consultants in many), combined with increased public awareness of the impact of court decisions, growing interest-group focus on courts and their make-up, and unusual events in particular states" (Brandenburg and Schotland 2008, 1236).

One key explanation suggested by judicial election specialists is the transformation surrounding "announce clauses." A component of codes of judicial conduct, announce clauses bar judicial candidates from announcing their views "on disputed legal or political issues" (*Republican Party of Minnesota v. White* 2002, 768). The use of these clauses was premised on the idea that judges and judicial candidates should avoid pronouncing their positions on issues because cases on those issues might later come before the judge. But in *Republican Party of Minnesota v. White* (2002), the U.S. Supreme Court declared Minnesota's announce clause unconstitutional. The Court's 5–4 decision ruled that the restriction on judicial candidates violates the First Amendment guarantee of free speech (*Republican Party of Minnesota v. White* 2002, 768). As a result of that holding, "judges, who at one time were forbidden from stating their positions on important political and legal issues, increasingly can and do run on these positions" (Canes-Wrone and Clark 2009, 38). Thus, although supreme court campaigns in some states had been "political" in tone prior to the Court's ruling, "*White* changed the electoral game by opening the door in all states to issue-based discourse, including attack advertising that can be part of aggressive, well-financed campaigns" (Hall 2014, 2).

Other experts emphasize the "increasing involvement of courts, particularly in recent decades, in addressing issues with far-reaching policy consequences" (American Bar Association Commission on the 21st Century Judiciary 2003, 17). This change stems from greater awareness of the role state courts—especially state supreme courts—can play in influencing public policy. Another probable factor driving the rise of interest-group participation in judicial campaigns is "contagion: when some groups seemed to achieve success in defeating judges, other groups on the same side of interest-group conflicts picked up the idea, and groups on the opposing side mobilized to counteract the influence they observed. This development has concentrated on state supreme courts, reflecting the relatively high stakes that groups perceive in decisions of the highest state courts and the more visible activism of state supreme courts since the 1970s" (Baum 2003, 33).

According to the ABA, among the multiple contributing factors that help explain the changes in judicial elections is the expanding docket of cases related to civil rights in America's courts. However, "increased judicial involvement with policy-laden social and political issues . . . has embraced a wide range of subjects, from environmental protection, to the rights of criminal defendants, abortion, political apportionment, education funding, and the liability of entire industries for toxic torts" (American Bar Association Commission on the 21st Century Judiciary 2003, 17).

While the commonly held view is one of dramatic changes in state judicial elections, a few researchers paint a somewhat different picture. Political scientist Melinda Gann Hall, for example, suggests that "extensive historical data show that state supreme court elections (partisan and nonpartisan) have been competitive by the standards of most visible elections in the United States during the entire post-World War II period" (Hall 2016, 437). Acknowledging that changes have occurred in judicial campaigns over recent years, she also points out that "contestation rates, defeat rates, and the vote shares of incumbents have been remarkably stable since the late 1940s, with the exception of the partisan transformation of the American South starting in the 1980s" (Hall 2016, 437).

Like Hall, political scientist Herbert Kritzer finds a considerable degree of stability over time when it comes to contestation and competitiveness in judicial elections. In particular, "there has been relatively little net change since the 1940s in terms of whether incumbents in state supreme court elections face competition or defeat, or whether open elections involve highly competitive races" (Kritzer 2015, 129). With the exception of partisan elections in southern states, where change did occur, Kritzer reports a story of relative stability. Political scientist Chris Bonneau praises Kritzer's findings, describing them as "an important corrective to the conventional (popular and scholarly) wisdom, which assumes that state supreme court elections became much different in the 1990s. Kritzer convincingly shows that this is not true" (Bonneau 2016, 235).

Still, the prevailing view is that, at the very least, judicial elections have become decidedly more issue-based, covering controversial topics like criminal justice, death penalty, tort reform, abortion, business regulation, and more. As Canes-Wrone and Clark argue, "interconnected changes to judicial contests—the increased involvement of interest groups, growth in political advertising, greater importance of campaign spending, and increased media scrutiny—have increased the electoral significance of judges' records on hot-button issues" (Canes-Wrone and Clark 2009, 33).

The role of interest groups in this politicization process is prominent. "Over the past twenty years, interest groups, many with national affiliations, like the Chamber of Commerce, have actively injected themselves into contested state supreme court elections," observes one analysis. "The playbook here is well known and proven: identify a state where control of the court could be at stake, identify a decision an incumbent has made that could resonate with voters (often criminal cases where a 'criminal goes free'), and run attack ads" (Clopton and Peters 2013, 340).

Worth noting is that among the chorus of those who find considerable increases in the politicization of judicial elections, there is not widespread agreement that this is a problem. To be sure, many observers argue that politicization of elections is detrimental to the independence and legitimacy of the courts, and, in turn, public faith in the American legal system. Others who say elections have become more political and politicized do not necessarily view this as problematic. They argue, instead, that there is insufficient evidence of harm to judicial independence or legitimacy, and, to the contrary, that benefits to voter information and participation accrue as a result of partisan judicial elections. In short, even if we grant that state judicial elections have become increasingly politicized, that does not automatically answer whether negative impacts on the judiciary and judicial independence ensue. Debates over that separate question are addressed in Q12 and Q13.

FURTHER READING

American Bar Association Commission on the 21st Century Judiciary. 2003. *Justice in Jeopardy.* American Bar Association. https://www .opensocietyfoundations.org/publications/justice-jeopardy-report -american-bar-assocation-commission-21st-century-judiciary

Baum, Lawrence. 2003. "Judicial Elections and Judicial Independence: The Voter's Perspective." *Ohio State Law Journal*, 64, no. 1: 13–42.

Baum, Lawrence. 2017. "Supreme Court Elections: How Much They Have Changed, Why They Changed, and What Difference It Makes." *Law & Social Inquiry*, 42, no. 3: 900–923.

Baum, Lawrence, David E. Klein, and Matthew J. Streb. 2017. *The Battle for the Court: Interest Groups, Judicial Elections, and Public Policy.* Charlottesville, VA: University of Virginia Press.

Bonneau, Chris W. 2007a. "Campaign Fundraising in State Supreme Court Elections." *Social Science Quarterly*, 88, no. 1: 68–85.

Bonneau, Chris W. 2007b. "The Dynamics of Campaign Spending in State Supreme Court Elections." In *Running for Judge: The Rising Political, Financial, and Legal Stakes of Judicial Elections*, ed. Matthew J. Streb, 59–72. New York: NYU Press.

Bonneau, Chris W. 2016. Review of *Justices on the Ballot: Continuity and Change in State Supreme Court Elections*, by Kritzer, Herbert M. *Perspectives on Politics*, 14, no. 1: 235–236.

Brandenburg, Bert, and Roy A. Schotland. 2008. "Justice in Peril: The Endangered Balance Between Impartial Courts and Judicial Election Campaigns." *Georgetown Journal of Legal Ethics*, 21, no. 4: 1229–1258.

Canes-Wrone, Brandice, and Tom S. Clark. 2009. "Judicial Independence and Nonpartisan Elections." *Wisconsin Law Review*, 2009, no. 1: 21–66.

Clopton, Andrew J., and C. Scott Peters. 2013. "Justice Denied: A County-Level Analysis of the 2010 Iowa Supreme Court Retention Election." *Justice System Journal*, 34, no. 3: 321–344.

Hall, Melinda Gann. 2014. *Attacking Judges: How Campaign Advertising Influences State Supreme Court Elections.* Stanford, CA: Stanford University Press.

Hall, Melinda Gann. 2016. "Partisanship, Interest Groups, and Attack Advertising in the Post-*White* Era, or Why Nonpartisan Judicial Elections Really Do Stink." *Journal of Law & Politics*, 31, no. 4: 429–456.

Hojnacki, Marie, and Lawrence Baum. 1992. "'New-Style' Judicial Campaigns and the Voters: Economic Issues and Union Members in Ohio." *Western Political Quarterly*, 45, no. 4: 921–948.

Kang, Michael S., and Joanna M. Shepherd. 2011. "The Partisan Price of Justice: An Empirical Analysis of Campaign Contributions and Judicial Decisions." *New York University Law Review*, 86, no. 1: 69–130.

Kritzer, Herbert M. 2015. *Justices on the Ballot: Continuity and Change in State Supreme Court Elections*. New York: Cambridge University Press.

Republican Party of Minnesota v. White, 536 U.S. 765 (2002).

Sample, James J., Charles Hall, and Linda Casey. 2010. "The New Politics of Judicial Elections." *Judicature*, 94, no. 2: 50–58.

Sample, James, Adam Skaggs, Jonathan Blitzer, and Linda Casey. 2010. "The New Politics of Judicial Elections 2000–2009: Decade of Change." Brennan Center for Justice. https://www.brennancenter.org/sites/default/files/legacy/JAS-NPJE-Decade-ONLINE.pdf

Shepherd, Joanna M. 2013. *Justice at Risk: An Empirical Analysis of Campaign Contributions and Judicial Decisions*. American Constitution Society for Law and Policy. https://www.acslaw.org/analysis/reports/justice-at-risk

Streb, Matthew J. 2007a. "Partisan Involvement in Partisan and Nonpartisan Trial Court Elections." In *Running for Judge: The Rising Political, Financial, and Legal Stakes of Judicial Elections*, ed. Matthew J. Streb, 96–114. New York: NYU Press.

Streb, Matthew J. 2007b. "The Study of Judicial Elections." In *Running for Judge: The Rising Political, Financial, and Legal Stakes of Judicial Elections*, ed. Matthew J. Streb, 1–14. New York: NYU Press.

Webster, Peter D. 1995. "Selection and Retention of Judges: Is There One Best Method?" *Florida State University Law Review*, 23, no. 1: 1–42.

Woodbury, Richard. 1988. "Is Texas Justice for Sale?" *TIME*, January 11, 1988.

Q10. ARE NONPARTISAN JUDICIAL ELECTIONS LESS POLITICAL THAN PARTISAN JUDICIAL ELECTIONS?

Answer: To some extent, yes, though perhaps not as much as might be expected.

The Facts: Competing views about whether and how to choose judges have produced a variety of approaches to judicial selection among the various states. Indeed, "[t]here are nearly as many different rules for selecting judges as there are states. Each state determines how their judges will be initially selected, the length of the judges' terms, and whether they will be reappointed or reelected, which leads to many different variations" (Streb 2007b, 6). What's more, some states employ different methods of judicial selection for different types of judges.

As of January 2022, the large majority of states relied on election in some form or other for at least some courts. Only seven states staffed their benches without any use of judicial elections. With respect to judges on state supreme courts, 13 opt for nonpartisan elections, eight rely on partisan elections, and Michigan combines the two, using partisan methods to select candidates followed by a nonpartisan general election. Other states use a combination of appointment and election for their high courts, with retention elections (sometimes uncontested) deployed following a term of office based on appointment.

Advocates of judicial elections emphasize the accountability theoretically afforded by giving voters a direct voice in picking judges. However, there is significant debate over whether judicial elections should be partisan or nonpartisan. On one side, growing criticism in recent decades over using partisan elections for judges has contributed to a move away from this method, with states adopting nonpartisan elections or appointment processes instead. In fact, "partisan elections have transitioned in recent decades from being the most popular method of selecting state supreme court justices (in nineteen states in 1960) to among the least utilized (in six states in 2016) as the result of intentional institutional reengineering by the judicial reform community" (Hall 2016, 431).

Some political science researchers, however, argue that the evidence does not warrant the move away from partisan elections. According to political scientist Melinda Gann Hall, "[o]n this issue, the chasm between political science scholars and the legal community is seemingly unbridgeable. Certainly not all political scientists favor electing state court judges, but a notable consensus has emerged among state judicial politics scholars that if judicial elections are to be held, the ballots should be partisan in format. This conclusion is grounded in a sizeable body of empirical scholarship over the past few decades demonstrating how partisan and nonpartisan elections actually work in practice. Much of this work stands in sharp contradistinction to the promises of judicial reform" (Hall 2016, 433).

Among the arguments against using partisan elections for the bench is that they politicize the electoral process. Partisan elections would seem, by definition, to be more partisan than nonpartisan elections, if only by the mere fact of the presence of party identification. The American Bar Association's (ABA's) Commission on the 21st Century Judiciary explains the concern this way: "partisan elections make party affiliation the single most salient feature of a judge's candidacy, by including it as the only information about the candidates on the ballot itself. Some states go even further by enabling voters to pull a single-party lever for all candidates in all branches of government, including judges" (American Bar Association Commission on the 21st Century Judiciary 2003, 102).

The problem, though, is that listing the party affiliations of candidates for judgeships can "further blur, if not obliterate the distinction between judges and other elected officials in the public's mind, by conveying the impression that the decision-making of judges, like that of legislators and governors, is driven by allegiance to party, rather than to law," states the American Bar Association. "It is therefore unsurprising that many of the most extreme examples of independence-threatening election related behavior have occurred in states that select their judges in either openly partisan elections, or elections that are non-partisan in name only" (American Bar Association Commission on the 21st Century Judiciary 2003, 102).

Some studies provide evidence for the claim that partisan judicial elections become more mired in politics than their nonpartisan counterparts. For example, political scientist Matthew J. Streb compared political party involvement in partisan and nonpartisan judicial elections using surveys of county party chairs. Focusing on state trial court elections and including 25 states in his analysis, Streb found "in every question examined, party organizations whose trial-court candidates ran in partisan elections were significantly more active than their counterparts whose candidates ran in nonpartisan races" (Streb 2007a, 102). This finding held across a wide range of activities.

Streb, however, also identified a considerable degree of political party involvement even in nonpartisan judicial elections. For instance, 67 percent of country party chairs reported "always," "most of the time," or "sometimes" arranging fundraisers for and contributing money to judicial candidates running in partisan elections. By comparison, 42 percent reported the same with respect to judicial candidates running in nonpartisan elections (Streb 2007a, 104–105). Similarly, 71 percent of party chairs reported endorsing candidates at least sometimes in partisan elections, whereas 52 percent reported doing so in nonpartisan elections (Streb 2007a, 108–109). These findings led Streb to conclude that "[w]hile parties are not equally active in all aspects of nonpartisan judicial elections (and not necessarily active in every election cycle), they seem to be especially important in terms of GOTV [get-out-the-vote] efforts and increasing name recognition, candidate recruitment, candidate endorsements, coordinating campaigns with candidates, and even raising and contributing money" (Streb 2007a, 102). Overall, his findings support the claim that partisan elections are, indeed, more partisan.

Other empirical research shows differences in the role money plays between partisan and nonpartisan judicial elections. For instance, in a 2007 analysis of state supreme court elections, political scientist Chris Bonneau found different levels of campaign spending. Excluding retention elections for judges, in "every election from 1990 to 2004, partisan elections were more expensive, on average, than nonpartisan elections. Indeed, in most years, partisan elections are *much* more expensive than their nonpartisan counterparts. Over the fifteen-year period examined here, contested partisan elections average spending of $885,177, while nonpartisan elections average $549,160" (Bonneau 2007, 63–64).

A study by political scientist Brent Boyea focused on individual campaign contributions made in state supreme court campaigns from 2000 through 2012, and found notable differences between partisan and nonpartisan elections. "The results suggest that contributors respond very differently to candidates seeking positions in professionalized courts according to whether the laws of a state allow explicit partisan information about candidates. Unlike contributions in states with nonpartisan systems, increased office status and authority to dictate the judicial agenda lead to larger contributions where states allow explicit partisan signals in elections" (Boyea 2017, 243).

Although their studies uncovered varying levels of campaign spending and campaign contributions, Bonneau and Boyea do not interpret these findings as necessarily harmful. Others, though, suggest more deleterious effects associated with the influence of campaign contributions from wealthy donors and organized interests. Indeed, as discussed further in Q12 and Q13, some evidence shows that judges elected in partisan contests are "more likely to decide in favor of business interests as the amount of campaign contributions received from those interests increases" (Kang and Shepherd 2011, 69).

Using data from all U.S. states, legal scholars Michael S. Kang and Joanna M. Shepherd showed a statistically significant relationship between campaign contributions and judicial decisions favoring the interests of those contributors in states with partisan judicial elections. That relationship does not exist, however, in states using judicial appointments or nonpartisan elections. Kang and Shepherd characterize the finding as "surprising because judges who run in nonpartisan elections need campaign money much like judges who run in partisan elections" (Kang and Shepherd 2011, 129). They also claim that "campaign money has a stronger connection to judicial decisions in states with partisan judicial elections because of the special brokering role that parties play in those states' judicial elections. Parties exercise discretion in candidate selection, connect judicial candidates with campaign contributors, and apply discipline to judicial candidates to a greater degree in states with partisan elections" (Kang and Shepherd 2011, 129).

By contrast, a line of recent research from political scientists suggests that parties make a difference, though not necessarily in a way that heightens polarization and partisanship. Though intuition might suggest that partisan cues in judicial elections would increase partisanship, the opposite may be true. Proponents of this argument claim that party identification communicates information to voters and serves as a basis to choose among candidates even when voters lack substantial information about the candidates themselves. Conversely, without partisan identification to delineate the competitors in electoral races, judicial candidates may need other ways of communicating with voters. That, in turn, can lead judicial candidates to campaign in ways that focus on issues, including hot-button and highly politicized topics. In other words, issue-based campaigning may be heightened in order to fill the void created by the lack of partisan cues, leading to greater politicization, polarization, and partisan division.

Within this line of analysis, researchers also challenge "the conventional wisdom that 'judges not identified by party will escape the ebb and flow of partisan tides'" (Hall 2016, 434). In so doing, researchers identify multiple potential indicators signaling the partisan character of nonpartisan judicial elections. Hall highlights empirical results showing that "the vote shares of supreme court candidates in nonpartisan elections closely correspond to patterns of state partisan competition and retrospective voting on the issue of violent crime. Similarly, county-level results in nonpartisan supreme court elections significantly track partisan voting patterns in gubernatorial elections. Finally, voters' partisan affiliations are still excellent predictors of their candidate choices in nonpartisan elections" (Hall 2016, 434).

Hall herself is among the most prominent researchers to counter the conventional wisdom that partisan elections are likely to be more partisan. Hall's 2016 study of televised campaign advertising, which examined all contested partisan and nonpartisan state supreme court elections from 2002 through 2008, is illustrative. On a race-by-race basis, Hall demonstrated a greater likelihood of attack ads in nonpartisan elections. In addition, she did not find organized interest groups sponsoring more attack ads in partisan as compared to nonpartisan elections. While interest groups sponsor negative ads, "their biggest relative influence has been in nonpartisan elections in which justices are seeking reelection" (Hall 2016, 452).

Finally, Hall found that "attack advertising takes a toll on justices seeking reelection only in nonpartisan elections" (Hall 2016, 452). That is, when incumbents who seek reelection face attack ads, their likelihood of reelection declines only in nonpartisan elections. Why might this be? "Partisan ballots shield incumbents from idiosyncratic forces, including attack ads, and make it easy for most citizens to select among candidates. Removing partisan labels significantly reduces the information available to voters while exposing incumbents to external threats, including attack ads. These disparaging messages then fill the information void and filter their way to the ballot box" (Hall 2016, 451). In other words, according to Hall, "[t]he damaging effects of attack advertising seem much more likely in relatively low-information elections using nonpartisan ballots than in the nation's most visible and salient elections" (Hall 2016, 451).

In addition to Hall's work, research by professors Brandice Canes-Wrone and Tom S. Clark counters the conventional wisdom about nonpartisan elections. Canes-Wrone and Clark found greater responsiveness to public opinion among state supreme court judges who face nonpartisan elections than those who face partisan ones. In particular, analyzing abortion-related cases from 1980 through 2006 in states with partisan or nonpartisan elections, they determined that "public opinion has a larger effect on judges facing nonpartisan elections than judges facing partisan ones." In the absence of partisan cues, "interest groups and others can more easily shape voters' perceptions of a judge by publicizing isolated rulings" (Canes-Wrone and Clark 2009, 25).

There is, in sum, a line of empirical research concluding that "nonpartisan elections are decidedly not immune to partisanship in multiple forms, the absence of the partisan ballot cue notwithstanding" (Hall 2016, 434). Furthermore, according to this line of research, "nonpartisan elections have only heightened the impact of some of the most pernicious aspects of modern campaign politics on state judiciaries and the justices seeking reelection" (Hall 2016, 432).

Debate thus continues over the degree of difference between partisan and nonpartisan judicial elections. Worth emphasizing, however, is one point of commonality that emerges even in the divergence: the presence and influence of party politics exists to some extent whether judicial elections are formally partisan or nonpartisan.

FURTHER READING

American Bar Association Commission on the 21st Century Judiciary. 2003. *Justice in Jeopardy*. American Bar Association. https://www .opensocietyfoundations.org/publications/justice-jeopardy-report -american-bar-assocation-commission-21st-century-judiciary

BallotPedia. 2022. "Judicial Election Methods by State." *Ballotpedia.* https://ballotpedia.org/Judicial_election_methods_by_state

Bonneau, Chris W. 2007. "The Dynamics of Campaign Spending in State Supreme Court Elections." In *Running for Judge: The Rising Political, Financial, and Legal Stakes of Judicial Elections,* ed. Matthew J. Streb, 59–72. New York: NYU Press.

Boyea, Brent D. 2017. "Individual Contributions to State Supreme Court Campaigns: Context and the Impact of Institutional Design." *State Politics & Policy Quarterly,* 17, no. 3: 227–250.

Canes-Wrone, Brandice, and Tom S. Clark. 2009. "Judicial Independence and Nonpartisan Elections." *Wisconsin Law Review,* 2009, no. 1: 21–66.

Hall, Melinda Gann. 2016. "Partisanship, Interest Groups, and Attack Advertising in the Post-*White* Era, or Why Nonpartisan Judicial Elections Really Do Stink." *Journal of Law & Politics,* 31, no. 4: 429–456.

Kang, Michael S., and Joanna M. Shepherd. 2011. "The Partisan Price of Justice: An Empirical Analysis of Campaign Contributions and Judicial Decisions." *New York University Law Review,* 86, no. 1: 69–130.

Streb, Matthew J. 2007a. "Partisan Involvement in Partisan and Nonpartisan Trial Court Elections." In *Running for Judge: The Rising Political, Financial, and Legal Stakes of Judicial Elections,* ed. Matthew J. Streb, 96–114. New York: NYU Press.

Streb, Matthew J. 2007b. "The Study of Judicial Elections." In *Running for Judge: The Rising Political, Financial, and Legal Stakes of Judicial Elections,* ed. Matthew J. Streb, 1–14. New York: NYU Press.

Q11. HAS POLITICIZATION OF JUDICIAL RETENTION ELECTIONS INCREASED?

Answer: Yes. Retention elections, designed to balance judicial independence and judicial accountability, have become increasingly contentious and overtly partisan in recent years. This is not a completely new phenomenon, and whether it will be sustained into the future remains to be seen. But the past two decades, especially in the 2010 election cycle, demonstrate how retention elections can inspire the types of campaign spending and attack advertising that have come to characterize regular competitive elections.

The Facts: A judicial retention election is an uncontested election used to decide whether or not an incumbent judge will continue to serve. Unlike regular contested judicial elections, the incumbent judge in a retention election does not face an opponent. Instead, the voter is asked to answer yes or no to whether the sitting judge should be retained for an additional term of office. Judges retain their seats if they receive a certain percentage of voters saying yes. The percentage of votes needed to retain the seat is typically a simple majority, but a few states require a higher percentage—57 percent and 60 percent in New Mexico and Illinois, respectively (Kritzer 2015, 205). Judges facing retention elections typically served their first term on the bench based on an appointment under a merit selection system. A few states adopt a model using contested partisan or nonpartisan elections for a judge's initial term of office and retention elections for subsequent terms.

As discussed in Q9, regular judicial elections, by most accounts, have entered a period of increased politicization over the past several decades. Because retention elections are uncontested, one might expect them to be less vulnerable to politicization. Indeed, advocates of retention elections often tout their use based on the idea that they provide a balance between judicial accountability and independence. Voters in retention elections have a way to check judges and remove them from the bench, thereby promoting judicial accountability. At the same time, the uncontested nature of these elections offers, at least in theory, a measure of judicial independence and insulation from the turbulence of contested electoral campaigns.

Have judicial retention elections, like their contested counterparts, been marked by rising politicization and partisanship? Are judges who stand for reelection in retention elections facing more politically based attacks? The consensus answer on both of these questions is yes. Though patterns vary across states and over different election cycles, most researchers agree that politicization and partisanship have steadily risen since the early 2000s. What were once "sleepy judicial retention elections have been turned into expensive partisan slugfests, as single-issue interest groups and political parties have subjected judges to the kind of rough-and-tumble treatment traditionally reserved [for] ordinary political candidates" (Bybee and Stonecash 2005).

Generally speaking, judicial retention elections have traditionally not attracted a lot of notice. One 2015 study, for example, found that of the 736 retention elections for state supreme courts held across the country from 1936 through 2013, voters removed only 11 sitting justices—1.5 percent of the total (Kritzer 2015, 203). Judges sitting on lower courts who faced retention elections had an even lower chance of being removed from the bench (Aspin 2011, 225; Kritzer 2015, 203).

Since 2010, though, a growing number of retention elections have been marked by increases in interest-group involvement, issue orientation, spending, partisanship, and television advertising—including attack ads. As one analysis puts it, retention elections "have become well-funded, hard-fought, politicized contests featuring increasingly strident partisan and special-interest attacks by those seeking to shape courts to their liking" (Pariente and Robinson 2016, 1530–1531).

The 2010 midterm elections produced a watershed moment. "Although only $2 million was spent on advertising in retention elections in the decade leading up to the 2010 midterm elections, $3 million was spent on state judicial-retention election advertising that year alone" (Pariente and Robinson 2016, 1535). Political scientist David Hughes explained the dramatic change: "[B]etween 2002 and 2009, 93 percent of incumbents on state courts of last resort spent no money whatsoever on their retention campaigns. Ninety-eight percent of all such elections had no television advertising affiliated with them. And 95 percent of all justices were unopposed by outside interests such as political action committees" (Hughes 2019a). But between 2010 and 2014, 35 percent of all justices on state high courts faced challenges to their retention. "Over one-quarter of these elections featured television advertising, thousands of which attacked justices in negative ads. And incumbents, looking to stave off the damage caused by these attacks, increased their campaign spending by over 400 percent compared to the previous decade" (Hughes 2019a).

That rise in campaign expenditures resulted from state supreme court retention candidates spending, on average, nearly $57,000, between 2010 and 2014. Over that same period, state supreme court retention campaigns became increasingly visible on television, with the average election attracting approximately 400 television advertisements either for or against the judge seeking retention (with attack ads accounting for about 30 percent of the total). By contrast, the average judicial retention election from 2002 to 2009 only had seven television advertisements (Hughes 2019b, 133).

What changed in 2010? Justices in multiple states, including Alaska, Colorado, Florida, Iowa, and Kansas, "all faced opposition by special-interest groups claiming to seek removal of 'activist' judges based on opinions they disagreed with rather than on the judges' qualifications" (Pariente and Robinson 2016, 1534–1535). This process played out, for instance, in Alaska, with a judge targeted over abortion rights, and in Colorado, with three justices targeted largely over their votes on punitive tort awards. "[N]ot only were judges facing greater opposition during this period, [but] that opposition was also better funded and coordinated, oftentimes by well-heeled outside interest groups" (Hughes 2019b, 134). Opposition came from state Republican parties, as well as conservative political action committees (PACs) and groups attached to the GOP-affiliated Tea

Party movement. In some cases, though not all, the judges facing attacks responded with their own campaigns and advertisements.

The 2010 retention elections for three state supreme court justices in Iowa are often held up as symbolic of the transformation of what were once relatively sleepy, low-key campaigns. Unlike opposition leveled against jurists in Alaska, Colorado, Florida, Illinois, and Kansas, the campaigns against the three Iowa justices resulted in their removal in what Hughes described as "the perfect storm of voter backlash, Tea Party activism, and special interest participation" (Hughes 2019b, 134).

In particular, the opposition campaigns stood out as issue-driven, targeting the supreme court justices for their votes in *Varnum v. Brien* (2009), which overturned Iowa's ban on same-sex marriage. Special-interest groups from outside Iowa dominated opposition campaign expenditures, accounting for more than $900,000 of the $1 million spent (Schotland 2009–2010, 120–121). "[T]hese organizations invested heavily in attack advertisements, blasting the justices' votes in *Varnum* and labeling them as 'activist' judges" (Hughes 2019b, 135). While the justices did not campaign, advertise, or raise money to counter the attacks, some organized interests did so in defense of judicial retention. They were, however, considerably outspent by those advocating removal (Brandenburg and Berg 2012, 710), and the subsequent voter turnout on election day was close to the highest ever seen in the state for retention elections (Schotland 2009–2010, 118). The results marked the first time that an appellate judge had ever lost a retention election in Iowa.

The shocking election results in Iowa attracted national attention because the removal of the justices was directly attributable to their 2009 decision striking down Iowa's ban on same-sex marriage (Pariente and Robinson 2016, 1534). According to law professor Roy Schotland, it "surely is one of the most significant judicial elections ever. It also was the highest-visibility judicial election since 1986, when Californians voted down the retention of Chief Justice Rose Bird and two of her colleagues" (Schotland 2009–2010, 118).

Following the Iowa elections, Bob Vander Plaats, one of the main architects of the removal campaign, said this: "We have ended 2010 by sending a strong message for freedom to the Iowa Supreme Court and to the entire nation that activist judges who seek to write their own law won't be tolerated any longer" (Brandenburg and Berg 2012, 712). Former Arkansas Governor Mike Huckabee predicted that the election would likely "give legs to a larger movement over the next few years" (Schotland 2009–2010, 118). Indeed, in the aftermath of the 2010 retention elections, "organized opposition campaigns have become more political and more strident, using television and mass-mail advertising based on issue-oriented attacks in response to decisions touching values sacred to voters. The organized opposition campaigns design the advertisements to tap into voters' moral outrage over the result in a particular court decision, without explaining whether the court was legally wrong" (Pariente and Robinson 2016, 1545).

While 2010 proved to be a remarkable and pivotal cycle for judicial elections, previous instances of politically contentious and issue-driven retention campaigns exist. Perhaps most notably, the 1986 California retention election resulted in the ousting of three supreme court justices. Along with the California election, in Nebraska and Tennessee in 1996, and Pennsylvania in 2005, "[i]nterest groups successfully targeted justices" (Clopton and Peters 2013, 325). The removal of the Pennsylvania justice in 2005 resulted from voter backlash, though not specifically against the judiciary. Angered by the state legislature's decision to give large pay increases to legislators and judges, voters took their frustrations out in the judicial retention elections. Their votes, including the ousting of one justice, served as "a proxy for the reformers to send a message to Harrisburg," home of the Pennsylvania state capitol (Barnes 2005). In a more direct referendum on the justices themselves, the "campaigns in California, Nebraska, and Tennessee revolved almost entirely around opposition to justices' rulings on matters of criminal law (the death penalty in California and Tennessee and the definition of second-degree murder in Nebraska)" (Clopton and Peters 2013, 325).

These earlier instances demonstrate that politicization of retention elections is not without precedent. What's more, political scientist Herbert Kritzer's analysis of judicial elections shows that partisanship in retention elections has been around for quite some time. Kritzer's study examines "the correlation between the county-level vote pattern in the gubernatorial election and the county-level vote pattern in the state supreme court election" (Kritzer 2015, 171). This metric showed only a modest increase in the correlation from 1960 through 2013. He also determined that "partisan patterns in voting in state supreme court retention elections are not limited to elections in which incumbents are defeated, nor are they limited to elections in which there are partisan-oriented campaigns challenging the incumbent" (Kritzer 2015, 204). While acknowledging "extreme examples of partisanship playing a role in such elections" as Iowa in 2010 and California in 1986, Kritzer nevertheless reported "a strong undercurrent of partisanship in a much larger number of state supreme court retention elections than previously assumed" (Kritzer 2015, 235).

Still, Kritzer noted some key changes in partisanship. "[T]he nature of the partisanship in retention elections varies from state to state in a way that links to the broad political context of the individual state. Where there has been change over time in the pattern of partisan correlations in a state using retention elections, the nature of that change tends to reflect the changing political context of that state" (Kritzer 2015, 236).

It is also worth noting that justices in retention elections face unusual vulnerability compared to those running in contested elections. This might seem counterintuitive given that judges in retention elections do not have a formal opponent. But "because opposition to a judge is not subject to time limits that exist in contested judicial elections, where a challenger must file before the qualifying deadline, there is a grave risk of a blindsiding attack by a politician or special-interest group just days before an election" (Pariente and Robinson 2016, 1545–1546).

It is unclear whether high spending, attack ads, issue orientation, and heavy involvement of special-interest groups will continue to characterize retention elections moving forward. According to Hughes, the rise in new-style campaigns for contested state supreme court elections slowed during the 2010s (Hughes 2019b, 148). If retention elections follow that pattern, it is possible that a similar downturn could occur in retention campaigns.

Also, like changes to regular judicial elections, the impact of the observed transformation in retention elections is disputed. Some observers bemoan these changes, arguing that they demonstrate that judicial elections—whether of the competitive or retention variety—are vulnerable to politicization and, as such, undermine the independence and legitimacy of the courts. Others say that changes to retention elections have democratic benefits, such as increasing the salience of elections and improving voter turnout. In other words, demonstrating that retention elections have become increasingly politicized does not, by itself, demonstrate negative impacts on the judiciary or its independence (see Q13).

FURTHER READING

Aspin, Larry. 2011. "The 2010 Judicial Retention Elections in Perspective: Continuity and Change from 1964 to 2010." *Judicature*, 94, no. 5: 218–232.

Barnes, Tom. 2005. "Voters Reject Supreme Court Justice Nigro." *Pittsburgh Post-Gazette*, November 9, 2005.

Brandenburg, Bert, and Matt Berg. 2012. "The New Storm of Money and Politics around Judicial Retention Elections." *Drake Law Review*, 60, no. 3: 703–714.

Bybee, Keith, and Jeff Stonecash. 2005. "All Judges Are Political Actors—Except When They Aren't." *Knight-Ridder/Tribune Information Services*, December 14, 2005.

Clopton, Andrew J., and Scott C. Peters. 2013. "Justices Denied." *The Justice System Journal*, 34, no. 3: 321–344.

Harris, Allison P. 2019. "Voter Response to Salient Judicial Decisions in Retention Elections." *Law & Social Inquiry*, 44, no. 1: 170–191.

Hughes, David. 2019a. "In Many States, Simple Elections to Keep or Fire Judges Have Become a Partisan Mess." *London School of Economics United States Politics and Policy*, February 27, 2019. https://blogs.lse.ac.uk /usappblog/2019/02/27/in-many-states-simple-elections-to-keep-or-fire -judges-have-become-a-partisan-mess

Hughes, David. 2019b. "New-Style Campaigns in State Supreme Court Retention Elections." *State Politics and Policy Quarterly*, 19, no. 2: 127–154.

Kritzer, Herbert M. 2015. *Justices on the Ballot: Continuity and Change in State Supreme Court Elections.* New York: Cambridge University Press.

Kritzer, Herbert M. 2018. "Judicial Elections in the 2010s." *DePaul Law Review*, 67: 387–424.

Pariente, Barbara J., and James Robinson. 2016. "A New Era for Judicial Retention Elections: The Rise of and Defense Against Unfair Political Attacks." *Florida Law Review*, 68, no. 6: 1529–1567.

Schotland, Roy A. 2009-2010. "Iowa's 2010 Judicial Election: Appropriate Accountability or Rampant Passion." *Court Review* 46, no. 4: 118–129.

Varnum v. Brien, 763 N.W.2d 862 (Iowa 2009).

Q12. DOES THE GROWTH OF CAMPAIGN SPENDING BY INTEREST GROUPS AFFECT JUDICIAL INDEPENDENCE?

Answer: It is commonly asserted that escalating campaign contributions in judicial elections are influencing rulings produced by the courts. How campaign contributions affect judicial independence is subject to more debate. Many accept and find evidence for the view that campaign contributions by special-interest groups pressure judges to rule in their favor, thereby directly undermining judicial independence. Others reject this contention, asserting instead that there is insufficient evidence to show that contributions or their increasing use amount to judicial vote buying.

The Facts: Multiple signs indicate growing politicization of judicial elections. Part of this politicization includes rising campaign contributions from special-interest groups (see Q9). In the opening decade of the 21st century, campaign fundraising in judicial elections more than doubled as compared to the previous decade, with interest groups accounting for a sizable portion of the contributions. Business groups, for instance, contributed about 30 percent of total contributions, while lawyers and lobbyists accounted for another 28 percent of the total (Shepherd 2013, 1). Television advertising by interest groups in state supreme court elections also soared during that decade, totaling $93.6 million for those elections between 2000 and 2009. Of that total, interest groups spent $27.5 million on television ads, with business groups accounting for more than 90 percent of that subtotal (Shepherd 2013, 1).

There has long been concern about the role of money in the elections of legislators and executives. That concern has now made its way into analysis of judicial elections, especially as campaigns for judges have grown more expensive and politicized. Disquiet about the effects of campaign contributions is particularly acute in the context of judicial selection. Maintaining an independent judiciary requires that judges have the ability "to issue decisions without fearing negative political consequences" (Canes-Wrone and Clark 2009, 22). The idea that judges face pressure to render decisions in ways that satisfy past or future contributors runs contrary to the rule of law and the ideal of an independent judiciary.

Is there good reason to worry that growing interest-group use of campaign contributions in judicial elections undermines judicial independence? Many court watchers say yes, though others express skepticism about claims that independence faces serious danger.

Legal scholars Michael S. Kang and Joanna M. Shepherd join those who warn about threats to judicial independence. Focusing on business groups and examining data from 1995 through 1998, they display a statistically significant relationship between campaign contributions and state supreme court decisions favoring the interests of those contributors. Specifically, they found that "every dollar of contributions from business groups is associated with increases in the probability that elected judges will decide for business litigants. Moreover, business groups' share of total contributions to judicial campaigns is also positively related to partisan-elected judges' voting for business litigants in many cases" (Kang and Shepherd 2011, 73). The research only detects this relationship in states with partisan judicial elections, not in states using judicial appointments or nonpartisan elections.

In a 2013 study, Shepherd confirmed "a significant relationship between business group contributions to state supreme court justices and the voting of those justices in cases involving business matters" (Shepherd 2013, 1). Based on more than 2,300 business-related state supreme court rulings from 2010 through 2012, the study observed that the "more campaign contributions from business interests justices receive, the more likely they are to vote for business litigants appearing before them in court. Notably, the analysis reveals that a justice who receives half of his or her contributions from business groups would be expected to vote in favor of business interests almost two-thirds of the time" (Shepherd 2013, 1). The research only showed this relationship in states with partisan and nonpartisan judicial elections, not in states using retention elections. Also, interestingly, the study demonstrated a stronger effect on Democratic justices than Republican justices. Shepherd explains this disparity by positing that given Republican predisposition to favor business interests, "additional business contributions may not have as large of an influence on them as they do on Democratic justices" (Shepherd 2013, 2).

In a forthcoming book, Kang and Shepherd turn their attention toward determining whether evidence demonstrates a causal link between campaign financing and judicial decisions that directly favor contributors. The analysis, previewed in a 2021 article, is based on comparisons between judges subject to reelection and "lame-duck" judges, those who are serving out their final terms of office when they are no longer eligible for reelection because of mandatory retirement. Because lame-duck judges face no reelection, they have no need to seek campaign contributions or to rule in ways that would encourage such contributions. In other words, "[i]f campaign finance money influences lame-duck judges differently from other judges, then it suggests that reelection may be the main source of money's influence" (Kang and Shepherd 2021, 1492). Kang and Shepherd find such a difference: judges facing reelection vote more substantially in favor of business interests, whereas campaign finance money produces only "a weak influence on lame ducks' judicial decisions" (Kang and Shepherd 2021, 1493).

Research by political scientist Damon Cann examined money flowing to judicial campaigns from lawyers and law firms by studying the Supreme Court of Georgia and its rulings in 2003. His analysis showed a statistically significant relationship between campaign contributions made by attorneys and law firms and the decisions rendered by judges. In addition, Cann found evidence of a causal link between contributions and judicial decision making, thus establishing "the existence of some circumstances under which *quid pro quo* electoral exchanges may occur even in the judicial branch" (Cann 2007b, 292).

A 2006 *New York Times* investigation further examined campaign contributions and judicial decision making, focusing on the Ohio Supreme Court. Based on 12 years of decision making, the investigation found that Ohio Supreme Court justices "routinely sat on cases after receiving campaign contributions from the parties involved or from groups that filed supporting briefs. On average, they voted in favor of contributors 70 percent of the time" (Liptak and Roberts 2006). The article noted that campaign contributors may not specifically aim to buy votes in particular cases, but rather seek to help elect judges with a general judicial philosophy beneficial to the contributor's interests. Still, the perception of vote buying and compromised independence may persist. According to said Justice Paul E. Pfeifer, a Republican member of the Ohio Supreme Court, "I never felt so much like a hooker down by the bus station in any race I've ever been in as I did in a judicial race" (Liptak and Roberts 2006).

Evidence that others share Justice Pfeifer's sentiments can be found in a 2002 survey of 2,400 state judges:

> Forty-five percent of trial judges expressed the view that campaign contributions influenced judicial decisions to at least some degree (4% said "a great deal," 21% said "some" and 20% said "just a little," as compared to 36% who reported "none"); an identical percentage of high court respondents thought likewise, although more thought that contributions exerted a greater degree of influence. That same survey revealed that 58% of trial judges—as compared to 55% of high court justices—supported the proposition that "judges should be prohibited from presiding over and ruling in cases when one of the sides has given money to their campaign." (American Bar Association Commission on the 21st Century Judiciary 2003, 50)

Perhaps part of the reason for the perception, if not the reality, that campaign contributions influence judicial decision making comes from a few high-profile cases. Among the most salient involves the 2004 election of Republican Brent Benjamin to the highest court of West Virginia. Benjamin's campaign for a seat on the court was funded to the tune of $3 million by the chief executive officer of Massey Coal. Massey Coal held a particular interest in the election's outcome because pending before the court was a $50 million liability judgment against the company. After Benjamin defeated an incumbent Democratic justice to win the seat, he refused to recuse himself from the Massey Coal case and voted with a slim majority to dismiss the $50 million liability judgment. In 2009, the U.S. Supreme Court weighed in, ruling that Justice Benjamin's refusal to recuse himself violated the Due Process Clause of the Fourteenth Amendment. According to the Supreme Court's ruling in *Caperton v. A.T. Massey Coal Co.*, "there is a serious risk of actual bias—based on objective and reasonable perceptions—when a person with a personal stake in a particular case had a significant and disproportionate influence in placing the judge on the case by raising funds or directing the judge's election campaign when the case was pending or imminent" (*Caperton* 2009, 884).

Some view the ruling in *Caperton* as giving "constitutional recognition to one of the most pressing concerns of American law and democracy— the influence of campaign money on the judiciary" (Kang and Shepherd 2011, 70). Coupled with evidence of the correlation between campaign spending and judicial decisions, *Caperton* bolsters the argument of those who assert that judicial independence is at risk. Other high-profile cases have also raised the specter of money's improper influence. For example, in Illinois in 2004, "the insurance and financial services giant State Farm spent millions (the actual amount of the firm's campaign spending is in dispute) to elect a justice who voted to overturn a $1 billion class-action verdict against the insurer" (Corriher 2012).

Still, some researchers caution against drawing the conclusion that interest-group spending on judicial elections jeopardizes independence. Take, for example, political scientist Melinda Gann Hall, who argues that we should expect to discover a correlation between the preferences of contributors and judicial decisions "simply because donors give money to those with whom they agree" (Hall 2016, 454). But the mere existence of correlation, Hall cautions, does not provide sufficient grounding to claim that spending on elections undermines judicial independence. "[S]tatistically significant relationships, even in multivariate models, are a far cry from quid pro quo relationships that impugn the integrity of the justices and the judicial selection process. In short, correlation is not causation, and claims to the contrary from project investigators do not change this fundamental fact" (Hall 2016, 454).

Research into the influence of campaign spending on the Ohio Supreme Court from the early 1980s through 2012 shows that judicial candidates supported by business interests held a funding advantage and a related electoral advantage (Baum, Klein, and Streb 2017, 101). However, the research does not find the kind of quid pro quo that jeopardizes judicial independence. Noting prior research showing that, in criminal justice cases, "the prospect of facing the voters does affect justices' choices," the researchers nevertheless noted that a similar effect does not show up with respect to tort law in Ohio (Baum, Klein, and Streb 2017, 101).

Even Damon Cann expresses skepticism, notwithstanding his own research on the Supreme Court of Georgia, which concluded that "an attorney's campaign contributions increase the probability that a judge rules in favor of that attorney's client" (Cann 2007b, 282). Cann argues that empirical studies, other than his own, "have failed to establish that campaign contributions lead judges to vote in a particular way" (Cann 2007a, 228). Disagreement thus persists over whether campaign contributions and their growing use effectively pressure individual judges to rule in certain ways. As legal scholar Lawrence Baum writes, "there is no direct evidence about whether growth in the costs of supreme court campaigns has given contributors more influence over the successful candidates they support" (Baum 2017, 915). The point holds true today—although critics of the current system often highlight circumstantial evidence of quid pro quo relationships between some elected judges and their most important financial supporters.

Broader agreement exists that campaign contributions have at least some influence on the composition of state judiciaries, even though contributors do not always succeed in getting their preferred candidates elected. What's more, even though division continues over how directly campaign contributions influence judicial independence, the appearance, rather than the fact, of influence may pose a problem for the legitimacy of the judiciary. That is, even if it remains unclear whether campaign contributions "effectively 'buy' judges' votes, it is possible that the very appearance of *quid pro quo* exchanges makes people uncomfortable" (Cann 2007a, 232). That possibility, along with the broader question of whether politicization of judicial elections undermines legitimacy, is taken up in this chapter's final question.

FURTHER READING

American Bar Association Commission on the 21st Century Judiciary. 2003. *Justice in Jeopardy.* American Bar Association. https://www.opensocietyfoundations.org/publications/justice-jeopardy-report-american-bar-assocation-commission-21st-century-judiciary

Baum, Lawrence. 2017. "Supreme Court Elections: How Much They Have Changed, Why They Changed, and What Difference It Makes." *Law & Social Inquiry*, 42, no. 3: 900–923.

Baum, Lawrence, David E. Klein, and Matthew J. Streb. 2017. *The Battle for the Court: Interest Groups, Judicial Elections, and Public Policy.* Charlottesville, VA: University of Virginia Press.

Canes-Wrone, Brandice, and Tom S. Clark. 2009. "Judicial Independence and Nonpartisan Elections." *Wisconsin Law Review*, 2009, no. 1: 21–66.

Cann, Damon. 2007a. "Beyond Accountability and Independence—Judicial Selection and State Court Performance." *Judicature*, 90, no. 5: 226–232.

Cann, Damon. 2007b. "Justice for Sale? Campaign Contributions and Judicial Decisionmaking." *State Politics & Policy Quarterly*, 7, no. 3: 281–297.

Caperton v. A.T. Massey Coal Co., 556 U.S. 868 (2009).

Corriher, Billy. 2012. "Partisan Judicial Elections and the Distorting Influence of Campaign Cash October." Center for American Progress. October 25, 2012. https://www.americanprogress.org/article/partisan-judicial-elections-and-the-distorting-influence-of-campaign-cash

Hall, Melinda Gann. 2016. "Partisanship, Interest Groups, and Attack Advertising in the Post-*White* Era, or Why Nonpartisan Judicial Elections Really Do Stink." *Journal of Law & Politics*, 31, no. 4: 429–456.

Kang, Michael S., and Joanna M. Shepherd. 2011. "The Partisan Price of Justice: An Empirical Analysis of Campaign Contributions and Judicial Decisions." *New York University Law Review*, 86, no. 1: 69–130.

Kang, Michael S., and Joanna M. Shepherd. 2021. "Judicial Campaign Finance and Election Timing." *Wisconsin Law Review*, 2021, no. 6: 1487–1510.

Liptak, Adam, and Janet Roberts. 2006. "Campaign Cash Mirrors a High Court's Rulings." *New York Times*, October 1, 2006.

Rebe, Ryan J. 2019. "Amici Curiae Campaign Contributions and Appellant Success in State Supreme Courts." *New England Journal of Political Science*, 11, no. 1: 88–113.

Shepherd, Joanna M. 2013. *Justice at Risk: An Empirical Analysis of Campaign Contributions and Judicial Decisions*. American Constitution Society for Law and Policy. https://www.acslaw.org/analysis/reports/justice-at-risk

Q13. DO POLITICIZED JUDICIAL ELECTIONS THREATEN THE LEGITIMACY OF STATE COURTS?

Answer: Probably, but analysts disagree about the extent to which they are affecting public perception and opinion.

The Facts: We have seen that research identifies a correlation between interest-group campaign spending and decisions issued by state courts. As discussed in Q12, many suggest that such evidence signifies a threat to judicial independence. Those who see rising campaign contributions as limiting independence also warn of associated risks to judicial legitimacy. More broadly, conventional wisdom holds that politicized judicial elections—especially partisan ones—undermine the legitimacy of courts with the broader American public. Calls to replace judicial elections with merit-based selection or to swap partisan elections with nonpartisan ones stem, in part, from concern that growing politicization and partisanship in elections harm the institutional legitimacy of the judiciary.

Indeed, the practice of electing judges has increasingly come under attack (Hall and Bonneau 2013, 117). The American Bar Association, the American Judicature Society, and the Brennan Center for Justice, among others, have all called for significant reforms to judicial elections. Retired U.S. Supreme Court Justice Sandra Day O'Connor has joined the reform efforts, waging "a campaign to curb state judicial elections" because they have "become so costly and confrontational as to potentially undermine judicial independence and the legitimacy of courts" (O'Brien 2016, 417).

The argument that using elections to seat judges weakens the judiciary's legitimacy runs as follows. Elections conflict with judicial impartiality and independence because they incentivize judges to issue decisions based not on law but on how their rulings affect public opinion, donors, and potential donors—and thus their future reelection prospects. As former California Supreme Court Justice Otto Kaus bluntly puts it, "[t]here's no way a judge is going to be able to ignore the political consequences of certain decisions, especially if he or she has to make them near election time. That would be like ignoring a crocodile in your bathtub" (Jolly 2017, 84). In light of such pressure, and even if judges may be able to resist it, some argue that "elected judges are incapable of maintaining perceptions of judicial fairness" (Jolly 2017, 83).

Empirical research provides some support for this concern. For one thing, judges report that the "fear of losing an election affects their judicial behavior," even in unopposed retention elections when losing "is highly unlikely" (Jolly 2017, 84). Moreover, as legal scholar Lawrence Baum noted, evidence related to state trial court decisions concerning criminal justice and the death penalty shows that "judges are influenced by the prospect of facing the voters in the near future" (Baum 2017, 914). For example, researchers Gregory Huber and Sanford Gordon found in a study of Pennsylvania trial court judges that sentences for aggravated assault, rape, and robbery "are significantly longer the closer the sentencing judge is to standing for reelection" (Huber and Gordon 2004, 248).

The general concern that judicial elections undermine the legitimacy of the courts has been around since the founding era. Alexander Hamilton famously addressed this worry in the *Federalist Papers* when defending the proposed structure of the federal judiciary and urging the need for insulation (Hamilton 2009). The recent emergence of the "new style" of judicial elections—discussed in Q9—amplifies this long-standing worry.

According to the American Bar Association's Commission on the 21st Century Judiciary, judicial election campaigns have become more and more issue-focused, covering such polarizing matters as products liability, medical malpractice litigation, criminal justice, abortion, and capital punishment. "But the message sent to the electorate is the same in each case: sitting judges should lose their jobs if they make a ruling of law in a particular case that a popular majority thinks is wrong. In the Commission's view, that message is antithetical to principles of judicial independence, impartiality, and the rule of law" (American Bar Association Commission on the 21st Century Judiciary 2003, 89).

Three aspects of the new style of judicial elections raise particular concern: growing campaign contributions, attack ads, and candidate policy declarations. First, critics of elections argue that rising campaign contributions from interest groups, litigants, and political parties threaten legitimacy by creating the impression that judges can be directly bought. As discussed in Q12, findings show at least a correlation between campaign contributions by interest groups and judicial outcomes, raising the specter, if not the fact, of influence. The increasing cost of judicial elections combined with the growing need to raise campaign funds seemingly creates enticements for judges to rule in ways that keep the money flowing for future campaigns and "to avoid taking positions that might be used against them in a future campaign" (Baum 2017, 914). Again, even if judges succeed in maintaining their independence in the face of such incentives, the public may be hard pressed to disassociate the deluge of money into campaigns from the resulting decisions produced by courts. High-profile cases of the sort addressed previously in this chapter add to this perception.

Second, critics of judicial elections contend that negative campaign advertisements have long-term consequences for public perceptions of legal system legitimacy. Casting candidates as ideological, partisan, minions for special-interest groups, or worse, such ads "portray judicial candidates as little different from any other political figure, thereby potentially undermining the distinctiveness of the judiciary, and thus contributing to the loss of judicial legitimacy" (Gibson 2008, 62).

Third, many argue that judicial candidates announcing their policy positions during campaigns further weakens the appearance of impartiality and, in turn, harms legitimacy. Consider here Minnesota's defense for its restriction on policy announcements by judicial candidates, which the U.S. Supreme Court overturned in *Republican Party of Minnesota v. White* (2002). "Minnesota contended that legitimacy requires the appearance of impartiality, that the appearance of partiality can undermine the confidence citizens have in their courts (legitimacy), and that legitimacy is crucial to the effective functioning of courts" (Gibson 2008, 60). Consider as well the comments offered by Justice Ruth Bader Ginsburg, dissenting along with three other justices from the majority decision in *White*:

> Prohibiting a judicial candidate from pledging or promising certain results if elected directly promotes the State's interest in preserving public faith in the bench. When a candidate makes such a promise during a campaign, the public will no doubt perceive that she is doing so in the hope of garnering votes. And the public will in turn likely conclude that when the candidate decides an issue in accord with that promise, she does so at least in part to discharge her undertaking to the voters in the previous election and to prevent voter abandonment in the next. The perception of that unseemly *quid pro quo*—a judicial candidates' promises on issues in return for the electorate's votes at the polls—inevitably diminishes the public's faith in the ability of judges to administer the law without regard to personal or political self-interest. (*Republican Party of Minnesota v. White* 2002, Ginsburg dissent, footnotes omitted, 818)

Ginsburg's argument did not carry the day in *White*. But even justices who joined the majority expressed reservations about the decision's impact. Justice O'Connor, who joined the majority in *White* on free speech grounds, nonetheless wrote a separate concurring opinion to warn that subjecting judges to regular elections gives them a personal stake "in the outcome of every publicized case," and "may leave judges feeling indebted" to campaign donors (*White* 2002, 789, 790, O'Connor concurring). She emphasized that even if judges resist the temptation to rule in ways that repay contributors or improve their chances in future elections, "the public's confidence in the judiciary could be undermined simply by the possibility that judges would be unable to do so" (*White* 2002, 789). O'Connor concluded by arguing that if Minnesota "has a problem with judicial impartiality, it is largely one the State brought upon itself by continuing the practice of popularly electing judges" (*White* 2002, 792). In her retirement, as noted earlier, O'Connor joined efforts to reform the judicial elections.

The argument that the new style of elections undercuts the judiciary's legitimacy with the public has intuitive appeal. It also has some empirical backing. Social science researchers seeking to test whether campaign contributions, attack ads, and policy pronouncements harm legitimacy have found substantiation for a few of these claims.

Concerning campaign contributions, political scientist James L. Gibson notes that, "[i]n some respects…it matters little if in fact contributions and votes are closely connected; what people believe about the connection may be of greater significance for the legitimacy of courts" (Gibson 2008, 62). Moreover, in the case of the judiciary, Gibson hypothesizes that "campaign contributions have a particularly corrosive influence on perceptions of impartiality. When contributions come from the very law firms and corporations that litigate before the judges whom they help elect, then the generally tawdry aura of contributions takes on an even more unseemly and sinister tint" (Gibson 2008, 62).

Gibson finds empirical support for this hypothesis in experiments conducted first in Kentucky and later using a nationally representative sample (Gibson 2008; Gibson 2009). The experiments presented respondents with vignettes containing different types of campaign activities and designed to test the effects on respondents' perceptions of judicial legitimacy. Gibson finds in the Kentucky experiment that "[w]hen groups with direct connections to the decision maker give contributions, legitimacy suffers substantially" (Gibson 2008, 69). He concludes "with considerable certitude that when candidates for public office receive campaign contributions from those with direct business interests before the institution, many (if not most) citizens perceive policy making as biased and partial and the policy-making institution as illegitimate" (Gibson 2008, 72). Gibson confirms these findings using the national sample, concluding that "the acceptance of campaign contributions significantly detracts from the legitimacy of the institution" (Gibson 2009, 1294).

Gibson also discovers some, albeit mixed, evidence supporting the contention that when "candidates for office, judicial or legislative, use attack ads, legitimacy suffers," though he notes that the effect "is moderate and is not nearly as large as the effect of campaign contributions" (Gibson 2008, 70). His national sample findings, though, do not show this effect for judicial elections, even while they demonstrate that attack ads in the context of legislative campaigns undermine the legitimacy of legislatures (Gibson 2009, 1295).

Other research on the effects of political advertising indicates that judges respond to attack ads. A study of roughly 1,000 cases in 40 state supreme courts covering 1990 through 2014 shows that in states "in which campaign advertisements attack a sitting justice over a previous environmental decision, the justices become responsive to public opinion in the years following the attack" (Canes-Wrone, Clark, and Semet 2018, 674). Although the study does not observe a similar effect for "general ads that do not reference specific judicial decisions," it does suggest that even in instances involving "a relatively low-salience issue, campaigns are associated with changes in judicial behavior" (Canes-Wrone, Clark, and Semet

2018, 696, 697). Though the study does not evaluate how this might affect judicial legitimacy, its conclusions lend weight to the argument that attack ads can make an impact.

Considerably less evidence exists that judicial candidates shake public faith in the courts when they announce policy positions. To the contrary, Gibson's research in Kentucky shows that, unlike with campaign contributions and attack ads, legitimacy does not suffer when judicial candidates engage in policy debates (Gibson 2008, 72). Similarly, Gibson's national study finds that "the data are unequivocal: When judges express their policy views during campaigns for elected judgeships, no harm is done to the institutional legitimacy of courts. The data reported in this article strongly disconfirm the fears of the minority in *Republican Party of Minnesota v. White*—as well as many if not most scholars—that policy talk would threaten judicial legitimacy. Indeed, the data even indicate that policy *promises* have no untoward effects on court legitimacy" (Gibson 2009, 1298).

Moreover, while certain research suggests harm to legitimacy caused by some aspects of elections, other studies cast doubt on the claim that "[c]ompetitive judicial elections, particularly hard-fought, expensive races with attack advertising . . . undermine citizen trust and confidence and thereby yield harsh consequences, including voter disaffection" (Hall and Bonneau 2013, 117). In fact, many scholars, especially within political science, supply evidence that partisanship and politics in judicial elections produce positive benefits.

For one thing, and contrary to the "conventional legal wisdom" that "judges cannot be perceived as respected arbiters of disputes while behaving like ordinary politicians in the electoral arena" (Hall 2016, 436), several commentators note the continued public support for judicial elections. Despite growing concerns about declining legitimacy, judicial elections endure as a common method for staffing the bench at the state level. Importantly, the American voting public has historically favored electing judges, with surveys showing that more than three-quarters of the public prefer judicial election over appointments (Shepherd 2013, 7), though not necessarily through partisan election processes (Streb 2007, 96). Also, as addressed in Q25, public confidence in state courts appears strong according to opinion polls, showing little decline in recent years.

Additionally, with respect to the new style of elections, some researchers contend that "the perceived negative consequences of this increasing politicization are exaggerated" (Baum, Klein, and Streb 2017, 105, citing Bonneau, Hall, and Streb 2011; Gibson 2012; Hall 2015). Others, though, acknowledge the politicization but emphasize its positive benefits. The asserted benefits include, among others, increased information, interest, engagement, choice, and voting, as well as enhanced judicial accountability (see, e.g., Bonneau 2018; Bonneau and Hall 2009).

For example, extant scholarship "finds that partisan, expensive, and even churlish campaigns for the bench educate and animate voters, leading to more competitive elections" (Hughes 2019, 128). According to political scientists Melinda Gann Hall and Chris Bonneau, existing empirical work documents that "the electorate in state supreme court elections is stimulated to participate by many of the same factors that mobilize voters in elections to nonjudicial offices. Generally, voter participation improves considerably in response to conditions that increase the salience of the races and enhance the information available to voters" (Hall and Bonneau 2013, 117). Hall and Bonneau emphasize that the new style of election helps generate these benefits: "Particularly relevant as agents of mobilization in state supreme court races are partisan elections, close contests, and big spending. . . . Indeed, hard-fought, expensive campaigns substantially improve voting in state supreme court elections" (Hall and Bonneau 2013, 117).

Bonneau sums up the argument for partisan elections in this way in another analysis from 2018: "Partisan judicial elections are controversial, but their benefits outweigh their problems. They are effective mechanisms for providing voters with relevant information about judicial candidates, meaningful choice in elections, and transparency in the selection process. Indeed, on all of these criteria, they are superior to other forms of elections (nonpartisan and retention) and appointment schemes. And partisan elections accomplish all this without suffering any decrease in the legitimacy of the courts, at least among those with knowledge of the courts" (Bonneau 2018, 6–7).

Finally, some observe that the alternative to regular judicial elections— that is, merit selection—does not necessarily remove politicization or provide more evidence of legitimacy. According to one study, for example, relying on state bar associations to select judges results in a judiciary that reflects the ideological preferences of lawyers rather than the public (Fitzpatrick 2009, 677). More broadly, some suggest that "appointment processes sometimes work in ways that would generally be considered undesirable, and considerations other than the merit of prospective judges have considerable weight in the selection of judges" (Baum 2017, 917). What's more, evidence presented by some research suggests "changes in appointment processes similar to changes in judicial elections, including growth in partisanship and greater scrutiny of incumbent judges who come up for reappointment" (Baum 2017, 918).

Alarm bells will almost surely continue to sound "announcing the immi-
nent demise of legitimacy in the country's elected state courts" (Gibson 2008,
60). In many ways, sounding the alarm appears warranted. "The confluence
of broadened freedom for judges to speak out on issues, the increasing importance of state judicial policies, and the infusion of money into judicial campaigns have produced what may be described as the 'Perfect Storm' of judicial
elections. . . . Many commentators fear the worst, arguing that the very legitimacy of the legal system may be eroded as people come to see law and courts
as little more than ordinary political institutions and therefore worthy of
their contempt and disrespect" (Gibson 2008, 60). On the other hand, however, it is possible that "experience with campaigning leads to acceptance of
it" (Gibson 2009, 1299). Perhaps, as Gibson speculates, "[p]oliticized judicial
campaigns may provide a 'shock' to an electorate, but that shock may not
have enduring consequences as citizens alter their expectations of proper
behavior for candidates. The perceived legitimacy of institutions may be
more resilient than is sometimes assumed" (Gibson 2009, 1299).

FURTHER READING

American Bar Association Commission on the 21st Century Judiciary.
    2003. *Justice in Jeopardy.* American Bar Association. https://www
    .opensocietyfoundations.org/publications/justice-jeopardy-report
    -american-bar-assocation-commission-21st-century-judiciary
Baum, Lawrence. 2017. "Supreme Court Elections: How Much They Have
    Changed, Why They Changed, and What Difference It Makes." *Law &
    Social Inquiry,* 42, no. 3: 900–923.
Baum, Lawrence, David E. Klein, and Matthew J. Streb. 2017. *The Battle
    for the Court: Interest Groups, Judicial Elections, and Public Policy.* Char-
    lottesville, VA: University of Virginia Press.
Bonneau, Chris W. 2018. "The Case for Partisan Judicial Elections: Part 1:
    State Judicial Selection Series." The Federalist Society, January 8, 2018.
    https://fedsoc.org/commentary/publications/the-case-for-partisan
    -judicial-elections-1
Bonneau, Chris W., and Melinda Gann Hall. 2009. *In Defense of Judicial
    Elections.* New York: Routledge Press.
Bonneau, Chris W., Melinda Gann Hall, and Matthew J. Streb. 2011.
    "White Noise: The Unrealized Effects of *Republican Party of Minnesota
    v. White* on Judicial Elections." *Justice System Journal,* 32, no. 3: 247–268.
Canes-Wrone, Brandice, Tom S. Clark, and Amy Semet. 2018. "Judicial
    Elections, Public Opinion, and Decisions on Lower-Salience Issues."
    Journal of Empirical Legal Studies, 15, no. 4: 672–707.

Fitzpatrick, Brian T. 2009. "The Politics of Merit Selection." *Missouri Law Review*, 74, no. 3: 675–710.

Gibson, James L. 2008. "Challenges to the Impartiality of State Supreme Courts: Legitimacy Theory and 'New-Style' Judicial Campaigns." *American Political Science Review*, 102, no. 1: 59–75.

Gibson, James L. 2009. "'New-Style' Judicial Campaigns and the Legitimacy of State High Courts." *Journal of Politics*, 71, no. 4: 1285–1304.

Gibson, James L. 2012. *Electing Judges: The Surprising Effects of Campaigning on Judicial Legitimacy*. Chicago, IL: University of Chicago Press.

Hall, Melinda Gann. 2007. "Voting in State Supreme Court Elections: Competition and Context as Democratic Incentives." *Journal of Politics*, 69, no. 4: 1147–1159.

Hall, Melinda Gann. 2015. *Attacking Judges: How Campaign Advertising Influences State Supreme Court Elections*. Stanford, CA: Stanford University Press.

Hall, Melinda Gann. 2016. "Partisanship, Interest Groups, and Attack Advertising in the Post-*White* Era, or Why Nonpartisan Judicial Elections Really Do Stink." *Journal of Law & Politics*, 31, no. 4: 429–456.

Hall, Melinda Gann, and Chris W. Bonneau. 2013. "Attack Advertising, the *White* Decision, and Voter Participation in State Supreme Court Elections." *Political Research Quarterly*, 66, no. 1: 115–126.

Hamilton, Alexander. 2009. "The Federalist No. 78." In *The Federalist Papers*, ed. Ian Shapiro, 391–397. New Haven, CT: Yale University Press.

Huber, Gregory A., and Sanford C. Gordon. 2004. "Accountability and Coercion: Is Justice Blind When It Runs for Office?" *American Journal of Political Science*, 48, no. 2: 247–263.

Hughes, David. 2019. "New-Style Campaigns in State Supreme Court Retention Elections." *State Politics and Policy Quarterly*, 19, no. 2: 127–154.

Jolly, Richard L. 2017. "Judges as Politicians: The Enduring Tension of Judicial Elections in the Twenty-First Century." *Notre Dame Law Review Online*, 92, no. 1: 71–86.

O'Brien, David M. 2016. "State Court Elections and Judicial Independence." *Journal of Law & Politics*, 31, no. 4: 417–428.

Republican Party of Minnesota v. White, 536 U.S. 765 (2002).

Sample, James, and Jesse Rutledge. 2006. "Once Courtly, Campaigns for America's High Courts Now Dominated by Television Attack Ads." Brennan Center for Justice, November 2, 2006. https://www.brennancenter.org/our-work/analysis-opinion/once-courtly-campaigns-americas-high-courts-now-dominated-television

Shepherd, Joanna M. 2013. *Justice at Risk: An Empirical Analysis of Campaign Contributions and Judicial Decisions.* American Constitution Society for Law and Policy. https://www.acslaw.org/analysis/reports/justice-at-risk

Streb, Matthew J. 2007. "Partisan Involvement in Partisan and Nonpartisan Trial Court Elections." In *Running for Judge: The Rising Political, Financial, and Legal Stakes of Judicial Elections*, ed. Matthew J. Streb, 96–114. New York: NYU Press.

3

Structures Affecting the Courts

Structural characteristics influence the way courts are staffed and how they operate. Some of these structural features are external to the courts themselves, giving other branches of government the power to shape the judiciary. Often by design, structures are put into place (or, at least, contemplated and debated) to act as an external institutional check on the courts. Some structures are modified or eliminated as exercises of partisan power by individuals or groups seeking to benefit a particular political party or to bolster an ideological position by gaining influence and control over the courts.

This chapter examines questions related to key external structures that shape and constrain the power of federal courts. Several of these questions have gained considerable attention in recent years in the partisan tug-of-war over control of the federal courts. Questions pertaining to the composition of the bench figure prominently in this chapter, including altering the size of the Supreme Court, imposing term limits on justices, and changing the use of the filibuster during Senate consideration of federal court nominees.

Q14. HAS CONGRESS OR THE PRESIDENT EVER SOUGHT TO ADJUST THE SIZE OF THE SUPREME COURT FOR POLITICAL GAIN?

Answer: Yes.

The Facts: Over the past few years, there have been growing calls from Democratic and independent voters to increase the number of justices on the U.S. Supreme Court. "Once considered taboo, court packing is now a topic at presidential debates, the subject of numerous op-eds and a trending hashtag on Twitter" (Frost 2020). Court packing has garnered a surprising level of approval from the public. According to a 2019 Marquette Law School poll, 43 percent of survey respondents expressed support for increasing the number of seats on the high Court, with Democrats and independents voicing the highest agreement (Franklin 2019, 21).

The idea gained particular momentum among Democrats in response to a number of developments. As discussed in Q5, many Democrats believe Republicans "stole" a Supreme Court seat from President Barack Obama in 2016 by refusing to consider his nomination of Merrick Garland for a vacancy on the Court left by the death of Associate Justice Antonin Scalia. Republicans refused to consider Garland, whom Obama nominated nearly eight months ahead of the 2016 election, asserting that "[t]he American people should have a voice in the selection of their next Supreme Court Justice. Therefore, this vacancy should not be filled until we have a new president" (Everett and Thrush 2016).

Democratic indignation increased when the Republican Party successfully confirmed Neil Gorsuch to that seat in 2017—changing Senate rules to eliminate the filibuster in Supreme Court confirmations. Without that rule change, the 54–45 vote in favor of Gorsuch would not have been enough to win confirmation.

The Republican response to the 2020 death of Justice Ruth Bader Ginsburg further propelled Democratic sentiment in favor of court packing. Republican President Donald Trump nominated Amy Coney Barrett to fill Ginsburg's seat just eight days after her death and 38 days prior to the November 2020 election. The Senate went on to confirm Barrett by a 52–48 margin eight days ahead of the election. This development incensed Democrats who remembered Republican obstruction of the Garland nomination four years earlier. "As soon as it became clear that the Republican-controlled Senate would almost certainly confirm Judge Amy Coney Barrett, creating a 6–3 conservative majority on the court, progressive Democrats—including prominent figures like Representative Alexandria Ocasio-Cortez of New York—argued that if Democrats won in November [2020 elections], they should seriously consider increasing the number of justices" (Herndon and Astor 2020).

Democrats did win the presidency in the 2020 election. They also maintained control of the House and gained control of the Senate by the narrowest of margins, holding 50 seats. Calls to expand the size of the Supreme Court continued, urged as a way to rectify what many saw as the GOP's hypocritical handling of the Garland and Barrett nominations. In April

2021, responding to those calls, President Biden formed the Presidential Commission on the Supreme Court of the United States to study the options. Staffed with lawyers, former federal judges, legal reform advocates, and scholars, Biden tasked the 36-member bipartisan Commission with providing "an analysis of the principal arguments in the contemporary public debate for and against Supreme Court reform, including an appraisal of the merits and legality of particular reform proposals" (White House 2021). Among other things, Biden included in the Commission's charge an analysis of "the length of service and turnover of justices on the Court" and "the membership and size of the Court" (White House 2021). Notably, Biden did not explicitly call on the Commission to offer specific recommendations for change.

Despite the strong support among some Democratic Party constituencies for expanding the Court, Biden has not proposed any changes as of 2022. Nor has Congress taken up legislation to expand the number of justices. Moreover, when the Commission released its report in 2021 it declined to take a stand on whether expansion would prove beneficial or detrimental.

The report noted that advocates of expansion view it as "necessary to address serious violations of norms governing the confirmation process." But the case for expanding the Supreme Court is not simply about restoring balance to the Court to remedy norms violations. It is also a response to what advocates perceive as "troubling developments in the Supreme Court's jurisprudence that they see as undermining the democratic system" (Presidential Commission on the Supreme Court of the United States 2021, 7). Indeed, strengthening democracy is central to the arguments offered by proponents of expansion. On their view, expansion is "required to ensure a Court more likely to uphold future voting rights and democracy-enhancing legislation constitutionally enacted by Congress and to prevent state legislatures from undermining or destroying the democratic process" (Presidential Commission on the Supreme Court of the United States 2021, 77). In addition, according to advocates of expansion, a larger Court would strengthen the institution by giving it the capacity to handle more cases and by providing the opportunity to increase the diversity of those who occupy the bench.

The report also stated, however, that opponents of expansion "contend that expanding—or 'packing'—the Court would significantly diminish its independence and legitimacy and establish a dangerous precedent that could be used by any future political force as a means of pressuring or intimidating the Court." For its part, the Commission's report specifically declared that it "takes no position on the validity or strength of these claims. Mirroring the broader public debate, there is profound disagreement among Commissioners on these issues" (Presidential Commission on the Supreme Court of the United States 2021, 7).

While profound disagreement indeed exists, changes to the size of the Court have been sought for political purposes by prior administrations and previous Congresses. In a few historical instances, changes to the size of the Court have been put into effect.

The U.S. Constitution does not specify how many justices are to serve on the Supreme Court, meaning that "[t]here is nothing sacrosanct about nine justices" (Noll 2020). In addition, a change to the size of the Court does not require a constitutional amendment. Instead, the Constitution delegates to Congress the legislative authority to structure the federal courts, authority that includes determining the number of judges who will serve on the bench. Passage of a congressional statute endorsed by the president or approved by enough votes to overcome a presidential veto would be enough to modify the number of seats on the Court and even the process by which the number of seats is determined.

Congress exercised its authority to determine the size of the Supreme Court during the founding era. In 1789, with the passage of the Judiciary Act, Congress put the number of Supreme Court justices at six, with one chief justice and five associate justices. In 1801, before Thomas Jefferson took over as president after beating President John Adams, the Federalist-controlled Congress passed legislation decreasing the future size of the Court; that change proved short-lived, reversed by the Democratic Republican Congress, which set the number of justices at six. Two more changes, in 1807 and 1837, increased the size of the Court, first to seven and then to nine. Several of these early reforms served, in part, to provide a sufficient number of justices to manage growing caseloads as the nation expanded. "But each expansion also served the interests of a political party," including ensuring "that a majority of Justices would be friendly to slavery" (Presidential Commission on the Supreme Court of the United States 2021, 68).

In the 1860s, Congress again exercised its power to adjust the size of the high Court. Congress increased the number of justices to 10 in 1863, dropped it down to eight in 1867, and bumped it up to nine in 1869, where it has since remained. The changes to the size of the Court enacted throughout the 1860s "are often said to have had a primarily political motivation" (Presidential Commission on the Supreme Court of the United States 2021, 68). In 1863, for example, Congress expanded the size of the Court in order to allow President Abraham Lincoln to appoint "a pro-Union, anti-slavery Justice" (Presidential Commission on the Supreme Court of the United States 2021, 69). In 1867, by contrast, Congress *decreased* the number of justices to stop President Andrew Johnson from selecting new justices.

Since 1869, there have been few serious efforts to alter the size of the Court. The most striking attempt was the failed proposal initiated by Franklin Delano Roosevelt in 1937. His controversial "court-packing plan," as it came to be known, would have given the president the authority to appoint new justices to the bench for every member of the Court over 70 years of age, up to a total Court membership of 15 justices. At that time, six justices met this age requirement; thus, if enacted, Roosevelt would have been in a position to dramatically and rapidly reshape the bench.

There is no doubt that Roosevelt's plan was politically inspired. While his surprise announcement of the plan on February 5, 1937, justified the legislation by arguing it would help the Court manage its workload, this efficiency argument was just the pretext under which Roosevelt could advance his main goal: to push through his New Deal agenda. This line of legislation, which sought to rebuild the economy after the massive dislocation created by the Great Depression, was substantially undercut by the Supreme Court during Roosevelt's first term of office. In 1937, coming off an overwhelming landslide victory in November 1936 that swept him into his second term, Roosevelt wanted to ensure the enactment of the New Deal by removing the roadblocks created by what he saw as a hostile Court. Consider historian William E. Leuchtenburg's description of Roosevelt's position.

> The [November 3, 1936] election-night jubilation was tempered, however, by an inescapable fear—that the U.S. Supreme Court might undo Roosevelt's accomplishments. From the outset of his presidency, FDR had known that four of the justices—Pierce Butler, James McReynolds, George Sutherland and Willis Van Devanter—would vote to invalidate almost all of the New Deal. They were referred to in the press as "the Four Horsemen," after the allegorical figures of the Apocalypse associated with death and destruction. In the spring of 1935, a fifth justice, Hoover-appointee Owen Roberts—at 60 the youngest man on the Supreme Court—began casting his swing vote with them to create a conservative majority. (Leuchtenburg 2005)

Sensational and hyperdramatized, the apocalyptic characterization of the justices nevertheless captured how substantially they demolished Roosevelt's agenda. Butler, McReynolds, Sutherland, and Van Devanter, joined by Roberts and "occasionally in concert with others, especially Chief Justice Charles Evans Hughes, struck down more significant acts of

Congress—including the two foundation stones, the NRA and the AAA, of Roosevelt's program—than at any other time in the nation's history, before or since. In May 1935, the court destroyed FDR's plan for industrial recovery. . . . Little more than seven months later, in a 6 to 3 ruling, it annihilated his farm program by determining that the Agricultural Adjustment Act was unconstitutional. Most of the federal government's authority over the economy derived from a clause in the Constitution empowering Congress to regulate interstate commerce, but the court construed the clause so narrowly that in another case that next spring, it ruled that not even so vast an industry as coal mining fell within the commerce power" (Leuchtenburg 2005).

Roosevelt devised his court-packing plan to confront and counteract this situation by diluting the power of the conservative justices through bench expansion. And while Roosevelt always maintained that the plan would make the Court more efficient and responsive, criticism of the proposal led him to take increasingly direct aim at the Court's conservative majority. In a fireside chat in March 9, 1937, Roosevelt emphasized the "overwhelming" electoral mandate given by the voters to Congress and the President to tackle the depression. "The Courts, however, have cast doubts on the ability of the elected Congress to protect us against catastrophe by meeting squarely our modern social and economic conditions," Roosevelt opined. "[W]e must take action to save the Constitution from the Court and the Court from itself. We must find a way to take an appeal from the Supreme Court to the Constitution itself. We want a Supreme Court which will do justice under the Constitution and not over it. In our courts we want a government of laws and not of men" (Roosevelt 1937).

Ultimately, Congress did not enact Roosevelt's plan, and the president took a substantial amount of heat for pressing it forward. He did, however, ultimately succeed in getting many of his economic New Deal policies enacted—in large measure because the Supreme Court stopped striking them down on legal grounds. It has long been argued, in fact, that the threat posed by Roosevelt's proposed court-packing plan was seen as so serious that it resulted in the so-called "switch in time that saved nine"—a decision by Justice Owen Roberts to swing to a position more favorable to Roosevelt's New Deal agenda. The validity of this longstanding argument, though, is disputed (see Q22).

Roosevelt eventually had the opportunity to pack the Court by ordinary means, namely by appointing justices to fill vacated seats. Justice Van Devanter, one of "the Four Horsemen," retired in the summer of 1937, giving Roosevelt his first appointment to the bench. By 1942, seven of the nine justices were Roosevelt appointments, and by the time of Roosevelt's death, he had appointed eight justices to the Court.

The legacy of Roosevelt's court-packing plan is substantial and bodes poorly for those who advocate changes to the current composition of the Court. Advocates offer strong arguments in favor of the institution-enhancing benefits of Court expansion—seeking to remedy earlier norms violations, stem the tide of antidemocratic developments, and strengthen the Court's institutional capacity and diversity. Nevertheless, they have to contend with claims that Roosevelt's 1937 court-packing plan has "long been regarded as one of the most disgraceful assaults on the Supreme Court in American history. Opponents of Court packing also emphasize that those who resisted Court packing in 1937—particularly those who stood up to the President and leader of their own party—are seen has having shown tremendous political courage" (Presidential Commission on the Supreme Court of the United States 2021, 81). Regardless of the accuracy of this narrative, it surely poses a barrier for those seeking Court reform.

FURTHER READING

Blake, Aaron. 2020. "How the GOP Is Trying to Justify its Supreme Court Reversal." *Washington Post*, September 21, 2020.

Everett, Burgess, and Glenn Thrush. 2016. "McConnell Throws Down the Gauntlet: No Scalia Replacement Under Obama." *Politico*, February 13, 2016.

Franklin, Charles H. 2019. "Public Views of the Supreme Court." Marquette Law School Poll: Complete Report. https://law.marquette.edu/poll/wp-content/uploads/2019/10/MULawPollSupremeCourtReportOct2019.pdf

Frost, Amanda. 2020. "Academic Highlight: The Past, Present and Future of Court Packing." *SCOTUSblog*, December 22, 2020. https://www.scotusblog.com/2020/12/academic-highlight-the-past-present-and-future-of-court-packing

Herndon, Astead W., and Maggie Astor. 2020. "Ruth Bader Ginsburg's Death Revives Talk of Court Packing." *New York Times*, September 19, 2020.

Leuchtenburg, William E. 2005. "When Franklin Roosevelt Clashed with the Supreme Court—and Lost." *Smithsonian Magazine*, May 2005.

Noll, David. 2020. "What Is Court Packing?" *Rutgers Today*, October 27, 2020. https://www.rutgers.edu/news/what-court-packing

Presidential Commission on the Supreme Court of the United States. 2021, December. "Draft Final Report." https://www.whitehouse.gov/wp-content/uploads/2021/12/SCOTUS-Report-Final-12.8.21-1.pdf

Roosevelt, Franklin Delano. 1937. "On 'Court-Packing.'" March 9, 1937: Fireside Chat 9. https://millercenter.org/the-presidency/presidential -speeches/march-9-1937-fireside-chat-9-court-packing

White House. 2021. "Presidential Commission on the Supreme Court of the United States." The White House, April 9, 2021. https://www .whitehouse.gov/pcscotus

Q15. CAN CONGRESS STRIP THE SUPREME COURT AND LOWER FEDERAL COURTS OF THEIR JURISDICTION?

Answer: It is widely agreed that Congress has the authority to limit jurisdiction of the lower federal courts. Whether Congress may limit the Supreme Court's jurisdiction is, however, unclear and subject to consider-able debate. Although Congress has frequently introduced legislation to strip the federal courts—and the Supreme Court in particular—of juris-diction, that legislation has rarely passed.

The Facts: Court jurisdiction—that is, a court's authority to hear and decide upon a particular matter or area of law—establishes the boundaries of which types of cases it can adjudicate. As Chief Justice Samuel Chase described it in 1868, "Without jurisdiction, the court cannot proceed at all in any cause. Jurisdiction is power to declare the law, and, when it ceases to exist, the only function remaining to the court is that of announcing the fact and dismissing the cause" (*Ex parte McCardle* 1869, 514). As such, a court's jurisdiction affects the reach of its power. If the legislative branch can alter the jurisdiction of the bench, it can broaden or curtail judicial authority.

Just as calls to expand the size of the U.S. Supreme Court have risen in recent years, so too have calls to modify the high Court's jurisdiction. For example, just ahead of the 2020 presidential election and again in May 2021, legal scholar Christopher Jon Sprigman urged progressives to push Congress to reduce federal judicial power through jurisdiction stripping (Sprigman 2020a; Sprigman 2020b; Sprigman 2021). Legal scholars Ryan Doerfler and Samuel Moyn recently advocated for jurisdiction changes, instead of court packing, as a "disempowering reform" that decreases judi-cial power by transferring it to other government bodies. This type of change is distinct from "personnel reforms," including efforts to increase the size of the Court or impose term limits. Unlike disempowering reforms, personnel reforms would not reduce the power of judges but merely alter the ideological composition of the jurists who exercise power (Doerfler and Moyn 2021, 1720–1721).

Moyn further pressed for jurisdiction changes and reduction of the Court's power in testimony before the Presidential Commission on the Supreme Court of the United States, a committee formed in 2021 by the Biden administration to evaluate options for reforming the Supreme Court (see Q14). Congress, Moyn suggested, could give itself the final say on whether a federal statute declared invalid by the Supreme Court would actually be invalidated. Congress could do so by passing a jurisdictional law that makes Court rejection of a federal statute conditional on congressional approval (Moyn 2021, 19). These and other takes from the left side of the political spectrum have emerged in response to the Supreme Court's growing power and conservatism. In particular, many Democrats express concern that an unchecked Court with a solidified conservative bloc will brazenly undermine voting rights, civil rights, abortion rights, LGBTQ+ rights, environmental protections, and more.

Pleas for jurisdiction stripping are neither new nor only the province of the left, however. For example, angered by the Supreme Court decision declaring racial segregation in public schools unconstitutional (*Brown v. Board of Education* 1954), Southern segregationists in Congress tried unsuccessfully to remove federal court jurisdiction over school desegregation cases. A related episode came in 1957 when two Republican senators introduced a bill to remove Supreme Court jurisdiction in matters relating to congressional investigations of those suspected of communism and subversive activity. That bill, motivated in part by lingering resentment of the ruling in *Brown*, also reflected expanding conflict between the Republican-controlled Congress and the liberal Warren Court over its decisions curtailing congressional investigations into alleged Communist sympathizers (Norton 2006; Rahnama 2020). Though approved by the Senate Judiciary Committee and debated in the full Senate, the jurisdiction-stripping bill was not brought to a formal vote.

In 1964, efforts to limit jurisdiction over cases involving apportionment of representation in state legislatures were precipitated by "decisions in *Baker v. Carr* [1962] and *Reynolds v. Sims* [1964]—two cases through which the court formally introduced the idea of 'one person, one vote' and prevented states from apportioning seats in their state legislatures in a way that clearly discriminated against their Black population" (Rahnama 2020). Fifteen years later, Republican Senator Jesse Helms put forward a jurisdiction-stripping measure that passed the Democratically-controlled Senate by a vote of 51 to 40. The legislation proposed "to remove Supreme Court and lower federal court jurisdiction over the issue of voluntary prayer in public schools" (Baucus and Kay 1982, 991). Senate Democratic leadership voted against the measure but let the bill go forward so conservative Democrats could show support for school prayer and with the expectation that the House of Representatives would kill the legislation, which it did (Oldmixon 2005, 106).

Jurisdiction-stripping efforts gained momentum in the 1980s when Republicans brought forward multiple such measures. In 1982 alone, Republicans in Congress introduced more than 20 bills that sought to strip the Supreme Court of its jurisdiction over a wide range of social issues including abortion, desegregation, and school prayer (Yaffe-Bellany 2020). Those bills ultimately failed, with President Ronald Reagan's Attorney General indicating the U.S. Department of Justice's (DOJ) reluctance to support jurisdiction stripping. Still, a memo written by then-DOJ lawyer— and current Chief Justice of the Supreme Court—John Roberts defended jurisdiction stripping as a lawful and constitutional exercise of legislative authority.

Because of the value commonly placed on judicial independence and America's historical emphasis on the separation of powers among the branches of government, the idea that a legislature could limit a court's jurisdiction for political purposes might seem odd or alarming. If Congress has authority to simply override Supreme Court decisions or remove particular subjects from the jurisdiction of the federal courts, that knowledge alone could dramatically diminish judicial power. The courts would have to be leery of making any legal rulings that might displease Congress to the point that it punishes the judges with jurisdiction stripping. Does Congress have such a prerogative?

The extent of congressional authority governing federal court jurisdiction—both over the Supreme Court and the lower federal courts—is grounded in the Constitution and, in turn, in the Supreme Court's interpretation of the Constitution. With respect to the lower federal courts, there is widespread consensus that Congress has authority to regulate jurisdiction. Article III explicitly gives Congress the power to "ordain and establish" the "inferior" federal courts. This explicit grant has been widely understood to include the implicit authority to determine the jurisdiction of the lower courts. As one legal scholar puts it, "Article III goes further than giving the Congress the all-or-nothing power to decide whether lower federal courts should exist. It leaves it to Congress to decide, having created lower federal courts, what their jurisdiction should be—that is, to decide *which* of the cases to which the federal judicial power extends should be litigated in the lower federal courts" (Bator 1982, 1030–1031).

The U.S. Supreme Court has concurred with this assessment, stating, for example, that "[c]ourts created by statute can have no jurisdiction but such as the statute confers" (*Sheldon v. Sill* 1850, 449). Simply put, the Court has accepted the logic that since Congress has substantial constitutional power to *not create* lower federal courts at all, that must also mean that Congress has the lesser power of choosing to create lower federal courts with specific or limited jurisdiction (Redish 1990, 1637).

There is, however, far less consensus and much more significant debate about whether Congress possesses the same governing authority over the jurisdiction of the Supreme Court. Article III of the Constitution specifies a few types of cases (e.g., cases involving ambassadors) as falling under the Court's original jurisdiction, that is, the authority to adjudicate a legal dispute on its first hearing. For all other "cases" and "controversies" identified in Article III, the Court has appellate jurisdiction, that is, the authority to hear and rule on a case on appeal from a lower court.

Importantly, though, Article III stipulates that "the supreme Court shall have appellate Jurisdiction, both as to Law and Fact, with such Exceptions, and under such Regulations as the Congress shall make." The wording of this so-called Exceptions Clause has led many to argue that Congress has near-absolute authority—also called "plenary" power—over the high Court's appellate jurisdiction. Others disagree.

Those who hold that Congress has extensive authority to determine the Supreme Court's appellate jurisdiction have the plain language of the Exceptions Clause on which to rely. As legal scholar William Van Alstyne put it in 1973, "[t]he power to make exceptions to Supreme Court appellate jurisdiction is a plenary power. It is given in express terms and without limitation" (1973, 260). Nearly four decades later, the same view is widely held, as legal scholar Tara Leigh Grove summarized: "Many commentators have concluded, based on the text and structure of Article III, that Congress has plenary power to restrict federal jurisdiction. . . . According to these scholars, this Exceptions Clause gives Congress broad power to remove cases from the [Supreme] Court's appellate oversight" (Grove 2011, 874–875).

The U.S. Supreme Court lent some support to this interpretation of congressional authority in a ruling in *Ex parte McCardle* (1869). In this case, William McCardle asked the Supreme Court to review his detention under the Habeas Corpus Act of 1867 after the lower federal courts denied his petition for habeas corpus, in which he claimed to have been unlawfully jailed for sedition. Among other things, the 1867 Habeas Corpus Act authorized the Supreme Court to hear appeals from Circuit Court rulings denying habeas corpus. That modified the Court's habeas corpus jurisdiction, which, under the 1789 Judiciary Act, permitted habeas review by the Supreme Court only when petitions were submitted to the Court originally, not on appeal.

But as the Court was reviewing McCardle's petition, Congress passed a provision withdrawing the Court's appellate jurisdiction under the Habeas Corpus Act. The Supreme Court, in turn, dismissed McCardle's appeal and acceded to the congressional authority delineated in Article III. In its unanimous opinion, the Court concluded that it is "quite clear . . . that this court cannot proceed to pronounce judgment in this case, for it has no longer jurisdiction of the appeal" (*Ex parte McCardle* 1869, 515).

Although the Court in *McCardle* did not challenge congressional authority to remove the jurisdiction allocated by the Habeas Corpus Act, the Court's ruling was notably narrow. Writing for the Court, Chief Justice Samuel Chase explained that the ruling does not imply "that the whole appellate power of the court, in cases of habeas corpus, is denied" (*Ex parte McCardle* 1869, 515). He emphasized that the ruling only takes away the Supreme Court's appellate jurisdiction in a limited class of legal cases—appeals from the Circuit Courts under the 1867 Act.

Still, scholars point to the *Ex parte McCardle* decision, along with other historical evidence and legal rulings, as grounds for the view that Congress has such plenary power over the jurisdictional reach of the Supreme Court. According to legal scholar Raoul Berger, "[c]ongressional control of the courts' jurisdiction under article III has the sanction of the First Congress, draftsmen of the Judiciary Act of 1789, and of an unbroken string of decisions stretching from the beginning of the Republic" (Berger 1983, 614).

Given that the vast majority of the cases heard by the Supreme Court get there by way of appeal rather than through original jurisdiction, Congressional authority to regulate appellate jurisdiction has the potential to serve as a substantial check on the Court. Advocates of jurisdiction stripping assert that disempowering the Court by curtailing its jurisdiction would make the institution "less central to our politics and our constitutional order" (Bouie 2021).

According to legal scholar Paul Bator, however, these calls to curtail the legal authority of the courts raise a troubling difficulty:

> If the Constitution means what it says, it means that Congress can make the state courts—or, indeed, the lower federal courts—the ultimate authority for the decision of any category of case to which the federal judicial power extends.
>
>   What is so troubling about that position, however, is that such a jurisdictional withdrawal would create a system inconsistent with

the structure that the Framers assumed to be appropriate. . . . Furthermore, even if one believes—as I do—that Congress has the raw power to do this, the argument that it would violate the spirit of the instrument to do so seems extremely powerful. (Bator 1982, 1038–1041)

In a related vein, some scholars argue that whatever authority Congress might be granted by the Exceptions Clause cannot interfere with the "essential appellate function" of the Supreme Court or the Court's position at the pinnacle of the federal judicial system. These scholars emphasize that "the Court has a unique role in the constitutional scheme and that Congress must provide the Court with sufficient jurisdiction to perform that role" (Grove 2011, 877). For example, legal scholar Leonard Ratner argued that if the Exceptions Clause is interpreted as giving Congress plenary control over the Supreme Court's appellate jurisdiction, that is tantamount to giving Congress the power to destroy. It would mean that

Congress can by statute profoundly alter the structure of American government. It can all but destroy the coordinate judicial branch and thus upset the delicately poised constitutional system of checks and balances. It can distort the nature of the federal union by permitting each state to decide for itself the scope of its authority under the Constitution. It can reduce the supreme law of the land as defined in article VI to a hodgepodge of inconsistent decisions by making fifty state courts and eleven federal courts of appeals the final judges of the meaning and Constitution, laws, and treaties of the United States. (Ratner 1960, 158–159)

Such an interpretation, according to Ratner, is untenable. Accordingly, Ratner argues that Congressional authority to make exceptions to the Court's appellate jurisdiction must be limited in order to allow the Court to operate consistent with the structure of the federal system established by the Constitution. He insists that Congress cannot remove particular subject matters from the Supreme Court's appellate jurisdiction because that would obstruct the Court's "essential appellate functions under the Constitution," which include providing a tribunal "for the ultimate resolution of inconsistent or conflicting interpretations of federal law by state and federal courts," and "for maintaining the supremacy of federal law when it conflicts with state law or is challenged by state authority" (Ratner 1960, 161).

Ratner is not alone in advancing this type of perspective on the limits of congressional authority even in the face of the unequivocal language of the Exceptions Clause. As law professor Henry Hart famously argued, exceptions made by Congress "must not be such as will destroy the essential role of the Supreme Court in the constitutional plan" (Hart 1953, 1365).

There are other reasons to think that congressional authority over the Supreme Court's appellate jurisdiction has considerable limits. First, there are stipulations in the Constitution outside of Article III that arguably constrain Congress's authority in this matter, and "most scholars agree that Congress's power is limited by constitutional sources other than Article III (known as 'external' limits)" (Grove 2011, 874).

Those external limits are beyond Article III but in the Constitution itself; namely, in the liberties and rights established elsewhere in the document. As Grove writes, "there is broad consensus that Congress may not enact a jurisdictional measure that violates the Equal Protection Clause or the Suspension Clause of Article I, Section 9. Although scholars dispute the precise scope of these external constraints, they generally agree that these provisions limit Congress's power" (Grove 2011, 874 n.11). Similarly, "if Congress provides that only Catholics may bring suits in the lower federal courts, this would be invalid, not because non-Catholics have a constitutional right of access to lower federal courts, but because the Constitution prohibits any Congressional action discriminating among religious denominations" (Bator 1982, 1034). Thus, even those who hold that the Exceptions Clause gives Congress broad authority concede that it does not give Congress absolute power—such as the power to violate other aspects of the Constitution.

Second, the debate surrounding the extent of congressional authority over the Supreme Court's jurisdiction emerges in part because of constitutional language contained in Article III. The Exceptions Clause seems pretty clear, to be sure. But Article III also says that the judicial power *shall* extend to *all* cases in law and equity arising under federal law. According to some analysts, this suggests that Article III does not give Congress much leeway to alter the jurisdiction of the federal courts. Rather, it suggests that Article III required jurisdiction to apply to all cases in law and equity arising under federal law. For example, legal scholar Robert N. Clinton asserts that

the framers, by providing that "[t]he judicial Power of the United States, *shall be vested* in one supreme Court and in such inferior Courts as the Congress may from time to time ordain and establish," intended to mandate that Congress allocate to the federal judiciary as a whole each and every type of case or controversy defined as part of the judicial power of the United States by section 2, clause 1 of article III, excluding, possibly, only those cases that Congress deemed to be so trivial that they would pose an unnecessary burden on both the federal judiciary and on the parties forced to litigate in federal court." . . . The powers over the federal judiciary that articles I and III gave to Congress thus involved authority over the distribution, organization, and implementation of the judicial power of the United States, not a license to curtail its exercise. (Clinton 1984, 749–750; see also Amar 1985)

Debate over whether Congress may strip the Supreme Court of jurisdiction is likely to continue, but the presence of such debates does not foreshadow the passage of jurisdiction-stripping laws. Indeed, Congress has "rarely enacted jurisdiction-stripping legislation" (Grove 2011, 880), though, as discussed earlier, it has tried. Although Congress has threatened to denude the Court of its power through jurisdiction stripping, and although considerable scholarly attention has been paid to whether this would be constitutional, much of the debate remains, as it were, academic.

FURTHER READING

Amar, Akhil Reed. 1985. "A Neo-Federalist View of Article III: Separating the Two Tiers of Federal Jurisdiction." *Boston University Law Review*, 65, no. 2: 205–274.

Baker v. Carr, 369 U.S. 186 (1962).

Bator, Paul M. 1982. "Congressional Power over the Jurisdiction of the Federal Courts." *Villanova Law Review*, 27, no. 5: 1030–1041.

Baucus, Max, and Kenneth R. Kay. 1982. "The Court Stripping Bills: Their Impact on the Constitution, the Courts, and Congress." *Villanova Law Review*, 27: 988–1018.

Berger, Raoul. 1983. "Insulation of Judicial Usurpation: A Comment on Lawrence Sager's Court-Stripping Polemic." *Ohio State Law Journal*, 44, no. 3: 611–648.

Bouie, Jamelle. 2021. "The Supreme Court Needs to Be Cut Down to Size." *New York Times*, July 23, 2021.

Brown v. Board of Education, 347 U.S. 483 (1954).

Clinton, Robert N. 1984. "A Mandatory View of Federal Court Jurisdiction: A Guided Quest for the Original Understanding of Article III." *University of Pennsylvania Law Review*, 132, no. 4: 741–866.

Clinton, Robert N. 1986. "A Mandatory View of Federal Court Jurisdiction: Early Implementation of and Departures from the Constitutional Plan." *Columbia Law Review*, 86, no. 8: 1515–1621.

Doerfler, Ryan D., and Samuel Moyn. 2021. "Democratizing the Supreme Court." *California Law Review*, 109, no. 5: 1703–1772.

Ex parte McCardle, 74 U.S. 506 (1869).

Grove, Tara Leigh. 2011. "The Structural Safeguards of Federal Jurisdiction." *Harvard Law Review*, 124, no. 4: 869–940.

Hart, Henry M., Jr. 1953. "The Power of Congress to Limit the Jurisdiction of Federal Courts: An Exercise in Dialectic." *Harvard Law Review*, 66, no. 8: 1362–1402.

Moyn, Samuel. 2021. "Written Statement: Presidential Commission on the Supreme Court of the United States." June 30, 2021. https://www
.whitehouse.gov/wp-content/uploads/2021/06/Moyn-Testimony.pdf

Norton, Helen. 2006. "Reshaping Federal Jurisdiction: Congress's Latest Challenge to Judicial Review." *Wake Forest Law Review*, 41: 1003–1043.

Oldmixon, Elizabeth Anne. 2005. *Uncompromising Positions: God, Sex, and the U.S. House of Representatives*. Washington, DC: Georgetown University Press.

Rahnama, Kia. 2020. "The Other Tool Democrats Have to Rein in the Supreme Court." *Politico*, October 26, 2020. https://www.politico.com
/news/magazine/2020/10/26/amy-coney-barrett-confirmation-court
-packing-jursidiction-stripping-432566

Ratner, Leonard G. 1960. "Congressional Power over the Appellate Jurisdiction of the Supreme Court." *University of Pennsylvania Law Review*, 109, no. 2: 157–202.

Redish, Martin H. 1990. "Text, Structure, and Common Sense in the Interpretation of Article III." *University of Pennsylvania Law Review*, 138, no. 6: 1633–1649.

Reynolds v. Sims, 377 U.S. 533 (1964).

Sheldon v. Sill, 49 U.S. 441 (1850).

Sprigman, Christopher Jon. 2020a. "A Constitutional Weapon for Biden to Vanquish Trump's Army of Judges." *The New Republic*, August 20, 2020.

Sprigman, Christopher Jon. 2020b. "Congress's Article III Power and the Process of Constitutional Change." *New York University Law Review*, 95: 1778–1859.

Sprigman, Christopher Jon. 2021. "Stripping the Courts' Jurisdiction." *The American Prospect*, May 5, 2021. https://prospect.org/justice
/stripping-the-courts-jurisdiction

Van Alstyne, William W. 1973. "A Critical Guide to Ex Parte McCardle." *Arizona Law Review*, 15, no. 2: 229–270.

Yaffe-Bellany, David. 2020. "Liberals Weigh Jurisdiction Stripping to Rein in Supreme Court." *Bloomberg News*, October 6, 2020.

Q16. WOULD TERM LIMITS MAKE THE
SUPREME COURT LESS POLITICIZED?

Answer: Maybe. Reducing politicization of the Supreme Court is among the main goals that advocates of judicial term limits assert in arguing their cause. The logic suggesting that term limits would decrease politicization is compelling, especially when term limits are combined with a regular appointment schedule. Moreover, the fact that almost all U.S. states, and all major democracies, employ term limits or mandatory retirement age for judges on their highest courts lends support to those who want to do the same thing for future U.S. Supreme Court justices. Still, whether term limits would actually decrease politicization—or just redirect it into other forms—remains the subject of debate and conjecture.

The Facts: In October 2020, 31 legal scholars signed a letter endorsing H.R. 8424, known as the Supreme Court Term Limits and Regular Appointments Act. Introduced in the House of Representatives, the bill would end life tenure for future justices appointed to the Supreme Court, replacing that tenure with an 18-year term on the Court. The term of each justice would be staggered, and a vacancy would automatically occur every two years (in nonelection years), giving each president two nominees for each term of office. The bill allows future justices to remain on the federal bench after the 18-year term is complete, serving on a lower court or temporarily filling in for unexpected vacancies in Supreme Court cases (H.R.8424–116th Congress 2019-2020). This allowance seeks to make the bill consistent with the stipulation in Article III of the Constitution that judges of both the supreme and inferior courts "hold their Offices during good Behaviour."

In their notably brief letter of endorsement—a mere 80 words, not including signatures—the signatories offered one argument in favor of term limits. "Though the bill is not perfect," they submitted, "we believe it to be a critical piece in prescribing how our country's leaders can work to depoliticize the Supreme Court and its confirmation process" (Campaign for Supreme Court Term Limits 2020).

Those advocating limits to the terms of Supreme Court justices cite a number of additional benefits as well. These include increasing accountability to the public; ending strategic retirements that give justices too much influence over who their successors will be; increasing the willingness of presidents to select more experienced jurists; and limiting the extent to which judges remain on the bench after their physical health or cognitive capacity decline. Still, advocates of term limits for the Supreme Court have placed their greatest focus on arguments that politicization of the Court has become so transparent that the Court's legitimacy in the public eye is in jeopardy. As a 2020 report by the American Academy of Arts and Sciences put it, the implementation of term limits and a regular appointment schedule would "go a long way toward depoliticizing the appointment process" and "help move the Court toward a less partisan future, restoring its legitimacy as an independent arbiter of justice" (American Academy of Arts and Sciences 2020, 31).

Would term limits diminish politicization of the Supreme Court? "The hope . . . is that by more regularly replacing longtime justices with newer ones, adding predictability to when those switches occur, the judicial-nomination process would become less divisive and disruptive" (Shapiro 2020). Regularizing the appointment of term-limited justices, the argument goes, would serve as a corrective to the current system, which is characterized by several features that routinely heighten partisan division and political conflict today.

First, under the current system, the timing of vacancies is unpredictable. Vacancies occur when justices depart, either by retirement, resignation, death, or, theoretically at least, impeachment. This means that openings on the bench can occur at any moment, including times of heightened partisan conflict. The death of Justice Ruth Bader Ginsburg 46 days ahead of the 2020 presidential election is a case in point.

Secondly, the unpredictable timing of Court vacancies can contribute to partisan imbalance over the nomination and confirmation process. For example, Democratic President Jimmy Carter made no nominations to the Supreme Court because there happened to be no vacancies in his four years as president, whereas Republican President George H. W. Bush made two nominations to the Supreme Court in his single term of office. Similarly, compare Democratic President Barack Obama and Republican President Donald Trump. Three vacancies on the bench occurred during each president's time in office, though Obama served as president for eight years and Trump only for four years (plus the Republican Senate refused to act on one of Obama's nominees). More broadly, through the end of 2020, "[a]cross the twenty-one presidential terms since 1937, Republican presidents have appointed twenty out of forty Justices. . . . In recent decades, however, a disparity has emerged. For instance, of the Justices appointed since Richard Nixon took office in 1969, fifteen out of nineteen Justices were appointed by Republicans" (Chilton et al. 2021, 16).

Third, justices can currently engage in the practice known as "strategic retirement," timing their departures to give control over the nomination to their preferred political party. As discussed in Q7, not all retirements are strategic. But there is both anecdotal evidence and empirical support showing that some justices make retirement decisions based on whether the party of their choice controls the White House. Even if justices do not engage in strategic retirement, rampant speculation and politically motivated encouragement to do so further underscores the sense that partisan politicization of the Court is a major factor in its operations.

Fourth, under the current system, justices serve for increasingly long periods of time. The justices appointed since 1990 and who have left the bench through the end of 2020 served an average of 26.3 years (Chilton et al. 2021, 13). This contrasts quite dramatically with earlier eras. For example, between 1789 and 1970, justices served an average of 14.9 years (Calabresi and Lindgren 2006, 770–771). The dramatic growth in the length of service is not just attributable to increasing life expectancy. A compounding factor is that "[l]ife tenure has motivated presidents to pick younger and younger justices. In the post-World War II era, presidents generally forgo appointing jurists in their 60s, who would bring a great deal of experience, and instead nominate judges in their 40s or 50s, who could serve on the court for many decades" (Collins and Ward 2021).

Fifth, with only nine justices serving on the bench, a single vacancy has the potential to dramatically shift the rulings of the Court. This is especially so when the Court is closely divided, as it often is. At the beginning of 2016, for instance, the Court was composed of four liberal justices, four conservative justices, and swing Justice Anthony Kennedy, who despite a generally conservative judicial philosophy often sided with liberals on social issues like gay rights and abortion. In February 2016, the sudden death of Justice Antonin Scalia, a staunchly conservative jurist who had been appointed by a Republican president, created a vacancy on the Court. Had the Republican-controlled Senate confirmed Obama's nomination of Merrick Garland, the Court would have shifted to a liberal majority. To avoid this shift, the Republican-controlled Senate took the blatantly partisan step of refusing to act on Obama's nomination, leaving Scalia's seat vacant for the winner of the next presidential election—Republican Donald Trump (Q5).

These five characteristics combine to amplify the political and partisan magnitude of each vacancy on the Court. "On the partisan chessboard, nailing down one of the nine spots is a major victory for any President, especially if you can install a young partisan who will serve for decades" (Hill 2020). As legal scholars Steven Calabresi and James Lindgren argue, "the combination of less frequent vacancies and longer tenures of office means that when vacancies do arise, there is so much at stake that confirmation battles have become much more intense" (Calabresi and Lindgren 2006, 771).

The aim of regularized appointments of term-limited justices is to "reduce the political incentives that have led to high-stakes, highly politicized appointments—the kind that could damage the Court's reputation over time. Quite simply, instituting term limits allows alternating presidents to each have a say on the Court's composition, ensuring more regularity and predictability in appointments" (Sen 2021, 4). Advocates of placing term limits on Supreme Court justices do not view it as a magic elixir that solves the problem of politicization. But they do say that it would tamp down the fervor that characterizes the selection process by making each appointment less consequential. "Term limits wouldn't remove politics from the court," the argument goes, "but they could make the confirmation process less high-stakes, where justices have to time their retirements and people in both parties spend time wondering which will be the next justice to die" (Waldman 2021).

There is not much available empirical evidence that either supports or rejects the logic linking term limits and declining politicization. However, some recent modeling suggests that terms limits would reduce "extreme ideological imbalance" on the Court. A group of law and public policy professors used simulations to estimate and assess the impact of term limits if they had been in effect between 1937 and 2020. They concluded that term limits would have cut the Court's extreme ideological imbalance of the past 80 years almost in half. Furthermore, "any of the major term-limits proposals are likely to produce similar, dramatic changes in the ideological composition of the Supreme Court" by *reducing* extreme ideological imbalance (Chilton et al. 2021, 6).

Even without such empirical support, though, the logic that links regularized appointments of term-limited justices with a decrease in politicization is self-evident—and it is especially compelling in the face of the increasing politicization of the Supreme Court and the partisanship that presently inundates the selection of justices.

However, not all court observers are persuaded that judicial term limits would produce a decrease in politicization. For one thing, proponents of term limits typically suggest applying them to future appointments, which leaves current justices on the Court for the time being. Opponents of term limits argue that whatever decrease in politicization might accrue from adding new, term-limited justices to the Court would take years to come to fruition.

In addition, opponents of term limits—and even some advocates— are dubious of the claim that regular, term-limited appointments would decrease politicization. Some who favor term limits for other reasons expect that politicization and partisanship would continue. Legal scholar

Orin Kerr argues that the selection of justices would remain "an inherently political process" even with term limits. "It would still," according to Kerr, "be one politician doing the nominating and 100 politicians doing the advising and consenting" (Boehm 2018).

Some opponents of term limits even assert that instituting such a measure could actually *increase* political and partisan conflict. According to Anthony Marcum, a fellow at the R Street Institute, a conservative think tank, "term limits will ensure that court vacancies are inextricably tied to every presidential race and has the potential to create abrupt ideological shifts on the highest court, only increasing the political scrutiny. In other words, term limits will not lower the temperature around nominations, they will leave the country scorched" (Marcum 2020). Professors Daniel Epps and Ganesh Sitaraman agree. They contend that a term-limits approach "is unlikely to depoliticize the Court or turn down the temperature of the nominations process. Indeed, if anything, it will make the politicization of the Court even worse by increasing the Court's prominence in every election cycle" (Epps and Sitaraman 2019, 173). Among the points that Epps and Sitaraman highlight in countering term limits is that Court appointments would be an election issue not just in presidential elections but in midterms as well, at least if party control over the Senate were in play. Furthermore, ideological battles around the Court would not dampen, as "activists on both sides would still jockey to make sure only the purest ideologues were appointed" (Epps and Sitaraman 2019, 174).

There is also some modeling suggesting that term limits could lead to shifting judicial doctrine, a decrease in the stability of precedent, and, in turn, further politicization. According to researchers at Vanderbilt University, "[a] Supreme Court that welcomes a new justice every two years, and turns over entirely over the course of every 18 years, could wreak havoc on doctrinal stability" (Sherry and Sundby 2019). That conclusion is based on a computer simulation modeling the effects of term limits on abortion rights, beginning in 1973 when the Court handed down its ruling legalizing abortion in *Roe v. Wade*. The simulation uses an 18-year term limit model, with a new justice added to the bench every two years, and runs from 1973 to 2019. According to the researchers, "[a]s our hypothetical Supreme Court changes every two years, we predict whether a majority of justices would vote to retain *Roe* or to overrule it; if an overruling is predicted, we then predict in subsequent years whether a majority would vote to reinstate it (and then whether it would be overruled again, reinstated again . . . you get the idea!)" (Sherry and Sundby 2019).

The simulation includes several additional assumptions about such things as the party of the nominating president and the Senate, and the likelihood that individual justices will be loyal to the nominating president and deferential to precedent. Running the simulations led the researchers to predict that *Roe* would have "suffered whiplash. Positing moderately loyal justices with no deference to precedent, *Roe* would have been overruled in 1987, reinstated in 2009 and overruled again in 2017. . . . Adding deference to precedent ameliorated some of the instability, but assuming that justices will uphold precedent is inconsistent with the primary justifications for imposing term limits" (Sherry and Sundby 2019). If term limits cause, or are seen as causing, dramatic swings in precedent, as the Vanderbilt researchers predict, that could further heighten politicization: "the chance for such a dramatic ideological shift in the highest court would only put a greater spotlight on it during presidential elections and judicial confirmations" (Marcum 2020).

In sum, while there is a rising tide of calls for the regularized appointment of term-limited justices, there is no consensus around the question of whether term limits would decrease politicization. Still, it is clear that retaining the status quo will not reduce the political character of the Court. Decisions about when (and whether) to retire are, themselves, politicized (see Q7). As editors of the *Boston Globe* explain, the death of Ruth Bader Ginsburg in 2020 was freighted with politics and partisanship:

> Justice Ruth Bader Ginsburg understood, more than anyone else, the enormous consequences of her death. "My most fervent wish," she said, in a statement dictated to her granddaughter before she died, in her Washington, D.C., home, "is that I will not be replaced until a new president is installed." . . . It was unseemly, to say the least, that our collective mourning of Ginsburg's extraordinary life and influential legacy was almost immediately eclipsed by the political implications of her death. But that's what Supreme Court confirmations have become: another venue for the country's poisonous partisanship. (*Boston Globe* 2020)

It is also clear from multiple public opinion polls that there is bipartisan public support for term or age limits, a point that advocates emphasize. For example, according to a 2021 survey of Americans, only 22% of respondents oppose using "term or age limits" for Supreme Court justices, while 63% indicated some or strong support for them. The same poll found that while Democrats were relatively more sanguine about these limits, a majority of Democrats (71%), Republicans (59%), and independents (63%) expressed either some or strong support (Ipsos 2021).

Support for term or age limits is manifest not only in public opinion polls but also in their widespread use at the state level. In fact, Rhode Island is the only one of the 50 states that does not have term limits or mandatory retirement ages in place for their state supreme court justices (Heintz and Peterson 2020). Moreover, all other major democracies around the world use term limits or mandatory retirement age for judges on their highest courts (Calabresi and Lindgren 2006, 819–820).

In short, even if the institution of term limits would not significantly lower the political temperature, there are other good reasons to consider this type of reform.

FURTHER READING

American Academy of Arts and Sciences. 2020. *Reinventing American Democracy for the 21st Century*. Cambridge, MA: Commission on the Practice of Democratic Citizenship.

Boehm, Eric. 2018. "Term Limits for Supreme Court Justices Won't Save Us. But They Might Be Worth Trying Anyway." *Reason*, October 3, 2018.

Boston Globe. 2020. "Set Term Limits for Supreme Court Justices." *Boston Globe*, September 22, 2020.

Calabresi, Steven G., and James T. Lindgren. 2006. "Term Limits for the Supreme Court: Life Tenure Reconsidered." *Harvard Journal of Law and Public Policy*, 29, no. 3: 769–877.

Campaign for Supreme Court Term Limits. 2020. https://fixthecourt.com /wp-content/uploads/2020/10/Endorsers-of-H.R.-8424-10.23.20f.pdf

Chilton, Adam, Daniel Epps, Kyle Rozema, and Maya Sen. 2021. "Designing Supreme Court Term Limits." *Southern California Law Review*, 95, no. 1: 1–72.

Collins, Paul M., Jr., and Artemus Ward. 2021. "Commentary: Should the Supreme Court Have Term Limits?" *Press Herald*, July 8, 2021.

Epps, Daniel, and Ganesh Sitaraman. 2019. "How to Save the Supreme Court." *Yale Law Journal*, 129: 148–206.

Heintz, Stephen B., and Pete Peterson. 2020. "Make the Supreme Court Less Political. Put Term Limits on Justices." *American Academy of Arts & Sciences*, October 5, 2020.

Hill, Steven. 2020. "Now How Do We Reform the U.S. Supreme Court?" *Salon*, October 27, 2020.

H.R.8424–116th Congress (2019-2020): Supreme Court Term Limits and Regular Appointments Act of 2020. Introduced September 29, 2020. https://www.congress.gov/bill/116th-congress/house-bill/8424

Ipsos. 2021. "Majority of Americans Support Placing a Term or Age Limit on Supreme Court Seats." *Ipsos*, April 19, 2021.

Leonhardt, David. 2018. "The Supreme Court Needs Term Limits." *New York Times*, September 18, 2018.

Marcum, Anthony. 2020. "Supreme Court Term Limits Would Increase Political Tensions Around Justices, Not Ease Them." *USA Today*, October 13, 2020.

Roe v. Wade, 410 U.S. 113 (1973).

Sen, Maya. 2021. "Written Testimony: Presidential Commission on the Supreme Court of the United States." June 30, 2021. https://scholar .harvard.edu/files/msen/files/sen-testimony-scotuscomission.pdf

Shapiro, Ilya. 2020. "Term Limits Won't Fix the Court." *The Atlantic*, September 22, 2020.

Sherry, Suzanna, and Christopher Sundby. 2019. "Academic Highlight: The Risks of Supreme Court Term Limits." *SCOTUSblog*, April 5, 2019. https:// www.scotusblog.com/2019/04/academic-highlight-the-risks-of-supreme -court-term-limits

Sundby, Christopher, and Suzanna Sherry. 2019. "Term Limits and Turmoil: *Roe v. Wade*'s Whiplash." *Texas Law Review*, 98, no. 1: 121–161.

Waldman, Paul. 2021. "Stephen Breyer Is Making a Strong Case for Supreme Court Term Limits." *Washington Post*, June 30, 2020.

Q17. WAS THE END OF THE FILIBUSTER IN FEDERAL JUDICIAL CONFIRMATIONS A HISTORIC RULE CHANGE?

Answer: Though noteworthy to be sure, the end of the filibuster in judicial confirmations may not be as historic as commonly claimed. At the very least, the magnitude of the change must be evaluated in its broader historic context. Three aspects of that context require special attention. First, the Senate has modified filibuster practice numerous times. Second, the Senate did not frequently use the filibuster to block judicial confirmations until the end of the 20th century. Third, the spike in filibuster use especially from 2003 to 2013 precipitated its demise; it can be argued, in fact, that the escalating use of the filibuster during this period was the more dramatic and historic change.

The Facts: Among the rules the Senate has used to govern itself are those that determine when debate among members ends and, in turn, when votes can be taken on proposed legislation. Under Senate practice of unlimited debate and unanimous consent, any member may demand continued debate and refuse to consent to holding a vote on bills being considered. Such a demand is commonly referred to as a filibuster. While often defended on the grounds that it encourages deliberation, this parliamentary maneuver is typically deployed by the minority party to stall or block Senate action.

Prior to 1975, the practice involved what has come to be called the "talking filibuster" of the sort memorably depicted in the 1939 film *Mr. Smith Goes to Washington*. This type of filibuster requires participating senators to speak continually on the Senate floor to keep a vote from being held. Prior to 1917, because Senate rules did not give the majority a mechanism to end debate in order to bring legislation or nominations to a vote, there was no formal countermeasure against the strategy of "talking a bill to death" (United States Senate 2021).

In 1917, however, the Senate finally adopted a countermeasure to override filibusters: the cloture rule. As first established, the rule permitted the invocation of cloture, a motion to bring debate to a close and allow senators to vote on the substance of the bill. Under the 1917 rule, cloture required a two-thirds vote of the 100-member Senate. The 1917 cloture rule applied only to legislative measures and could not be invoked during Senate confirmation processes of any presidential nomination, judicial or otherwise. It was not until 1949 that cloture was put into place in the context of the Senate's "advise and consent" authority. That does not mean that use of the filibuster was unavailable in confirmation processes before 1949; rather, it means that the formal cloture mechanism was not available to stop filibusters of presidential nominees until 1949.

In 1975, the Senate further modified its cloture rule for both legislation and nominations. The change reduced the number of senators required for a cloture vote to three-fifths of the chamber—that is, from 67 to 60 senators. Although this change made it easier to override a filibuster, other modifications to the practice simultaneously made it much easier to initiate and sustain filibusters. In particular, "the Senate leadership began agreeing to allow measures that were facing a filibuster to be put aside while the chamber acted on other bills" (Cornwell 2021). This effectively brought the requirement of a talking filibuster to an end, though some senators occasionally continued to use the talking filibuster "for dramatic effect" (Fortin 2021). Furthermore, modern Senate rules permit a filibuster to occur in any instance when a senator simply declares the intent to debate a particular bill. "That senator does not actually have to debate the bill; they need merely announce their intention to do so" (Olsen 2021).

Taken together, these and other changes created the modern Senate filibuster and cloture rules, which have effectively mandated a supermajority of 60 votes to pass legislation. Though it only takes a majority vote to *pass* a bill, it takes 60 votes to actually bring that same bill up for a vote. In other words, "if 40 Senators oppose something, they can prevent a majority vote on the merits" (Adler 2018).

From the mid-1970s through 2017, this state of affairs applied to the Senate's consideration of presidential nominations. However, in 2013 and in 2017, the Senate further modified its cloture rule. As noted in Q8, the Democrats who controlled the Senate in 2013 lowered from three-fifths to a simple majority the number of votes required for cloture for all presidential nominees, except for appointments to the U.S. Supreme Court. They made this controversial move—deploying what has come to be called "the nuclear option"—after Republicans repeatedly delayed and blocked President Obama's judicial nominations. That change applied to all judicial appointments to the federal district and circuit courts, but left the filibuster in place for the high Court.

Four years later, the Republicans who controlled the Senate went a step further, making the same rule change for consideration of nominees to the Supreme Court. This deployment of the nuclear option came because Democrats were filibustering President Trump's nomination of Neil Gorsuch to the Supreme Court. The demise of the filibuster for presidential nominees was ironically brought about by a simple majority vote, as Republican leadership employed a parliamentary procedure to establish a new interpretation of the Senate cloture rule (Reynolds 2020).

These facts are not disputed. Subject to question, however, is whether the recent changes to cloture and, accordingly, the end of the filibuster in judicial nominations constitute a historic rule change.

Defenders of the filibuster who bemoan its recent demise in the judicial context often appeal to its place as longstanding practice and tradition. This reversal of tradition, the objection goes, amounts to a historic departure from longstanding Senate norms and practice.

The change to the filibuster is certainly noteworthy and significant; however, a closer look at the use of the filibuster in general and in the context of nominations suggests that criticisms of the change as a violation of longstanding political norms is overstated.

First, critics of the recent changes often misleadingly paint the filibuster as an unadulterated feature that sits at the heart of the Senate's design and uniqueness. But as already discussed, the Senate has on multiple occasions changed its filibuster rules and practice. Second, the filibuster is thought of as a commonly used fixture of Senate history. However, since the founding era, the Senate has used the filibuster quite sparingly when considering presidential appointments to the federal bench. Third, declaring the reversal a historic departure from longstanding Senate norms obscures an arguably more significant change in filibuster practice: namely, the dramatic increase in the Senate's use of the filibuster in judicial nominations from 2003 to 2013. If anything, that increase, which precipitated the 2013 and 2017 rule changes and was made possible by earlier rule changes, should be considered the historic departure from Senate practice.

Considerable lore has developed around the filibuster. "No activity in the United States Congress captures the attention of political practitioners, pundits, and the public like filibustering in the Senate. . . . [T]he filibuster is deeply ingrained in the political culture of the United States" (Wawro and Schickler 2006, 6). Touted in this fashion, the filibuster is proffered as a centerpiece of the chamber's uniqueness. Take that away, the argument goes, and the Senate becomes just a typical legislative body.

Part of the common wisdom undergirding the filibuster and its place in history is that "the upper chamber was designed [by the founders] to be a slow-moving, deliberative body that cherished minority rights. In this version of history, the filibuster was a critical part of the framers' Senate" (Binder 2010). But the Constitution does not even mention the filibuster or anything like it. More importantly, according to several scholarly accounts, this received wisdom about the framers' design is incorrect (see, e.g., Binder and Smith 1997). According to one account, in fact, the filibuster was erroneously created in 1806 as part of a wider effort to clean up and update the Senate rule book (Binder 2010). That included removing a rule permitting a simple majority vote to end debate. According to another account, the 1806 rule change was not motivated by a desire to institutionalize the filibuster by removing obstacles to free debate, "but rather by the belief that the rule's infrequent use made it unnecessary" (Beeman 1968, 421).

Whether or not the founders intended to install the filibuster as a central feature of the Senate, the history of its practice suggests that its use was limited. There is some debate as to when the first Senate filibuster took place, though some researchers put it as early as 1831 (see Koger 2010). "Even then, the filibuster was not widely used until the second half of the 19th century, as the parties, and thus the Senate, grew more polarized along party lines" (Bouie 2021). According to political scientist Gregory Koger, "Classic filibusters were contests of endurance, not votes. They were dramatic and unscripted marathons. *And they were exceedingly rare*" (Koger 2010, 4, emphasis in the original).

Despite the lore over the filibuster and its entrenchment in the popular imagination, disaffection with the tactic is not new. Indeed, consternation over its growing use in the late 1800s and early 1900s—and the political gridlock it caused—contributed to the creation of the cloture rule in the first place. In short, the 1917 rule change that introduced cloture reflected dissatisfaction with the filibuster.

Moreover, if historical use of the filibuster has been relatively rare, it *appears* to have been rarer still in the context of nominations. Determining the extent to which the Senate filibustered nominations prior to 1949, however, is difficult because little information about such filibusters is available. "One reason is that until 1929, the Senate normally considered nominations in closed session" (Beth, Rybicki, and Greene 2018, 5). In addition, filibusters themselves, and certainly the threat of filibusters, are not necessarily recorded as such. The creation of the cloture rule improved the ability to identify filibusters, since cloture is often invoked to end a filibuster. Still, cloture votes and filibusters are not interchangeable. "Although cloture affords the Senate a means for overcoming a filibuster, it is erroneous to assume that cases in which cloture is sought are always the same as those in which a filibuster occurs. Filibusters may occur without cloture being sought, and cloture may be sought when no filibuster is taking place" (Beth, Rybicki, and Greene 2018, 2). That said, cloture can help serve as an indicator of the presence of filibusters. But because the cloture rule did not exist in the Senate before 1917, and did not apply to nominations until 1949, it was not a tool available to senators who wished to filibuster a nomination (Beth, Rybicki, and Greene 2018, 5).

That caveat aside, however, three studies suggest the rarity of filibusters in Senate consideration of judicial appointees prior to 1949. As noted earlier, Gregory Koger's detailed study of the history of the filibuster concludes that they were exceedingly rare (Koger 2010, 4). That assessment applies to all filibusters, and because almost all of the filibusters examined by Koger occurred in the context of legislation, those occurring in the context of nominations are rarer still.

Another key study of the use of cloture in nominations, produced by the Congressional Research Service, concludes that there is "some reason to think that in earlier periods, filibustering on nominations was, indeed, infrequent" (Beth, Rybicki, and Greene 2018, 5). As the analysis explains, consultation between presidents and members of the Senate ahead of nominations may have contributed to the scarce filibuster use. Also dampening filibuster use were customs like senatorial courtesy, "under which the Senate would decline to consider a nomination to a position in the home state of a Senator who declared the nomination 'personally obnoxious' to him" (Beth, Rybicki, and Greene 2018, 5).

Clearer evidence of filibuster use and nonuse in the confirmation process becomes available starting in 1949 with the cloture rule change. Even from this period forward, we see that filibustering judicial nominees remained a rarity.

Indeed, following the 1949 rule change, "[t]he first time a cloture motion was even filed for a judicial nomination was in 1968, when President Lyndon Johnson's attempt to elevate Associate Justice Abe Fortas to Chief Justice foundered in the face of bipartisan opposition. Over the next 35 years, cloture motions would only be filed on six more judicial nominations, none of which were blocked. (Two of these nominations were for the Supreme Court. The others were for lower courts.)" (Adler 2018).

A more comprehensive analysis of the period from 1949 through 2013 shows the pattern of cloture invocation in all presidential nominees, including those to the federal bench. That pattern is one of limited use prior to the turn of the 21st century, and then a significant upward spike. With one exception, no Congress from 1949 through 2002 had more than five motions for cloture in nominations for judges and executive branch officials, and almost all sessions had three or fewer. The one exception during that 53-year span was the 103rd Congress (1993–1994), which accounted for 12 such cloture motions. The exception became the rule beginning in 2003 and running through 2013. According to the analysis, only the 110th Congress (2007–2008) used cloture sparingly in nominations, with just one cloture motion. The other Congresses during this 10-year span moved cloture between 14 and 33 times (Beth, Rybicki, and Greene 2018, 6–7).

This increase applied to both judicial and executive branch nominees, with cloture sought on 74 executive and 69 judicial candidates. But judicial nominations accounted for most of the cloture motions in the 108th Congress (2003–2004), the 112th Congress (2011–2012), and before 2003, except in the 103rd Congress (1993–1994). In addition, the study shows the results of these particular invocations of cloture. For all but the 108th Congress, "when almost 80% of nominations subjected to cloture attempts (mostly judicial) were not confirmed," nominations that faced cloture motions were confirmed more than 75% of the time (Beth, Rybicki, and Greene 2018, Summary).

In sum, exercising the nuclear option and thereby foreclosing the use of the filibuster in nominations is, without question, a noteworthy move. But it can only be fully understood in the broader historic context in which the change took place.

FURTHER READING

Adler, Jonathan H. 2018. "The Mythical History of Nomination Filibusters." *Reason*, July 9, 2018.

Beeman, Richard R. 1968. "Unlimited Debate in the Senate: The First Phase." *Political Science Quarterly*, 83, no. 3: 419–434.

Beth, Richard S., Elizabeth Rybicki, and Michael Greene. 2018. "Cloture Attempts on Nominations: Data and Historical Development through November 20, 2013" (CRS Report No. RL32878). Congressional Research Service. https://fas.org/sgp/crs/misc/RL32878.pdf

Binder, Sarah A. 2010. "The History of the Filibuster: Testimony Before the U.S. Senate Committee on Rules and Administration." April 22, 2010. https://www.brookings.edu/testimonies/the-history-of-the-filibuster

Binder, Sarah A., and Steven S. Smith. 1997. *Politics or Principle? Filibustering in the United States Senate*. Washington, DC: Brookings Institution Press.

Bouie, Jamelle. 2021. "I'm Not Actually Interested in Mitch McConnell's Hypocrisy." *New York Times*, January 29. 2021.

Chafetz, Josh. 2011. "The Unconstitutionality of the Filibuster." *Connecticut Law Review*, 43, no. 4: 1003–1040.

Cornwell, Susan. 2021. "What Is the U.S. Senate Filibuster and Why Is Everyone Talking About It? *Reuters*, March 17, 2021.

Fortin, Jacey. 2021. "The Senate's 'Talking Filibuster' Might Rise Again." *New York Times*, March 19, 2021.

Jacobson, Louis. 2021. "Would a 'Talking Filibuster' Get the Senate Moving?" *PolitiFact*, March 9, 2021.

Koger, Gregory. 2010. *Filibustering: A Political History of Obstruction in the House and Senate*. Chicago, IL: University of Chicago Press.

Olsen, Henry. 2021. "A Talking Filibuster Will Not Help Democrats as Much as Some Might Think." *Washington Post*, March 17, 2021.

Reynolds, Molly E. 2020. "What Is the Senate Filibuster, and What Would It Take to Eliminate It?" *Brookings Institution*, September 9, 2020. https://www.brookings.edu/policy2020/votervital/what-is-the-senate-filibuster-and-what-would-it-take-to-eliminate-it

Smith, Steven S. 2014. *The Senate Syndrome*. Norman, OK: University of Oklahoma Press.

United States Senate. 2021. "About Filibusters and Cloture: Historical Overview." https://www.senate.gov/about/powers-procedures/filibusters-cloture/overview.htm

Wawro, Gregory J., and Eric Schickler. 2006. *Filibuster: Obstruction and Lawmaking in the U.S. Senate*. Princeton, NJ: Princeton University Press.

Q18. IS THE END OF THE FILIBUSTER IN FEDERAL JUDICIAL CONFIRMATIONS LIKELY TO INCREASE POLARIZATION ON THE FEDERAL COURTS?

Answer: Maybe. There is little doubt that increasing partisanship and polarization in the Senate contributed to the end of the filibuster for judicial confirmations. Whether the end of the filibuster will in turn produce greater polarization on the federal courts, including the Supreme Court, remains uncertain. Nevertheless, empirical research conducted since the 2013 change to the cloture rule provides support for claims that the change has increased political polarization.

The Facts: Because the seating of judges to the federal bench requires Senate confirmation, the Senate functions as a constraint on who the president nominates. Presidents cannot act unilaterally, installing candidates who align with their own policy interests and ideological predilections. Given the Senate's "advise and consent" authority, presidents are "assumed to choose nominees that move policy output in a way that maximizes the president's ideological preferences while still gaining the support of enough senators to achieve confirmation" (Boyd, Lynch, and Madonna 2015, 628).

If confirmation of presidential nominees requires a supermajority vote of senators, the constraint on the president is greater because the president has to garner a greater level of support. As detailed in Q17, formally speaking, a simple majority of the 100-member Senate is needed to confirm presidential nominees. But the availability of the filibuster had, in effect, upped the requirement for confirmation to a supermajority. From 1949 to 2013, filibusters of lower federal court nominations could be overridden by 60 votes, and from 1949 to 2017, the same vote margin was needed to override a filibuster against a Supreme Court nominee. Under such rules, and because the ideological views of 60 members of the Senate do not usually coincide with those of the president, "[t]o pick up the support of the pivotal sixtieth senator, presidents must also choose judicial nominees such that their political ideologies are more moderate than the ideology of the president" (Boyd, Lynch, and Madonna 2015, 628). If, in contrast, confirmation only requires a simple majority vote, the level of support the president must rally is reduced, as is the constraint on the president. In other words, if the bar for Senate support is lower, presidents are arguably freer to maximize ideological preferences in their choices (see, e.g., Nash and Shepherd 2020).

As explained in Q8 and Q17, the deployment of the so-called "nuclear option" reduced the cloture vote needed to end debate on judicial nominees from 60 to a simple majority of the Senate, first in 2013 for lower courts and again in 2017 for the Supreme Court. In theory, the implications of eliminating the filibuster are that "presidents should be able to nominate more ideologically-extreme judicial nominees and still gain the support of the Senate's median voter. This would, theoretically, lead presidents to make fewer concessions on nominee ideology since a liberal (conservative) president now only needs to gain the approval of the fiftieth most liberal (conservative) senator to gain confirmation for his nominees" (Boyd, Lynch, and Madonna 2015, 628–629).

Even though there is not much evidence that the filibuster was frequently used for judicial nominations in earlier eras (see Q17), it could be that the prospect or threat of a filibuster in earlier periods operated as incentive to nominate less polarizing candidates. Existing research supports this supposition (see, e.g., Johnson and Roberts 2005; Wawro and Schickler 2006).

In short, it is commonly predicted that the end of the filibuster would likely produce more ideologically extreme judges. The logic of this prediction sounds quite plausible, and many court observers have warned, based on this logic, that polarization is a likely outcome of the filibuster's demise. Though it is a bit soon to tell whether this prediction will be borne out, a handful of studies have offered preliminary insights about the post-filibuster landscape.

In one such study, political scientists Christina Boyd, Michael Lynch, and Anthony Madonna asked whether the ideology of judicial nominees changed following the 2013 adjustment to the cloture rule. They also studied whether more nominations are confirmed, and whether the speed of confirmations increases. Their search for answers led them to examine all district and circuit court nominations made by President Obama from 2009 through the end of 2014. Comparing the nominations made before and after the lowering of the cloture vote, their research used data on the ideology of the nominees, whether they won confirmation, and how long it took successful nominees to be confirmed.

Contrary to the prediction that presidents would nominate more ideologically extreme candidates, the findings suggest that the ideology of the selected judges did not change notably. However, what did change was the pace of securing confirmations, with quicker action from the Democrat-controlled Senate (Boyd, Lynch, and Madonna 2015, 626). Thus, although the study does not confirm the prediction that presidents will act to install more ideologically extreme candidates in the face of a reduced cloture bar, it nevertheless suggests that the impact on the federal judiciary is notable. "Obama has not, as formal theory predicts and some had feared, taken advantage of the altered gridlock interval to push forward increasingly liberal nominees. Despite this, however, through increased confirmation rates, decreased time to confirmation, and the overall efficient filling of vacancies, Obama and Senator Reid [Democratic Senate Majority Leader Harry Reid] have been able to overcome past hurdles regarding minority party confirmation obstruction tactics and quickly affect the overall ideological composition of the lower federal judiciary" (Boyd, Lynch, and Madonna 2015, 636–637).

One key caveat to this finding is that this impact could well be muted when the executive branch and the Senate are controlled by different political parties. Under this type of divided government, the lower cloture does not change the fact that the majority leader of the Senate can stall confirmation processes by refusing to schedule votes on nominees. With respect to the finding that Obama did not nominate more ideologically extreme candidates, another caveat is that other presidents may act differently and show more willingness to press forward with such nominees.

A second empirical study by legal scholars Jonathan Remy Nash and Joanna Shepherd also found an even greater impact on the federal judiciary resulting from the filibuster elimination. Nash and Shepherd theorized that removing the filibuster might alter the ideology and other characteristics of the selected and confirmed candidates. As such, they hypothesized that more liberal judges would find their way to the federal appeals courts. In addition, sitting judges hoping to gain a promotion to a higher court, the researchers hypothesized, might act differently with the filibuster no longer in place. In particular, Nash and Shepherd posited that decisions by federal district court judges would increasingly align with the partisan ideology of the president who appointed them—leading to more liberal behavior for judges selected by a Democrat and more conservative decisions for those chosen by a Republican. Such behavior would "signal" to a sitting president that the judge would "match the preferences of the newly relevant pivotal senator—that is, the senator ideologically closest to the president whose support the president requires to obtain a successful confirmation vote" (Nash and Shepherd 2020, 649).

Comparing appeals court candidates nominated by Obama before and after 2013, Nash and Shepherd found the filibuster removal to have had statistically significant effects. Judges nominated to the federal appeals courts after 2013, though not as racially diverse, were somewhat younger and more likely to be female. In addition, the post-2013 nominees, who held more liberal ideologies and were more likely to have served as a law clerk for a liberal judge, voted more liberally in abortion and death penalty cases once they had received confirmation to the appellate bench (Nash and Shepherd 2020, 649).

The study also presents evidence about the impact of the cloture rule change on sitting district court judges. In opinions on abortion cases after 2013, district court judges appointed by a Democratic president used more liberal language, whereas those appointed by a Republican president relied on conservative language. "These effects are greatest for younger district judges, suggesting that judges with a greater chance of promotion are more likely to alter their signaling behavior in response to the change in the filibuster rule" (Nash and Shepherd 2020, 649).

Nash and Shepherd caution that their data is limited in terms of sample size. Because Obama nominated 39 judges to the appellate bench before the cloture rule change compared to 14 judges between the change and the time that Republicans regained Senate control, the data set is small. Moreover, with respect to the content analysis of the opinions of district court judges, the research only covers abortion cases. Still, Nash and Shepherd concluded that removal of the filibuster in lower court nominations increases polarization of the judiciary.

More studies would be needed to confirm the effects of the filibuster change. Importantly, the two studies discussed here focus—understandably—on Obama nominees to the bench. That, too, is a notable limitation to the findings.

In addition, it is worth emphasizing that there are other factors in play that may well be contributing to polarization of the courts. Legal scholars Neil Devins and Lawrence Baum, for example, argue that the rising polarization of political elites has shaped the polarization of the Supreme Court. Among other things, their research suggests that partisan sorting among political elites—in which conservatives identify with the Republican Party and liberals gravitate to the Democratic Party—helps explain how the ideological blocs on the Supreme Court have come to be so closely aligned with party lines. According to Devins and Baum, presidents have both more motivation to select and ability to identify judicial candidates with ideologies congruent to those of the president's party. "Partisan polarization has affected the Justices as well, reducing the likelihood that they will stray from the ideological positions that brought them to the Court in the first place" (Devins and Baum 2016, 361).

If other factors like those identified by Devins and Baum have heightened polarization of the judiciary, then it may not be the lack of the filibuster that is responsible for polarization on the courts. It may, instead, be that the end of the filibuster is a symptom of the widening divide between the political parties.

On this view, the deployment of the nuclear option evidences the widening partisan divide and breakdown in cooperation and compromise. As legal scholars Tom Donnelly and Jeffrey Rosen assert, "the end of the filibuster is a symptom of the death spiral of the Senate into permanent polarization, not its cause" (Donnelly and Rosen 2017). Citing the growing use of the filibuster in the late 20th and early 21st century, and its turn into a de facto 60-vote requirement, they argue that "it's time to acknowledge that the cause of the breakdown in the Senate isn't the end of the filibuster, but polarization in the country. . . . And, if polarization is, indeed, the cause of the Senate's problems, then there is no easy solution" (Donnelly and Rosen 2017).

This does not necessarily mean that the filibuster's demise will not further exacerbate polarization. Indeed, there is good reason and evidence to think it will. But it serves as a reminder that the change in the filibuster did not occur in a vacuum, and that it may be far from the only or primary factor shaping the politicized and polarized character of the federal judiciary.

FURTHER READING

Boyd, Christina L., Michael S. Lynch, and Anthony J. Madonna. 2015. "Nuclear Fallout: Investigating the Effect of Senate Procedural Reform on Judicial Nominations." *The Forum*, 13, no. 4: 623–641.

Devins, Neal, and Lawrence Baum. 2016. "Split Definitive: How Party Polarization Turned the Supreme Court into Partisan Court." *Supreme Court Review*, 2016: 301–366.

Donnelly, Tom, and Jeffrey Rosen. 2017. "Political Polarization Killed the Filibuster." *The Atlantic*, April 8, 2017.

Johnson, Timothy R., and Jason M. Roberts. 2005. "Pivotal Politics, Presidential Capital, and Supreme Court Nominations." *Congress & the Presidency*, 32: 31–48.

Nash, Jonathan Remy, and Joanna Shepherd. 2020. "Filibuster Change and Judicial Appointments." *Journal of Empirical Legal Studies*, 17, no. 4: 646–695.

O'Connell, Anne Joseph. 2015. "Shortening Agency and Judicial Vacancies Through Filibuster Reform? An Examination of Confirmation Rates and Delays from 1981 to 2014." *Duke Law Journal*, 64: 1645–1715.

Wawro, Gregory J., and Eric Schickler. 2006. *Filibuster: Obstruction and Lawmaking in the U.S. Senate*. Princeton, NJ: Princeton University Press.

4

Decisions and Decision Making

Despite assertions that judges make decisions based only on law—a claim often made by judges themselves—studies suggest otherwise. Numerous influences, including political ones, have been found by researchers to inform, shape, and constrain court rulings. This chapter identifies some of those purported influences and, more broadly, the debates suggesting that judicial decision making often reflects not just legal behavior but also human behavior. Much of the focus of this chapter rests on how politics might influence Supreme Court justices and the legal opinions they forge.

Q19. ARE SUPREME COURT JUSTICES INFLUENCED BY PUBLIC OPINION?

Answer: Probably. Most research suggests a link between public opinion and Supreme Court decisions. There is, however, no clear consensus on what explains the connection, and at least one recent study questions whether there is, in fact, a correlation between Court rulings and public opinion at all. Moreover, even if a correlation exists, there is no consensus that Supreme Court decision making is directly, rather than indirectly, responsive to public sentiment. Still, most concur that public opinion exerts at least an indirect influence on the Court. Even some justices have admitted that the institutional insulation of the Court does not create an impervious barrier against the influence of public opinion.

The Facts: In *The Authority of the Court and Peril of Politics*, Supreme Court Justice Stephen Breyer argues that judges "should not, and virtually never do, pay particular attention to public opinion" (Breyer 2021, 59). But he qualified this assessment by identifying occasions when the Court felt obligated to consider public sentiment in its deliberations. Breyer points out that when the Supreme Court handed down its landmark decision in *Brown v. Board of Education* (1954), the Court worried that states would refuse to abide by the unanimous decision, which declared racial segregation in public schools unconstitutional. Because of this worry, the Court "carefully chose which cases to take, sometimes avoiding ones that might thwart its ambitions in *Brown*" (Breyer 2021, 59–60). Indeed, the 13-year interval between *Brown* and the Court's decision in *Loving v. Virginia* (1967) to overturn laws banning interracial marriage was no accident. According to Breyer, that delay was "a calculated part of the Court's enforcement strategy," which "reflected its views about the state of public opinion" (Breyer 2021, 60).

Breyer's explanation of the delay between *Brown* and *Loving* highlights a direct and causal connection between public opinion and judicial decision making. In particular, it exemplifies "strategic institutional maintenance theory," one of several theories that seeks to answer whether the Supreme Court responds to public opinion. While arguing that this type of direct causal influence is rare, Breyer acknowledges justices are neither oblivious nor completely unresponsive to public opinion.

Other justices have conceded the influence of public sentiment. As Justice Benjamin N. Cardozo famously asserted, "[t]he great tides and currents which engulf the rest of men, do not turn aside in their course, and pass the judges by" (Cardozo 1921, 168). Like Cardozo, Chief Justice William Rehnquist observed the potential influence of the tides of public opinion, especially when they are "sufficiently great and sufficiently sustained" (Rehnquist 1986, 768). After acknowledging that the work of judges is relatively insulated from the public, Rehnquist admits that "these same judges go home at night and read the newspapers or watch the evening news on television; they talk to their family and friends about current events. . . . Judges, so long as they are relatively normal human beings, can no more escape being influenced by public opinion in the long run than can people working at other jobs" (Rehnquist 1986, 768). Justice Sandra Day O'Connor indicated that attentiveness to public opinion could even be salutary: "We [Supreme Court justices] don't have standing armies to enforce opinions, we rely on the confidence of the public in the correctness of those decisions. That's why we have to be aware of public opinions and of attitudes toward our system of justice, and it is why we must try to keep and build that trust" (Greenhouse 2012, 72).

Because justices on the Supreme Court are unelected and hold life tenure, their institutional setting makes them far more insulated from public pressure and sentiment than elected government officials. But how insulated are they? The longstanding interest surrounding this question has generated a copious body of research exploring the purported link between public opinion and Supreme Court decision making. This research shows widespread, albeit not universal, agreement of correlations between public opinion and judicial decisions. As political scientists Ben Johnson and Logan Strother note, "the idea that the Court moors itself in the mainstream of public opinion is well established in the literature" (Johnson and Strother 2021b, 19).

A main line of research in this area by political scientist Robert Dahl posits an *indirect* link achieved through the judicial selection process: "policy views dominant on the Court are never for long out of line with the policy views dominant among the lawmaking majorities of the United States" (Dahl 1957, 285). This is because Supreme Court justices are appointed by the president and confirmed by the Senate, and typically selected because they are thought to share the appointing president's views. Accordingly, as one examination of data from the Warren and Burger-Rehnquist eras concludes, "[w]hatever influence public opinion exercises on the Court occurs indirectly, through the choice of justices by presidents chosen by the people" (Norpoth and Segal 1994, 711).

If Dahl's theory is useful in explaining the connection between public opinion and judicial decisions—and most researchers agree it is—it likely applies more in a context when justices are replaced with sufficient regularity to keep their decisions aligned with changes in the public mood. Dahl found that on average, a new justice was appointed to the Court every two years from the beginning of the Court's history to 1957 (Dahl 1957, 284). But that pace of appointment has slowed in the modern era. From 1972 to 2004, appointments of new justices occurred on average only every four years, a pattern that may persist with longer life expectancy and the trend of selecting younger justices (Giles, Blackstone, and Vining Jr. 2008, 293).

With justices being appointed at younger ages and serving longer (see Q16), the indirect link Dahl posited may be diminished, and the possibility of justices becoming out of step with public sentiment increases. Still, most researchers concur that "the process of appointment and confirmation induces indirect responsiveness to public opinion through the slow process of judicial replacement" (Johnson and Strother 2021b, 19).

In contrast with this indirect explanation, numerous studies analyzing Supreme Court decision making find more direct lines of influence. One strand among these studies is sometimes called "drift" theory (Johnson and Strother 2021a) or the "attitude change hypothesis" (Mishler and

Sheehan 1996, 174). These terms are used to describe the idea that judicial attitudes do not necessarily remain exactly as they were when justices arrived on the bench. Instead, they may drift over time. For example, as public opinion on same-sex marriage changes, so too may judicial dispositions. Consistent with the observation Justice Cardozo made a century ago about the pull of public sentiment, this drift may be influenced by the common set of forces that shape public opinion and produce the prevailing public mood (Giles, Blackstone, and Vining Jr. 2008, 295). As such, the theory does not suggest that justices are "weathervanes, always changing direction with the wind" (Flemming and Wood 1997, 494), or "political chameleons who continually adjust their attitudes and decisions to reflect short-term changes in public sentiment" (Mishler and Sheehan 1996, 175). Rather, justices simply come to hold different views on issues over the passage of years, just as the rest of us often do as we acquire new life experiences and information.

Several researchers find evidence of this type of attitude change in examining judicial decision making. Political scientists William Mishler and Reginald S. Sheehan, for example, hypothesize that "the attitudes of some justices occasionally may change, consciously or not, in response to either fundamental, long-term shifts in the public mood or to the societal forces that underlie them" (Mishler and Sheehan 1996, 175). Studying the responsiveness of individual justices from 1953 to 1992, Mishler and Sheehan find that "public opinion has significant, and for some, very strong effects on the behavior of upward to half of all justices who served," with the impact of public opinion being most pronounced for the more moderate justices (Mishler and Sheehan 1996, 197). Research by political scientists Roy B. Flemming and B. Dan Wood finds an even stronger and broader link. Examining Court terms from 1956 to 1989, they conclude that individual justices shift with the public mood, that the response is quick and occurs over multiple issue areas, and that the shift is not limited to certain justices (Flemming and Wood 1997, 493).

A second strand of research finding a direct link between public opinion and Court rulings is known as "strategic institutional maintenance theory" (Johnson and Strother 2021b, 20). This explanation of judicial behavior does not suppose that the *preferences* of justices change in direct response to public sentiment. Instead, it suggests that the direct influence of public opinion results in justices altering their behavior *strategically* (Giles, Blackstone, and Vining Jr. 2008, 295). "The logic of strategic behavior is that judges conform their voting to public opinion to avoid negative public reactions and to protect the institutional integrity of the Court" (Giles, Blackstone, and Vining Jr. 2008, 296). As exemplified in

Justice Breyer's discussion of the Court avoiding segregation cases after *Brown*, "a Court that cares about its perceived legitimacy must rationally anticipate whether its preferred outcomes will be respected and faithfully followed by relevant publics. Consequently, a Court that strays too far from the broad boundaries imposed by public mood risks having its decisions rejected" (McGuire and Stimson 2004, 1019).

Researchers testing strategic institutional maintenance theory across multiple studies have found empirical support for it. For example, one study using time-series models to analyze data from 1953 to 1996 found that "the Court's policy outcomes are not only affected by public opinion, but to a degree far greater than previously documented" (McGuire and Stimson 2004, 1033). Another study examining Supreme Court decisions from the 1956 to 2000 terms also identified important direct effects of public opinion on the strategic behavior of justices in some cases. However, the study found these effects to be less evident in salient cases—that is, cases that attract substantial public and media attention—than in nonsalient cases (Casillas, Enns, and Wohlfarth 2011).

The line of research suggesting the existence of direct linkages does not necessarily deny that the judicial selection process creates an indirect tether between public opinion and the Court's rulings. Indeed, "virtually all the studies demonstrate an *indirect* effect of public opinion via the appointments process" (Epstein and Martin 2010, 270). Some even concede that the Dahlian explanation is "the primary link," while finding evidence that "the impact of public opinion via presidential election/judicial selection is not the only source of public influence on the Court" (Mishler and Sheehan 1996, 198).

Aside from attitude change theory and strategic institutional maintenance theory, researchers put forward other explanations for a direct link between public opinion and judicial decisions. For example, a social psychology approach suggests that justices may be motivated to respond to public opinion because they care what others think of them. "The desire to be liked and respected by other people is a fundamental psychological motivation, and self-esteem depends heavily on the esteem in which one is held by others. We would hardly expect Supreme Court Justices to be immune to this motivation. Indeed, it is likely to be especially salient to them" (Baum and Devins 2010, 1532).

This theory suggests that justices could be swayed by broad public sentiment, but political science and legal scholars Lawrence Baum and Neal Devins argue that the influence is narrower. In particular, the audience justices care about is composed of elites, that is, "individuals and groups that have high socioeconomic status and political influence" (Baum and

Devins 2010, 1516). Because justices have elite status, "they are likely to care a great deal about their reputations among other elites, including academics, journalists, other judges, fellow lawyers, members of other interest groups, and their friends and neighbors" (1516–1517). Although they admit their empirical analysis is more suggestive than definitive, Baum and Devins find it reasonable to conclude that justices "are more susceptible to influence from elite groups than from the mass public" (1580).

The growing line of research citing empirical evidence for the claim that public opinion directly affects judicial decisions is not without its critics. Political scientists Helmut Norpoth and Jeffrey Segal, for example, draw on data from the Warren and Burger-Rehnquist eras to conclude that there is "no evidence for a direct path of influence from public opinion to Court decisions" (Norpoth and Segal 1994, 711). A 2021 study using data from 1952 to 2017 found "no statistically significant relationship between public mood and Court outputs" (Johnson and Strother 2021b, 30). That same study concluded that "prior studies actually provide very little empirical support for any theory of judicial responsiveness" to public opinion (Johnson and Strother 2021b, 30).

Moreover, even among the studies concluding that public opinion directly influences court rulings, no widespread agreement exists as to the extent of that influence or the mechanisms by which the influence operates. To the contrary, "[o]nce we venture beyond the concern for institutional legitimacy, theories diverge sharply and often contradict one another—as do the empirical results presented as supporting evidence for these assorted theories" (Johnson and Strother 2021b, 20). As political scientists Kevin T. McGuire and James A. Stimson explained, though most recent studies find that individual justices respond to public sentiment, "the extent to which the Court's policies represent popular opinion is indeterminate, at best" (McGuire and Stimson 2004, 1018).

FURTHER READING

Barnum, David. 1985. "The Supreme Court and Public Opinion: Judicial Decision Making in the Post-New Deal Period." *Journal of Politics*, 47, no. 2: 652–666.

Baum, Lawrence, and Neal Devins. 2010. "Why the Supreme Court Cares about Elites, Not the American People." *Georgetown Law Journal*, 98: 1515–1581.

Breyer, Stephen. 2021. *The Authority of the Court and Peril of Politics.* Cambridge, MA: Harvard University Press.

Brown v. Board of Education of Topeka, 347 U.S. 483 (1954).

Bryan, Amanda C., and Christopher D. Kromphardt. 2016. "Public Opinion, Public Support, and Counter-Attitudinal Voting on the US Supreme Court." *Justice System Journal*, 37, no. 4: 298–317.

Cardozo, Benjamin N. 1921. *The Nature of the Judicial Process*. New Haven, CT: Yale University Press.

Casillas, Christopher J., Peter K. Enns, and Patrick C. Wohlfarth. 2011. "How Public Opinion Constrains the U.S. Supreme Court." *American Journal of Political Science*, 55, no. 1: 74–88.

Collins, Todd A., and Christopher A. Cooper. 2016. "The Case Salience Index, Public Opinion, and Decision Making on the US Supreme Court." *Justice System Journal*, 37, no. 3: 232–245.

Dahl, Robert A. 1957. "Decision-Making in a Democracy: The Supreme Court as a National Policymaker." *Journal of Public Law*, 6: 279–295.

Epstein, Lee, and Andrew D. Martin. 2010. "Does Public Opinion Influence the Supreme Court? Possibly Yes (But We're Not Sure Why)." *University of Pennsylvania Journal of Constitutional Law*, 13, no. 2: 263–282.

Epstein, Lee, and Jack Knight. 1998. *The Choices Justices Make*. Washington, DC: CQ Press.

Flemming, Roy B., and B. Dan Wood. 1997. "The Public and the Supreme Court: Individual Justice Responsiveness to American Policy Moods." *American Journal of Political Science*, 41, no. 2: 468–498.

Flemming, Roy, B. Dan Wood, and John Bohte. 1999. "Attention to Issues in a System of Separated Powers: The Macrodynamics of American Policy Agendas." *Journal of Politics*, 61, no. 1: 76–108.

Franklin, Charles, and Liane Kosaki. 1989. "Republican Schoolmaster: The U.S. Supreme Court, Public Opinion, and Abortion." *American Political Science Review*, 83, no. 3: 751–771.

Friedman, Barry. 2009. *The Will of the People: How Public Opinion Has Influenced the Supreme Court and Shaped the Meaning of the Constitution*. New York: Farrar, Straus and Giroux.

Giles, Micheal, Bethany Blackstone, and Richard L. Vining Jr. 2008. "The Supreme Court in American Democracy: Unraveling the Linkages between Public Opinion and Judicial Decision Making." *Journal of Politics*, 70, no. 2: 293–306.

Greenhouse, Linda. 2012. *U.S. Supreme Court: A Very Short Introduction*. New York: Oxford University Press.

Hall, Matthew E. K. 2014. "The Semiconstrained Court: Public Opinion, the Separation of Powers, and the U.S. Supreme Court's Fear of Nonimplementation." *American Journal of Political Science*, 58, no. 2: 352–366.

Hoekstra, Valerie. 2000. "The Supreme Court and Local Public Opinion." *American Political Science Review*, 94, no. 1: 89–100.

Johnson, Ben, and Logan Strother. 2021a. "Does the US Supreme Court Respond to Public Opinion?" In *Open Judicial Politics* (Version 2.0, 08/18/2021), ed. Rorie Spill Solberg and Eric Waltenburg. https://open.oregonstate.education/open-judicial-politics/chapter/supreme-court-public-opinion

Johnson, Ben, and Logan Strother. 2021b. "TRENDS: The Supreme Court's (Surprising?) Indifference to Public Opinion." *Political Research Quarterly*, 74, no. 1: 18–34.

Link, Michael W. 1995. "Tracking Public Mood in the Supreme Court: Cross-Time Analyses of Criminal Procedure and Civil Rights Cases." *Political Research Quarterly*, 48, no. 1: 61–78.

Loving v. Virginia, 388 U.S. 1 (1967).

McGuire, Kevin T., and James A. Stimson. 2004. "The Least Dangerous Branch Revisited: New Evidence on Supreme Court Responsiveness to Public Preferences." *Journal of Politics*, 66, no. 4: 1018–1035.

Mishler, William, and Reginald Sheehan. 1993. "The Supreme Court as a Countermajoritarian Institution? The Impact of Public Opinion on Supreme Court Decisions." *American Political Science Review*, 87, no. 1: 87–101.

Mishler, William, and Reginald Sheehan. 1996. "Public Opinion, the Attitudinal Model, and Supreme Court Decision Making: A Micro-Analytic Perspective." *Journal of Politics*, 58, no. 1: 169–200.

Norpoth, Helmut, and Jeffrey A. Segal. 1994. "Popular Influence on Supreme Court Decisions." *American Political Science Review*, 88, no. 3: 711–724.

Rehnquist, William R. 1986. "Constitutional Law and Public Opinion." *Suffolk University Law Review*, 20, no. 4: 751–770.

Stimson, James A., Michael B. MacKuen, and Robert S. Erikson. 1995. "Dynamic Representation." *American Political Science Review*, 89, no 3: 543–565.

Q20. DO JUDGES' POLITICAL ATTITUDES AND IDEOLOGIES INFLUENCE THEIR LEGAL DECISIONS?

Answer: Judges routinely say no, but a long line of social science research supports the claim that political attitudes and ideologies are among the factors that influence judicial decision making. There is less consensus about how and to what extent attitudes and ideologies shape legal judgments and opinions. Research commonly notes that the influence of political attitudes and ideology varies across multiple contexts and operates in the face of numerous constraints.

The Facts: During his 2017 Senate confirmation hearings to the U.S. Supreme Court, Neil Gorsuch addressed the role of personal, political, and partisan attitudes in judicial decision making. "My personal views . . . I leave those at home," Gorsuch said (Barnes and O'Keefe 2017). He further explained that, as a judge, "I have no difficulty ruling against or for any party other than based on what the law and the facts of a particular case require. . . . And I'm heartened by the support I have received from people who recognize that there's no such thing as a Republican judge or a Democratic judge—we just have judges in this country" (Barnes and O'Keefe 2017). In a 2021 speech, Supreme Court Justice Clarence Thomas warned that critics who accuse justices of making legal decisions to advance their own political ideologies jeopardize public faith in the Court: "I think the media makes it sound as though you are just always going right to your personal preference. So if they think you are antiabortion or something personally, they think that's the way you always will come out. They think you're for this or for that. They think you become like a politician" (Berardino and Marimow 2021).

The remarks offered by Gorsuch and Thomas reflect a familiar and prevailing characterization of how judges should and do act. According to this aspirational view, commonly called legal formalism, judges act as disinterested umpires, coming to each case in a neutral fashion. They are guided not by their own personal preferences, interests, ideologies, or political views, but only by the facts presented as interpreted through governing law and jurisprudence. Unlike politicians, judges are to set aside their partisan and private predilections, removed from the political fray. Symbolized by the blindfold covering the eyes of Lady Justice and the robes judges wear, this take conceives of judges as "value-free technicians who do no more than discover 'the law'" (Murphy and Tanenhaus 1972, 13).

As prevalent as this asserted view is—at least among legal practitioners—research into judicial decision making tells another story. By and large, social scientific research finds that judicial behavior does not occur in a sealed vacuum that contains only relevant law, jurisprudence, and case facts. Scholarship dating back to the emergence of "legal realism" at the turn of the 20th century and to the behavioral revolution in the social sciences in the mid-20th century has adopted a more realistic view. Under the broad umbrella of research into judicial behavior, scholars have identified multiple "extralegal" factors said to influence decisions made by courts. Among these factors are political attitudes and ideologies held by judges.

The research does not, however, offer a unified or uncomplicated account of the influencing factors. While a realist account sees judges as actors driven by an interest in advancing their own policy agendas, "the extent to which judges *choose* to act in such a manner and the extent to which they *can realize their goals* by acting in such a manner is the subject of much debate" (Segal 2011, 275). Indeed, those who find that apolitical judging is unrealistic and believe that extralegal factors influence judges offer different theories to explain how judges act. The main competing theories are called the attitudinal model, the strategic or rational choice model, and historical institutionalism (see, e.g., Maveety 2003, 5; Banks and O'Brien 2008, 297).

The attitudinal model, applied most commonly in study of the Supreme Court, says that justices rule as they do because of the ideological attitudes and policy preferences they hold. "Simply put, Rehnquist votes the way he does because he is extremely conservative; Marshall voted the way he did because he [was] extremely liberal" (Segal and Spaeth 1993, 65). According to this approach, law, precedent, and jurisprudence do not determine the outcomes of cases, nor do they even pose much of a constraint on justices' decision making. Instead, justices decide cases largely based on their pre-established preferences, and, in turn, vote and write opinions that directly coincide with those preferences. It is true that justices present interpretations of law and precedent in their written opinions. But according to the attitudinal model, those "provide no more than convenient rationalizations" in support of justices' individual preferences (Songer 2012, 340).

Political scientists Jeffrey Segal and Harold Spaeth exemplify this approach in *The Supreme Court and the Attitudinal Model Revisited*. There, they tested the theory by coding the attitudes of justices using newspaper editorial assessments that characterize the ideologies of Supreme Court nominees "as liberal or conservative" on civil rights and liberties issues (Segal and Spaeth 2002, 321). They then examined the outcomes in Fourth Amendment search-and-seizure cases and concluded that judicial attitudes alone predicted 70 percent of outcomes (325).

Multiple studies by a broad range of political scientists show that political attitudes factor into judicial decision making and especially Supreme Court decision making. As political scientist Donald Songer summarizes, "At this point, there is little doubt that the political attitudes and ideology of the justices on the United States Supreme Court have a substantial effect on many of the outcomes adopted by the Court and on the votes of individual justices" (Songer 2012, 340).

The special focus on the Supreme Court given by the attitudinal model acknowledges that not all jurists are equally free to decide cases based on their preferences. Supreme Court justices encounter fewer constraints on their decisions than their lower court counterparts and, as a result, are generally thought to have considerable leeway to let their preferences drive their votes. Lower court judges, meanwhile, might have aspirations to higher court appointment or might worry that their decisions will be reversed by the higher courts. Because promotion to a higher federal court requires a presidential nomination and Senate confirmation, lower court judges would understandably be concerned about whether their decisions are reversed on appeal or viewed as based solely on politics or ideology. These lower court judges thus may be more likely to be restrained in their decision making and less likely to rule in ways that single-mindedly advance their political preferences.

When it comes to examining Supreme Court decisions, some advocates of the attitudinal model insist that it's not only that attitudes matter, it's that they matter more than anything else in almost all circumstances (see, e.g., Segal and Cover, 1989; Segal and Spaeth 1994, 2002). However, even though the attitudinal model remains a dominant approach in political science research, not all accept the proposition that attitudes explain everything about judicial decision making.

An alternative approach, commonly referred to as the strategic choice account, accepts that political attitudes figure into judicial decision making and that judges may, indeed, be driven by their ideology rather than the law. At the same time, however, justices seeking to achieve their preferences may have to make *strategic* calculations and decisions to achieve their policy goals. According to this alternative approach, the attitudinal account tells part of the story, but, by itself, is too simple because it downplays other influences that shape and constrain judicial decision making (Epstein, Landes, and Posner 2013, 29).

In particular, the strategic model sees justices as "strategic actors who realize that their ability to achieve their goals depends on a consideration of the preferences of other actors, the choices they expect others to make, and the institutional context in which they act" (Epstein and Knight 1998, 10). On this view, exemplified in the work of political scientists Lee Epstein and Jack Knight, there is not a simple and straight line between a justice's preferences and the votes that a jurist casts. Justices seeking to achieve their preferences may have to rely on strategic decision making, which requires an "*interdependent* choice: an individual's action is, in part, a function of her expectations about the actions of others" (Epstein and Knight 1998, 12).

Sometimes, this allows justices to vote and behave in ways that directly align with their attitudes. Other times, engaging in strategic and sophisticated calculations, justices will compromise so as to avoid their least preferred outcomes (Epstein and Knight 1998, 13). For example, in the context of Supreme Court decision making, the individual justice does not act in solitude but with eight other justices—not only to vote on outcomes but also to select cases and craft opinions that produce legal tests and standards. For a case to receive the full review of the Court, at least four justices must support hearing the case. In addition, determining who writes the opinion for the Court has consequences, and studies of opinion assignment "demonstrate that the Chief Justice frequently bases opinion assignments on strategic considerations" (Maltzman, Spriggs II, and Wahlbeck 1999, 54).

Strategic considerations may also play a role in the drafting of opinions, which often requires negotiation among the justices. After a drafted opinion is circulated among the justices, the justice writing the opinion may have to compromise by adding or removing language to ensure that a majority of justices are willing to sign onto the final version. Justice Antonin Scalia, for instance, was pressed by another justice to add significant language in *District of Columbia v. Heller* (2008), the landmark Second Amendment case holding that the Constitution protects an individual's right to own a gun for personal use. In that 5–4 ruling, Justice Anthony Kennedy "insisted—as the price of his vote" in favor of gun rights—that the majority opinion nevertheless incorporate language permitting states to pass reasonable gun regulations (Totenberg 2019). Without Kennedy's vote to join the opinion, the Court ruling would not have garnered a majority of justices and would have been weakened as a result.

These types of internal institutional constraints, some researchers find, can lead justices to engage in collegial and strategic coalition building. As political scientists Forrest Maltzman, James F. Spriggs II, and Paul J. Wahlbeck argue, "[p]erhaps the most important institutional feature of the Court is its collegial character" (Maltzman, Spriggs II, and Wahlbeck 1999, 51). Individual judicial preferences matter, as the attitudinal model claims. But "preferences alone do not dictate the choices justices make" (Maltzman, Spriggs II, and Wahlbeck 2000, 149).

The behavior of judges and resulting strategic choices are thought to be constrained not only internally by the expected behavior of others on the bench, but also by broader institutional structures and dynamics. According to Epstein and Knight, justices "must also consider the preferences of other political actors, including Congress, the president, and even the public" (Epstein and Knight 1998, 13).

Consider, again, Justice Stephen Breyer's explanation for why it took 13 years for the Court to overturn prohibitions against interracial marriages in *Loving v. Virginia* (1967) after declaring racial segregation in public schools unconstitutional in *Brown v. Board of Education* (1954) (see Q19). That explanation offers a strategic account for why justices—who sought to end racial discrimination—delayed doing so. Rather than quickly pressing forward in line with their own attitudes and policy preferences, they waited, worried that public and political backlash might derail the achievement of their preferences. According to Breyer, selectively choosing which cases to hear and, in some instances, avoiding cases, were part of the judicial calculus (Breyer 2021, 60).

In addition to the attitudinal and strategic models, another main strand of social science studies into judicial behavior suggests that attitudes and ideology matter but that they should be examined less as the cause of behavior and more as the product of the history and institutions in which judges act. This framework—called new institutionalism (or historical institutionalism)—approaches the question of how political attitudes and ideologies shape judicial decision making in a different way than do attitudinalist or strategic choice theories. While not denying that ideology and attitudes play a role in decision making, new institutionalists resist the idea that judges are purely instrumental actors seeking to advance their policy preferences or moved by sophisticated calculations to maximize their preferences. In addition, they do not assume that judges come to their jobs with fully formed and fixed perspectives, attitudes, and preferences.

Instead, new institutionalists suggest that judicial ideology and attitudes are shaped as judges do the job of judging. They are shaped by such things as the judiciary as an institution, by the professional role of judges, by the place of the courts within the political system, and by historical context. What matters, then, to understanding judicial behavior is "how judicial attitudes are themselves constituted and structured by the Court *as an institution* and by its relationship to other institutions in the political system at particular points in history" (Clayton and Gillman 1999, 2).

Consider, for example, how playing the unique role of a judge might influence both a judge's behavior and attitudes. Judicial role perceptions include "the institutional actors' sense of duty, obligation, or recognition that their actions are inherently meaningful" (Macfarlane 2013, 31). Judicial role orientations are framed by what judges "think they ought to do" (Gibson 1983, 9), and by the belief that the judicial role "imposes upon them an obligation to act in accordance with particular expectations and responsibilities" (Gillman and Clayton 1999, 4). A Supreme Court justice might, based on role orientation, think that their job is to simply call balls and strikes. Or the justice might think that their job is restricted to making decisions based on a felt obligation to follow prior legal precedent, even if that means coming to a conclusion that is in conflict with the justice's political preferences.

An emphasis on role perception would, on the surface, seem more sympathetic to the idea that judges set aside their personal predilections in order to act in accordance with their role as a judge and fulfill their legal responsibilities. However, those who posit this approach typically emphasize how the very conceptualizations of the judicial role are themselves created and influenced by political and institutional contexts. As such, a new institutionalist suggests that it is important to explore what historical, political, and cultural factors influence justices to adopt particular jurisprudential theories or particular views about when to follow precedent and when to overturn it.

Divergence among alternative theories that seek to explain judicial behavior remains. That divergence should not be seen as demonstrating that ideology and attitudes do not play a role in decision making. Even granting that research "provides evidence of the existence of constraints . . . on freewheeling ideologically motivated judicial behavior," legal scholarship confirms "that ideology plays a significant role in judicial behavior" (Epstein, Landes, and Posner 2013, 66). And it may be, as political scientist James Gibson argues, that at least a partial integration of predominant frameworks offers the most useful explanation of behavior (Gibson 1983, 7). In a classic characterization combining attitudinal theory, role theory, and "a host of group-institution theories," Gibson asserts that "judges' decisions are a function of what they prefer to do, tempered by what they think they ought to do, but constrained by what they perceive it feasible to do" (Gibson 1983, 9).

In any case, whether finding that judicial preferences and attitudes are dominant, constrained by context, or operating in conjunction with other variables, the bulk of existing research belies the claim that judges—especially those who occupy the high bench—leave their personal views aside when donning their official robes.

FURTHER READING

Banks, Christopher P., and David O'Brien. 2008. *Courts and Judicial Policymaking.* Upper Saddle River, NJ: Prentice Hall.

Barnes, Robert, and Ed O'Keefe. 2017. "Supreme Court Nominee Gorsuch Stresses His Independence from President Trump." *Washington Post*, March 21, 2017.

Berardino, Mike, and Ann E. Marimow. 2021. "Justice Thomas Defends the Supreme Court's Independence and Warns of 'Destroying our Institutions.'" *New York Times*, September 16, 2021.

Brenner, Saul, and Marc Stier. 1996. "Retesting Segal and Spaeth's Stare Decisis Model." *American Journal of Political Science*, 40, no. 4: 1036–1048.

Breyer, Stephen. 2021. *The Authority of the Court and Peril of Politics*. Cambridge, MA: Harvard University Press.

Brown v. Board of Education of Topeka, 347 U.S. 483 (1954).

Clayton, Cornell, and David A. May. 1999. "A Political Regimes Approach to the Analysis of Legal Decisions." *Polity*, 32, no. 2: 233–252.

Clayton, Cornell, and Howard Gillman. 1999. "Introduction: Beyond Judicial Decision Making." In *The Supreme Court in American Politics: New Institutionalist Interpretations*, ed. Howard Gillman and Cornell Clayton, 1–14. Lawrence, KS: University Press of Kansas.

District of Columbia v. Heller, 554 U.S. 570 (2008).

Epstein, Lee, and Jack Knight. 1998. *The Choices Justices Make*. Washington, DC: CQ Press.

Epstein, Lee, William M. Landes, and Richard A. Posner. 2013. *The Behavior of Federal Judges: A Theoretical and Empirical Study of Rational Choice*. Cambridge, MA: Harvard University Press.

Gibson, James L. 1983. "Judicial Behavior: Theory and Methodology." *Political Behavior*, 5, no. 1: 7–49.

Gillman, Howard, and Cornell W. Clayton. 1999. "Beyond Judicial Attitudes: Institutional Approaches to Supreme Court Decision Making." In *Supreme Court Decision-Making: New Institutionalist Approaches*, ed. Cornell W. Clayton and Howard Gillman, 1–14. Chicago, IL: University of Chicago Press.

Kritzer, Herbert M., and Mark J. Richards. 2005. "The Influence of Law in the Supreme Court's Search-and-Seizure Jurisprudence." *American Politics Research*, 33, no. 1: 33–55.

Loving v. Virginia, 388 U.S. 1 (1967).

Macfarlane, Emmett. 2013. *Governing From the Bench: The Supreme Court of Canada and the Judicial Role*. Vancouver, BC: UBC Press.

Maltzman, Forrest, James F. Spriggs II, and Paul J. Wahlbeck. 1999. "Strategy and Judicial Choice: New Institutionalist Approaches to Supreme Court Decision Making." In *Supreme Court Decision-Making: New Institutional Approaches*, ed. Cornwell W. Clayton and Howard Gillman, 43–64. Chicago, IL: University of Chicago Press.

Maltzman, Forrest, James F. Spriggs II, and Paul J. Wahlbeck. 2000. *Crafting Law on the Supreme Court: The Collegial Game*. New York: Cambridge University Press.

Maveety, Nancy. 2003. *The Pioneers of Judicial Behavior*. Ann Arbor, MI: University of Michigan Press.

Murphy, Walter F., and Joseph Tanenhaus. 1972. *The Study of Public Law*. New York: Random House.

Richards, Mark J., and Herbert M. Kritzer. 2002. "Jurisprudential Regimes in Supreme Court Decision Making." *American Political Science Review*, 96, no. 2: 305–320.

Robertson, David. 1982. "Judicial Ideology in the House of Lords: A Jurimetric Analysis." *British Journal of Political Science*, 12, no. 1: 1–25.

Robertson, David. 1998. *Judicial Discretion in the House of Lords*. New York: Oxford University Press.

Schubert, Glendon. 1965. *The Judicial Mind*. Evanston, IL: Northwestern University Press.

Segal, Jeffrey A. 2011. "Judicial Behavior." In *The Oxford Handbook of Political Science*, ed. Robert E. Goodin, 275–288. New York: Oxford University Press.

Segal, Jeffrey A., and Albert D. Cover. 1989. "Ideological Values and the Votes of U.S. Supreme Court Justices." *American Political Science Review*, 83, no. 2: 557–565.

Segal, Jeffrey A., and Harold J. Spaeth. 1993. *The Supreme Court and the Attitudinal Model*. New York: Cambridge University Press.

Segal, Jeffrey A., and Harold J. Spaeth. 1994. "The Authors Respond." *Law and Courts*, 4: 10–12.

Segal, Jeffrey A., and Harold J. Spaeth. 2002. *The Supreme Court and the Attitudinal Model Revisited*. New York: Cambridge University Press.

Songer, Donald R. 2012. "The Dog That Did Not Bark: Debunking the Myths Surrounding the Attitudinal Model of Supreme Court Decision Making." *Justice System Journal*, 33, no. 3: 340–362.

Songer, Donald R., and Stephanie A. Lindquist. 1996. "Not the Whole Story: The Impact of Justices' Values on Supreme Court Decision Making." *American Journal of Political Science*, 40: 1049–1063.

Totenberg, Nina. 2019. "From Cover-Ups to Secret Plots: The Murky History of Supreme Justices' Health." *National Public Radio*, January 23, 2019. https://www.npr.org/2019/01/23/686208930/from-cover-ups-to-secret-plots-the-murky-history-of-supreme-justices-health

Zorn, Christopher, and Jennifer Barnes Bowie. 2010. "Ideological Influences on Decision Making in the Federal Judicial Hierarchy: An Empirical Assessment." *Journal of Politics*, 72, no. 4: 1212–1221.

Q21. DID THE SUPREME COURT'S "SWITCH IN TIME THAT SAVED NINE" OCCUR IN DIRECT RESPONSE TO EXTERNAL POLITICAL PRESSURE?

Answer: There has long existed a general consensus that the Supreme Court's remarkable shift—from hostility to acceptance—regarding the New Deal programs and policies of President Franklin Delano Roosevelt was a response to the president's so-called "court-packing plan" to expand the size of the Court with hand-picked judges. Many scholars also believe the Court became sensitive to the disapproval of an American public that regularly gave Roosevelt high marks as president. However, more recent scholarship has challenged this consensus. Though there is agreement that the Court did, in fact, substantially alter its jurisprudence in the mid-1930s, considerable disagreement remains over whether this change was a result of the Court "caving" to external political pressure.

The Facts: The conflict between President Franklin Delano Roosevelt and the U.S. Supreme Court that unfolded in the 1930s ranks among the most dramatic political episodes ever to engulf the high Court. Roosevelt and the Court repeatedly clashed over the President's massive New Deal legislative agenda, an ambitious effort to lift the American people out of the Great Depression. In particular, the Court declared unconstitutional several key provisions of the New Deal, including the National Industrial Recovery Act and the Agricultural Adjustment Act. "By the end of 1936, the Court had struck down a series of legislative efforts by the Roosevelt administration to extend the federal government's role in shaping and regulating economic life. The president and his allies feared that the justices were on the verge of dismantling the New Deal's achievements altogether" (Brinkley 2005, 1046). Roosevelt became so frustrated with the Supreme Court that he proposed legislation to increase the number of justices on the Court. If passed, that legislation would have given Roosevelt the opportunity to pack the Court with new appointees likely to be supportive of his New Deal agenda.

Roosevelt's court-packing plan did not come to pass. Instead, one of the justices on the Court who had previously voted to overturn New Deal legislation—Justice Owen Roberts—appeared to switch his legal position. In *West Coast Hotel v. Parrish* (1937), a Supreme Court decision that was handed down in the midst of the court-packing fight, Roberts toggled in favor of the Roosevelt administration's challenged legislation, becoming the pivotal vote in a slim 5–4 majority that upheld a Washington state minimum wage law. The prior year, in *Morehead v. New York ex rel. Tipaldo*, Roberts had voted against a nearly identical law.

That surprising shift by Roberts, famously dubbed "the switch in time that saved nine" (because it preserved a nine-seat Supreme Court), helped seal the fate of the court-packing plan. Roosevelt did not succeed in getting Congress to pass his plan and in fact encountered heavy criticism for making the proposal. But his agenda succeeded nevertheless. Once the Court became more favorably disposed toward his New Deal legislation, the main components of Roosevelt's legislative agenda went into effect.

Did the external pressure placed on the Court by an enormously popular president who had just won a landslide election lead a key swing justice to cave and suddenly switch sides?

"Scholars have battled for decades—and with increasing intensity in the past years—over the role of Justice Roberts," disputing whether he switched sides suddenly or evolved his legal thinking gradually (Ho and Quinn 2010, 71). As historian Alan Brinkley noted, the increasingly heated debate came

> as something of a surprise to many historians, most of whom had long accepted the arguments of Roosevelt's contemporaries and of the first great historians of the New Deal—most notably William E. Leuchtenburg—that there was a reasonably simple, political explanation for the Court's change of course. . . . The [court-packing] plan created a political firestorm and did considerable damage to the president's standing within his own party and among the public. But according to more than a generation of scholars, it also frightened the justices themselves, at least one of whom, Owen Roberts, appeared to switch positions in response to growing political pressure and to begin supporting New Deal legislation. (Brinkley 2005, 1046–1047)

Some scholars felt that the simple political explanation did not take into consideration other developments and shifts in jurisprudence that were already taking place. According to this alternate theory, the major change in constitutional jurisprudence that led the Court to find New Deal legislation constitutional in 1937 and later years was the result of "an intellectual evolution within the judicial world itself over the proper relationship between the state and the national economy, evidence of which was the narrow balance of many of its decisions in the 1930s. Roberts's apparent shift in 1937 was a logical continuation of a change in his legal thinking, and the thinking of others, that had been in progress for some time" (Brinkley 2005, 1047).

Among the most prominent and early advocates of this "internalist" theory is legal historian Barry Cushman. In his book *Rethinking the New Deal Court: The Structure of a Constitutional Revolution* (1998), Cushman argued that there is internal consistency between a line of rulings handed down by the Court prior to *West Coast Hotel v. Parrish* and the ruling in *Parrish* itself. As evidence for this view, Cushman pointed to several cases, including *Nebbia v. New York* in 1934, as markers of jurisprudential change that was underway.

Cushman also asserted that a significant change in the Court's jurisprudence took place in the early 1940s—well after the court-packing threat—in the Court's decisions interpreting the interstate commerce clause. By that time, retirements from the bench had occurred and Roosevelt had the opportunity to replace justices who had remained opposed to his New Deal legislation with others who favored a broader interpretation of the interstate commerce clause (Cushman 1998).

"Externalists," meanwhile, subscribe to the longstanding view that external political influences—rather than internal evolution of the Court's legal doctrine—led Justice Roberts to make a pragmatic, political switch with his vote in 1937. The externalists cite, among other things, Roosevelt's landslide 1936 election, growing legislative pressure against and criticism of the Court, and the court-packing threat as among the main factors that compelled Roberts to change sides. But internalists argue that although the decision in *Parrish* was announced after Roosevelt threatened to pack the Court, the vote in the case took place before Roosevelt released his court-packing plan. They also argue that additional rulings handed down later in the 1937 term and following the *Parrish* decision came after the court-packing threat had already subsided.

Still, externalists insist that Roberts's vote in *Parrish* cannot be reconciled with the jurisprudential positions he had presented in earlier cases. For example, political scientists Daniel Ho and Kevin Quinn provided evidence to support the externalist position by analyzing nonunanimous cases decided in the Court's 1931 to 1940 terms. They concluded that Justice Roberts "shifted sharply (and statistically significantly)," though only temporarily, to the left in the 1936 term when *Parrish* was decided (Ho and Quinn 2010, 72). Although Roberts's shift was short-lived, it didn't matter because Roosevelt's own appointments over the ensuing years moved the Court to the left. This "drastic realignment of the Court. . . . quickly marginalized Roberts, who in three terms would be left as the single most conservative justice on the Court" (Ho and Quinn 2010, 72).

The theory that the announced court-packing plan, by itself, precipitated the switch in time that saved nine seems to have fewer adherents these days than it did in the past. Even those scholars who conclude that the sea change in the Court's jurisprudence can be explained largely by external political factors concede that the threat of court packing was not decisive. Historian William Leuchtenburg, for example, whose research on the Court during the New Deal era was strongly influential in expounding the externalist argument, conceded the point. He wrote that while it initially seemed reasonable to assume that Roberts shifted in response to the court-packing threat, "we have known for decades that, though the *Parrish* decision was announced in March, the vote had been taken prior to FDR's thunderbolt, and hence Court-packing legislation could not have influenced Roberts on that case" (Leuchtenburg 2005, 1081).

Though debate continues over whether the switch was a direct result of external pressure, the episode nevertheless clearly marks the intense political context in which the Court is embedded. It also, perhaps, suggests that there may be truth to both perspectives on the debate. According to historian Alan Brinkley, "[j]udicial decisions are almost always a result of both 'internal' constitutional principles and 'external' social, cultural, and political influences. Stark disagreements in scholarly discourse, much like stark disagreements in popular political discourse, often mask a far more complex reality in which two seemingly opposed positions are in fact more compatible with one another than they seem" (Brinkley 2005, 1049).

FURTHER READING

Ackerman, Bruce. 1998. *We the People: Transformations*. Cambridge, MA: Harvard University Press.

Brinkley, Alan. 2005. "The Debate Over the Constitutional Revolution of 1937: Introduction." *The American Historical Review*, 110, no. 4: 1046–1051.

Cushman, Barry. 1994. "Rethinking the New Deal Court." *Virginia Law Review*, 80: 201–261.

Cushman, Barry. 1998. *Rethinking the New Deal Court: The Structure of a Constitutional Revolution*. New York: Oxford University Press.

Friedman, Richard D. 1994. "A Reaffirmation: The Authenticity of the Roberts Memorandum, or Felix the Non-Forger." *University of Pennsylvania Law Review*, 142: 1985–1995.

Ho, Daniel E., and Kevin M. Quinn. 2010. "Did a Switch in Time Save Nine?" *Journal of Legal Analysis*, 2, no. 1: 69–113.

Kalman, Laura. 1999. "Law, Politics, and the New Deal(s)." *Yale Law Journal*, 108: 2165–2213.

Kalman, Laura. 2005. "The Constitution, the Supreme Court, and the New Deal." *The American Historical Review*, 110, no. 4: 1052–1080.

Leuchtenburg, William E. 1995. *The Supreme Court Reborn: The Constitutional Revolution in the Age of Roosevelt*. New York: Oxford University Press.

Leuchtenburg, William E. 2005. "Comment on Laura Kalman's Article." *The American Historical Review*, 110, no. 4: 1081–1093.

Morehead v. New York ex rel. Tipaldo, 298 U.S. 587 (1936).

Nebbia v. New York, 291 U.S. 502 (1934).

Ross, William G. 2005. "When Did the 'Switch in Time' Actually Occur?: Rediscovering the Supreme Court's 'Forgotten' Decisions of 1936–1937." *Arizona State Law Journal*, 37: 1153–1220.

West Coast Hotel v. Parrish, 300 U.S. 379 (1937).

White, G. Edward. 2005. "Constitutional Change and the New Deal: The Internalist/Externalist Debate." *The American Historical Review*, 110, no. 4: 1094–1115.

Q22. IS THE INFLUENCE OF AMICUS BRIEFS ON THE SUPREME COURT GROWING?

Answer: There has been a clear and substantial increase in the number of amicus briefs submitted to the Supreme Court. *Briefs* are written documents elaborating legal arguments in favor of a particular position. In cases reviewed by the Supreme Court, the direct parties to the cases submit legal briefs that seek to persuade the Court to find in their favor. Beyond the direct parties, other interested parties may seek to present written legal arguments to the Court. These are called amicus curiae, or "friend of the court," briefs.

Most legal observers agree that the increase in amicus brief filings submitted to the Court signals their growing influence. But, like other factors thought to affect the Court, there is less agreement about how and to what extent amicus briefs shape judicial decisions.

The Facts: In September 2021, the Women's National Basketball Players Association, the National Women's Soccer League Players Association, Athletes for Impact, and more than 500 women athletes submitted an amicus curiae brief to the U.S. Supreme Court in a case involving abortion rights (Streeter 2021). At issue in the case of *Dobbs v. Jackson Women's Health Organization* (2021) was whether a Mississippi law banning most abortions after 15 weeks of pregnancy violates the Constitution.

The particular brief in question asserted that access to abortion is vital for female athletes, and it was one of many submitted briefs urging the Court to hold that the Mississippi law violates the Constitution (*Dobbs v. Jackson Women's Health Organization* Brief of Amicus Curiae 2021). On the opposite side, other amicus briefs filed in the case encouraged the Court to affirm the law, with some arguing that the Court should fully reverse *Roe v. Wade*, the 1973 ruling establishing a constitutional right to choose abortion.

"[A]mici curiae—nonparties who are nevertheless advocates, who are not bound by rules of standing and justiciability, or even rules of evidence, and who can present the court with new information and arguments—occupy a unique place in the appellate courts" (Anderson 2015, 361–362). Interested individuals, groups, or organizations—like the Women's National Basketball Players Association, for instance—can submit amicus briefs if given permission by both parties to the litigation or the Court.

The unique place of amici curiae has been taking up considerably more space in recent years. Together, more than 140 amici curiae submitted briefs in *Dobbs v. Jackson Women's Health Organization*, representing not only athletes but also "professors, politicians, states, and interest groups from across the ideological spectrum" (Erskine 2021). This level of amicus involvement approached the record of 147 briefs submitted in *Obergefell v. Hodges*, the 2015 case in which the Court held that the Constitution protects a right to same-sex marriage. Though this volume of briefs in a single case is unusually high, it nevertheless reflects a trend of rising amicus activity in the modern era of Supreme Court decision making.

According to Supreme Court Rule 37, "[a]n *amicus curiae* brief that brings to the attention of the Court relevant matter not already brought to its attention by the parties may be of considerable help to the Court" (Rules of the Supreme Court of the United States 2019, 51). Rule 37 also warns, however, that an amicus brief "that does not serve this purpose burdens the Court, and its filing is not favored" (Rules of the Supreme Court of the United States 2019, 51). Notwithstanding this warning, for at least the past 50 years, the Court has adopted an open-door disposition toward granting permission to those seeking to file as a friend of the court, allowing "essentially unlimited amicus participation" (Caldeira and Wright 1990, 784). Moreover, the U.S. government, as well as state governments, may elect to file amicus briefs.

As documented by legal scholars Joseph D. Kearney and Thomas W. Merrill, the growth in friend-of-the-court briefs marks a major transformation in Supreme Court practice. Rare in the 19th century and infrequent in the first part of the 20th century, amicus participation rose considerably in the 50 years following World War II. The change was so substantial that "at the close of the twentieth century, cases without amicus briefs have become as rare as cases with amicus briefs were at the beginning of the century" (Kearney and Merrill 2000, 744).

By Kearney and Merrill's count, the total number of amicus briefs filed with the Supreme Court over the five decades they studied rose remarkably. For each decade from 1946 to 1955, 1956 to 1965, 1966 to 1975, 1976 to 1985, and 1986 to 1995, the number of amicus briefs filed was, respectively, 531, 743, 2042, 4182, and 4907. Among the cases reviewed by the Court with oral arguments, the percentage that included amicus briefs also swelled. In each of the five decades studied, the percent of cases argued that included one or more amicus brief rose as follows: 23%, 33%, 54%, 73%, and 85%, respectively (Kearney and Merrill 2000, 752–753).

In addition, as a measure of the intensity of amicus participation, Kearney and Merrill found that over the entire five decades of their study, in cases with amicus briefs, the median number of briefs filed increased from one to three (Kearney and Merrill 2000, 754). The study notes that large numbers of friend-of-the-court briefs have been filed not only in hot-button cases adjudicating laws and policies pertaining to abortion, death penalty, and affirmative action, but also in lower-profile cases involving copyright law, punitive damages, and apportionment of state taxes (Kearney and Merrill 2000, 756).

More recent studies show that the rising participation of amici curiae has persisted into the 21st century. For example, 98 percent of cases filed in the U.S. Supreme Court 2014–15 term featured amicus curiae filings, with a total of almost 800 briefs (Franze and Anderson 2015). This constituted an 800% rise from the 1950s, and from 1995 alone a jump of 95% (Larsen and Devins 2016, 1902).

Another analysis of the 10 years of Supreme Court decision making beginning with the 2010–11 term confirms the continuing rise in amicus participation. "Over ten terms, amici cumulatively filed more than 8,000 briefs, participated in 96 percent of all argued cases, and were cited by the justices in more than half of their rulings." Moreover, the final record-breaking term of the decade "had more than 900 amicus briefs filed in argued cases, the highest average number of amicus briefs per case ever. The justices cited briefs in 65 percent of cases—another record" (Franze and Anderson 2020).

While there is no disputing the remarkable rise in amicus participation, the sheer volume is not, by itself, determinative of whether and how the information they present influences the final decisions of the Supreme Court. Many research findings suggest that amicus activity does influence the Court. The hypotheses and findings, though, often diverge with respect to identifying the main paths and types of influence. Thus, while most scholars conclude that amici are influential, there is far less agreement about how *much* influence amicus curiae briefs have on the outcomes of cases, and on the language and legal arguments used by the justices. There is also less consensus about what factors explain amici influence and variation in that influence.

For example, researchers have variously found that (a) parties that have more amicus support are more likely to win on the merits (Collins Jr. 2008a; Kearney and Merrill 2000); (b) the presence of amicus briefs increases the chances that justices will write concurring or dissenting opinions (Collins Jr. 2008b); (c) judicial support for the outcomes favored in briefs is likely to increase when the amicus briefs come from groups connected to, and that collaborate with, other well-connected interest groups (Box-Steffensmeier, Christenson, and Hitt 2013); (d) justices view briefs more favorably when they come from amici reputed to submit high-quality briefs (Box-Steffensmeier, Christenson, and Hitt 2013); (e) justices incorporate language from those briefs submitted by amici that align ideologically with the justices' ideological positions (Collins Jr., Corley, and Hamner 2015); and (f) amicus briefs get more attention if they come from government or academics, or if they provide new information not included in the briefs submitted by the parties to the case (Franze and Anderson 2020).

Though research findings on the pathways and explanations of impact are not unified, there is consensus on at least three avenues of influence. The first concerns the influence of amicus briefs in determining which cases the Court agrees to hear. "Cert-stage" amicus briefs are those filed at the time when parties petition the Court for a writ of certiorari—when petitioners ask the Court to hear their case. Friend-of-the-court briefs at this stage are less common than those filed after the Court agrees to grant certiorari. Still, amicus briefs filed at this stage are correlated with a higher rate of cert grants. According to one study, for example, in the 2014 term, friends of the court filed a total of 403 briefs prior to cert decisions in 177 out of 7,006 cases. Almost 18 percent of these 177 cases were granted cert, as compared to the 1 percent rate of all filed petitions (Feldman 2016).

Another study found that for cert petitions with a reasonable chance of acceptance in the first place, "amicus curiae briefs can mark the difference between success and failure. . . . When a case involves real conflict or when the federal government is petitioner, the addition of just one amicus curiae brief in support of certiorari increases the likelihood of plenary review by

40%–50%" (Caldeira and Wright 1988, 1122). Still other research suggests that while the effects of amici participation at this stage is hardly uniform across petitioners, the presence of amici is "most beneficial to resource-poor petitioners and primarily allows those petitions to have a chance at having their case discussed, even if the Court is no more likely to grant review in it" (Black and Boyd 2013, 1141).

The second avenue of influence concerns whether amicus briefs actually have an impact on the outcome of the cases heard by the Court. Here, research shows that a particular friend of the court—the United States solicitor general—has special influence on achieving a favorable outcome. The U.S. solicitor general is the federal government's chief lawyer and serves as the legal representative for the federal government in Supreme Court cases. The solicitor general's unique relationship to the Supreme Court has been well documented—so much so that the solicitor general has been dubbed the "Tenth Justice" (Caplan 1987).

In the area of amici influence, multiple scholars have studied the impact of solicitor general briefs in particular. For example, political scientist Jeffrey A. Segal's study of the Warren and Burger Courts, covering cases between 1952 and 1982, concluded that roughly three-quarters of the time, the solicitor general's amicus briefs supported the party that won (Segal 1988). A similar level of success for the solicitor general was found in a study of the Court covering cases from 1959 to 1986 (Salokar 1992). Kearney and Merrill's study of cases from 1946 through 1995 similarly concluded that the solicitor general's success rate as an amicus filer is dramatic (Kearney and Merrill 2000). So too did research conducted by political scientists Ryan C. Black and Ryan J. Owens on Supreme Court rulings from 1950 through 2010. That data showed that when the solicitor general participates as a friend of the court, the success rate at the merits stage tends to be between 70 and 80 percent (Black and Owens 2012, 26).

Third, legal researchers have confirmed that justices regularly cite friend-of-the-court briefs in their opinions. To be clear, citing briefs does not necessarily constitute concurrence with those briefs. Indeed, justices often cite briefs to reject the arguments made therein (Franze and Anderson 2020). Nevertheless, citing amici is a common and growing phenomenon.

In terms of the magnitude of citations (and not including the handful of instances in which the Court appointed a friend of the court to submit briefs), the 2019–20 term marked a recent high. Beating out the previous nine terms, justices cited amici "in 65 percent of argued cases with amicus participation and signed majority opinions" (Franze and Anderson 2020). Amicus briefs submitted by the solicitor general received the most attention. Justices cited 10 percent of nongovernmental amicus briefs while citing 63 percent of briefs submitted by the Office of the Solicitor General (Franze and Anderson 2020).

Citations to amicus briefs are not unique to the past decade or to the Roberts Court. According to political scientists Ryan J. Owens and Lee Epstein, in the nearly 700 cases heard by the Rehnquist Court during the 1986 through 2003 terms, the Court's opinion referenced at least one amicus in 38 percent of cases that had amicus participation (Owens and Epstein 2005, 130). But this level of citation—which does not include concurring and dissenting opinions—diverges from the terms running from 1946 through 1985. As Kearney and Merrill found, "majority, plurality, concurring, and dissenting opinions *combined* cited to *amicus curiae* briefs in just 24 percent of the cases" (Owens and Epstein 2005, 130, citing Kearney and Merrill, 2000).

Whether the brief submitted by athletes in *Dobbs* will be cited or in another way influence the justices in their consideration of the right to abortion is, at the time of this writing, unclear. What is clear is that unless the Court changes the rules governing amicus briefs, we should expect amicus participation to remain robust, even if we cannot pinpoint precisely how influential that participation is.

FURTHER READING

Anderson, Helen A. 2015. "Frenemies of the Court: The Many Faces of Amicus Curiae." *University of Richmond Law Review*, 49, no. 2: 361–416.

Black, Ryan C., and Christina L. Boyd. 2013. "Selecting the Select Few: The Discuss List and the U.S. Supreme Court's Agenda-Setting Process." *Social Science Quarterly*, 94, no. 5: 1124–1144.

Black, Ryan C., and Ryan J. Owens. 2012. *The Solicitor General and the United States Supreme Court: Executive Branch Influence and Judicial Decisions*. New York: Cambridge University Press.

Box-Steffensmeier, Janet M., Dino P. Christenson, and Matthew P. Hitt. 2013. "Quality Over Quantity: Amici Influence and Judicial Decision Making." *American Political Science Review*, 107, no. 3: 446–460.

Caldeira, Gregory A., and John R. Wright. 1988. "Organized Interests and Agenda Setting in the U.S. Supreme Court." *American Political Science Review*, 82, no. 4: 1109–1127.

Caldeira, Gregory A., and John R. Wright. 1990. "Amici Curiae Before the Supreme Court: Who Participates, When, and How Much?" *Journal of Politics*, 52, no. 3: 782–806.

Caplan, Lincoln. 1987. *The Tenth Justice: The Solicitor General and the Rule of Law*. New York: Vintage Books.

Collins, Paul M., Jr. 2008a. *Friends of the Supreme Court: Interest Groups and Judicial Decision Making.* New York: Oxford University Press.

Collins, Paul M., Jr. 2008b. "Amici Curiae and Dissensus on the U.S. Supreme Court." *Journal of Empirical Legal Studies,* 5: 143–170.

Collins, Paul M., Jr., Pamela C. Corley, and Jesse Hamner. 2015. "The Influence of Amicus Curiae Briefs on U.S. Supreme Court Opinion Content." *Law & Society Review,* 49, no. 4: 917–944.

Dobbs v. Jackson Women's Health Organization. 2021. Brief amicus curiae of Over 500 Women Athletes, the Women's National Basketball Players Association, the National Women's Soccer League Players Association, and Athletes for Impact. September 20, 2021. https://www.supremecourt .gov/DocketPDF/19/19-1392/193300/20210921171646329_19 -1392%20Amici%20Curiae.pdf

Dobbs v. Jackson Women's Health Organization, Docket Number 19-1392 (2021).

Erskine, Ellena. 2021. "We Read All the Amicus Briefs in Dobbs So You Don't Have To." Blog. *SCOTUSblog,* November 30, 2021. https://www.scotusblog .com/2021/11/we-read-all-the-amicus-briefs-in-dobbs-so-you-dont -have-to

Feldman, Adam. 2016. "Successful Cert Amici 2014." Blog. *Empirical SCOTUS,* March 15, 2016. https://empiricalscotus.com/2016/03/15 /certamici-2014

Franze, Anthony J., and R. Reeves Anderson. 2015. "Record Breaking Term for Amicus Curiae in Supreme Court Reflects New Norm." *The National Law Journal,* August 19, 2015.

Franze, Anthony J., and R. Reeves Anderson. 2020. "Amicus Curiae at the Supreme Court: Last Term and the Decade in Review." *The National Law Journal,* November 18, 2020.

Kearney, Joseph D., and Thomas W. Merrill. 2000. "The Influence of Amicus Curiae Briefs on the Supreme Court." *University of Pennsylvania Law Review,* 148, no. 3: 743–855.

Larsen, Allison Orr, and Neal Devins. 2016. "The Amicus Machine." *Virginia Law Review,* 102, no. 8: 1901–68.

Obergefell v. Hodges, 576 U.S. 644, 135 S. Ct. 2584 (2015).

Owens, Ryan J., and Lee Epstein. 2005. "Amici Curiae During the Rehnquist Years." *Judicature,* 89: 127–133.

Roe v. Wade, 410 U.S. 113 (1973).

"Rules of the Supreme Court of the United States." 2019. https://www .supremecourt.gov/ctrules/2019RulesoftheCourt.pdf

Salokar, Rebecca Mae. 1992. *The Solicitor General: The Politics of Law.* Philadelphia, PA: Temple University Press.

Segal, Jeffrey A. 1988. "Amicus Curiae Briefs by the Solicitor General During the Warren and Burger Courts: A Research Note." *Western Political Quarterly*, 41, no. 1: 135–144.

Streeter, Kurt. 2021. "Why Scores of Female Athletes Are Speaking Out on Abortion Rights." *New York Times*, September 27, 2021.

Q23. IS THE SUPREME COURT USING THE "SHADOW DOCKET" MORE FREQUENTLY?

Answer: Yes. Whether we should be concerned about the Supreme Court's growing use of the so-called "shadow docket"—emergency orders and summary reversals of lower court rulings—it is clear that it is being used more frequently and controversially than in the past.

The Facts: When we think of the rulings handed down by the U.S. Supreme Court, we typically think of cases handled under the Court's "merits docket." The merits docket includes the roughly 60 to 70 cases a year that tend to receive the most attention from the Court, legal scholars, media, and political pundits. The rulings in cases that comprise the merits docket are considered as being especially impactful when they establish *precedent*—principles and rules that lower courts and future Supreme Courts are generally expected to follow.

However, the Supreme Court handles far more than the cases on the merits docket. Roughly 7,000 petitions arrive at the Court each year and almost all of these are disposed of without oral arguments and without the signed (and typically lengthy) opinions issued in cases handled under the merits docket. Most of the cases on the "orders docket" are petitions asking for the Court to hear the case on its merits. Most are denied, however, with little more than an unsigned order from the Court.

Among the cases that comprise the orders docket are petitions seeking "emergency relief." Although the name insinuates that all such petitions involve emergency situations, applications for emergency relief often relate to relatively mundane matters, such as seeking extra time to file court documents. In some instances, however, they involve life-or-death requests, as happens when an application asks the Supreme Court to halt an execution. In other cases, emergency relief applications ask the Court to act while a case is winding its way through the appeals process. For instance, an application may ask the Supreme Court to temporarily halt—or "stay"—the implementation of a ruling issued by a lower court, or to remove a lower court stay or injunction. These latter types of requests essentially ask the justices to take an action before the case makes its way to the high Court through the normal appeals process.

There have long been such emergency applications to the Court, and there is good reason to have an avenue for submitting petitions seeking emergency relief and for the Court to manage those petitions with due haste—that is, without the slower deliberative process used in other cases that the Court addresses on the merits docket. There are also petitions for Court action that take place when the Court is in recess, between the end of June/early July and the first Monday in October. In addition, the Court can issue, without oral arguments and signed opinions, summary orders reversing lower court decisions. Summary reversals, as well as orders issued in cases seeking emergency relief, are among the cases that comprise the "shadow docket."

In its broadest definition, the *shadow docket* refers to the orders docket: that is, to "the significant volume of orders and summary decisions that the Court issues without full briefing and oral argument" (Vladeck 2019, 125). As such, the term references longstanding procedural aspects of how the Supreme Court has managed the orders docket. But the phrase itself is relatively new, first used in 2015 by University of Chicago Law Professor William Baude to connote the lack of transparency and information concerning Court actions involving cases on the orders docket (Baude 2015).

More recent attention to the Court's handling of emergency petitions and summary reversals shows that something new is taking place with respect to the shadow docket. Legal scholars have documented a significant increase in the Court's reliance on the shadow docket. Legal analysts have also suggested that use of the shadow docket has not merely increased, but that the Court's handling of the cases has changed in character, including more reversals of lower court rulings. As Stephen I. Vladeck, a law professor and leading expert on the shadow docket, said in 2021, "there is simply no dispute, even anecdotally, that the shadow docket has become increasingly prominent over the past four years" (Vladeck 2021, 3).

The Court's use of the shadow docket surged during the administration of President Donald Trump. In response to lower court rulings striking down a series of executive orders, Trump's solicitor general turned to the shadow docket with a record of 41 emergency appeals (Satter 2021). By comparison to previous presidential administrations, this was a marked increase. In the four years of the Trump presidency, the federal government filed shadow docket applications with the Supreme Court "at 20 times the rate of each of the two previous eight-year administrations" (Hurley, Chung, and Allen 2021). For the Trump administration, this "dramatic increase in application paid dividends," with the Court granting "24 of the 36 applications in full and four in part," not including four applications that were withdrawn and one temporarily on hold (Vladeck 2021, 5). These applications, seeking "to stay a lower-court ruling or lift a lower-court stay," included "14 alone during the October 2019 term" (Vladeck 2020).

While the Supreme Court showed receptiveness to the Trump administration's aggressive use of emergency appeals, the Court's growing openness to issuing notable orders from cases on the shadow docket has continued since Trump's term ended. And, to be clear, emergency petitions handled on the shadow docket do not have to come from the Justice Department. "To get on the shadow docket, any litigant can apply to a single justice, who decides whether to forward the dispute to the full court. Five votes among the nine justices are needed to grant a request" (Hurley, Chung, and Allen 2021). While the Trump administration made noteworthy use of emergency applications, it is also clear that the recent Court has "has entertained emergency relief petitions from more and more litigants" (Donegan 2021).

The increasing influence of the shadow docket is demonstrated not simply in quantity of cases. Indeed, one of the more notable aspects of the growing reliance on the shadow docket is its use in controversial contexts. To be sure, as Vladeck explains, controversial orders have been issued in the past from shadow docket cases, "from the execution of the Rosenbergs to Justice Douglas halting Nixon's bombing of Cambodia to the stay of the Florida recount in what became *Bush v. Gore*" (Vladeck 2021, 2). However, such high-profile decisions coming from the shadow docket have historically been relatively rare; in Vladeck's estimation, significant rulings from the shadow docket have tended to amount to no more than three or four each term (Vladeck 2021, 3).

By contrast, more recent shadow docket cases have addressed multiple controversial subjects. During the Trump administration, these cases included, for example, orders on Trump's travel ban and efforts to change the U.S. Census. Multiple COVID-19 regulations have been handled within the shadow docket, including several noteworthy cases following Trump's term of office. In February 2021, the Court blocked California from enforcing most of its COVID regulations on indoor religious services, and in April 2021, the Court did the same with respect to private religious gatherings in people's homes. In August 2021, the Court blocked the Center for Disease Control's extension of a COVID-related emergency moratorium on eviction.

Among the Court's recent and controversial shadow docket rulings is one on abortion that garnered substantial national attention. On September 1, 2021, the Court let stand a Texas law banning almost all abortions after the detection of a fetal heartbeat, which usually occurs around six weeks of pregnancy. A ban on abortions that early in pregnancy ran counter to the standing legal precedent that, at the time of the law's passage, held that women retain a constitutional right to abortion prior to fetal viability. Allowing the ban to take effect meant that for almost all women seeking an abortion in Texas after six weeks of pregnancy, the procedure was no longer available. Nonetheless, and over the objection of four dissenting justices, the Court issued a brief order permitting the abortion prohibition to take effect, citing procedural matters as grounds for not issuing an injunction.

What makes the growing reliance on the shadow docket especially notable is that the Court is using it

> to change the status quo—where the Court's summary action disrupts what was previously true under rulings by lower courts. . . . In both absolute and relative terms, there have been far more of these kinds of rulings in cases seeking emergency relief—granting injunctive relief; granting stays of lower-court rulings; or, as in a surprising number of capital cases, *lifting* stays of lower-court rulings—than at any prior point in the Court's history. In that respect, part of the significance of the shadow docket of late has been in how often the Justices are using it to disrupt the state of affairs as a case reaches the Court. (Vladeck 2021, 4)

It is also clear that more and more cases handled on the shadow docket are generating strongly worded dissents from justices. Although the orders issued by the Court in shadow docket cases do not typically include written judicial opinions, dissents are becoming more common. Consider the 36 emergency applications filed by the Trump Justice Department: at least one dissent was issued in 27 of the 36 cases. This compares with only one dissent in the eight emergency applications sought by the Justice Department during the presidential terms of George W. Bush and Barack Obama.

The increasing number of dissents displays growing contentiousness around the use of the shadow docket. That contentiousness is perhaps best exemplified by Justice Elena Kagan's dissent in the case that let the Texas abortion ban go into effect. In a blistering criticism of the Court's one-paragraph, unsigned opinion, Justice Kagan wrote that "the majority's decision is emblematic of too much of this Court's shadow-docket decisionmaking—which every day becomes more unreasoned, inconsistent, and impossible to defend" (*Whole Woman's Health v. Jackson* 2021, 2500 Kagan dissenting).

Kagan's dissent highlights some of the main concerns about the Court's shadow docket rulings. While concerns are often expressed about the substance of the Court's orders, that is also true of many rulings handed down on the merits docket. Of particular concern to those criticizing shadow docket rulings, however, is the process itself—and the increased willingness of the Court's conservative majority to use it to make consequential rulings that affect the lives of millions of Americans. As Kagan detailed in her dissent concerning the Texas law, the Court order

> illustrates just how far the Court's "shadow-docket" decisions may depart from the usual principles of appellate process. That ruling, as everyone must agree, is of great consequence. Yet the majority has acted without any guidance from the Court of Appeals—which is right now considering the same issues. It has reviewed only the most cursory party submissions, and then only hastily. And it barely bothers to explain its conclusion—that a challenge to an obviously unconstitutional abortion regulation backed by a wholly unprecedented enforcement scheme is unlikely to prevail. (*Whole Woman's Health v. Jackson* 2021, 2500 Kagan dissenting)

In these ways, the Court is increasingly handling cases on the shadow docket in ways that "defy its normal procedural regularity" and "lack the procedural transparency that we have come to appreciate in its merits cases" (Baude 2015, 1). Rulings from the shadow docket stand in stark contrast to cases handled on the merits docket, which have procedural consistency and far greater transparency. In the latter cases, "[o]bservers know in advance what cases the Supreme Court will decide, and they know how and when the parties and others can be heard. We know what the voting rule is; we know that the results of the voting rule will be explained in a reasoned written opinion; and we know that each Justice will either agree with it or explain his or her disagreement" (Baude 2015, 12).

In addition, cases on the merits docket "receive at least two full rounds of briefing; are argued in public at a date and time fixed months in advance; and are resolved through lengthy written opinions handed down as part of a carefully orchestrated tradition beginning at 10:00 a.m. EST on pre-announced 'decision days'" (Vladeck 2021, 2).

The shadow docket cases are far more shrouded in mystery. Court decisions in these cases "typically come after no more than one round of briefing (and sometimes less); are usually accompanied by no reasoning (let alone a majority opinion); invariably provide no identification of how (or how many of) the Justices voted; and can be handed down at all times of day—or, in some exceptional cases, in the middle of the night. Owing to their unpredictable timing, their lack of transparency, and their usual inscrutability, these rulings come both literally and figuratively in the shadows" (Vladeck 2021, 2).

Not everyone agrees that use of the shadow docket is of concern or marked by procedural irregularity. Among those resisting the growing expressions of concern over the shadow docket is Justice Samuel Alito. In his own scorching critique of criticism of the shadow docket, Alito described the phrase as "loaded" and "misleading," saying that it was unfairly "used to portray the court as having been captured by a dangerous cabal that resorts to sneaky and improper methods to get its ways" (Liptak 2021). He further complained that the "portrayal feeds unprecedented efforts to intimidate the court and to damage it as an independent institution" (Liptak 2021).

Still, Alito does not deny the rising use of the emergency applications. Moreover, the growing attention to the Court's use of the shadow docket, along with the divisiveness and tension it has produced within the Court itself, is further evidence of its growing influence.

FURTHER READING

Baude, William. 2015. "Foreword: The Supreme Court's Shadow Docket." *New York University Journal of Law and Liberty*, 9, no. 1 (2015): 1–47.

Brosnahan, James. 2021. "SCOTUS 'Shadow Docket' Decisions Impact Americans' Liberties." *Bloomberg Law*, September 23, 2021.

Donegan, Moira. 2021. "The US Supreme Court Is Deciding More and More Cases in a Secretive 'Shadow Docket.'" *The Guardian*, August 31, 2021.

Fawbush, Joseph. 2021. "SCOTUS Ends CDC Eviction Moratorium Through 'Shadow Docket.'" *FindLaw*, August 31, 2021.

Hurley, Lawrence, Andrew Chung, and Jonathan Allen. 2021. "The 'Shadow Docket': How the U.S. Supreme Court Quietly Dispatches Key Rulings." *Reuters*, March 23, 2021.

Liptak, Adam. 2021. "Alito Responds to Critics of the Supreme Court's 'Shadow Docket.'" *New York Times*, September 30, 2021.

Satter, Andrew. 2021. "The Shadow Docket and How the Supreme Court Uses It Now" [video]. *Bloomberg Law*, November 3, 2021. (Transcript available at https://aboutblaw.com/0jz)

Vladeck, Stephen I. 2019. "Essay: The Solicitor General and the Shadow Docket." *Harvard Law Review*, 133: 123–163.

Vladeck, Stephen I. 2020. "Symposium: The Solicitor General, the Shadow Docket and the Kennedy Effect." *SCOTUSblog*, October 22, 2020.

Vladeck, Stephen I. 2021. "The Supreme Court's Shadow Docket: Hearing Before the Subcommittee on Courts, Intellectual Property, and the Internet of the House Committee on the Judiciary." Thursday, February 18, 2021. https://judiciary.house.gov/calendar/eventsingle .aspx?EventID=4371

We the People Podcast. 2021. "The Supreme Court's 'Shadow Docket.'" National Constitution Center, October 7, 2021.

Whole Woman's Health v. Jackson, 141 S. Ct. 2494 (2021).

5

Public Perceptions of the Judiciary

Confidence in governing institutions is important for well-functioning democracies, and support of the judiciary is thought to be especially important for maintaining the rule of law. Historically, measures of public attitudes show that the judiciary has tended to outperform other governing institutions in terms of job performance and trust. In addition, positive public perceptions about a well-functioning judiciary have historically been associated with confidence that the courts are sufficiently insulated from politics. Indeed, the idea that judicial institutions are largely apolitical and make decisions in nonpartisan ways has been thought to be a bedrock of the legitimacy of the courts. However, public perceptions of the courts appear to be in flux in the face of increasing political polarization and partisan divide in the United States.

Q24. IS PUBLIC FAITH AND CONFIDENCE IN THE SUPREME COURT IN DECLINE?

Answer: With respect to the U.S. Supreme Court, evidence shows a noteworthy decline of approval and confidence between 2011 and 2017, and a record low in 2021. Whether public approval of lower federal courts and state courts is in decline is less clear because most studies of public attitudes about the courts focus on the Supreme Court.

The Facts: When analyzing public attitudes toward the judiciary, scholars and court observers often highlight "the reservoir of goodwill courts typically enjoy" (Gibson 2008, 59). The value of confidence in the judicial system—and the risks associated with declining confidence—are notable. As political scientist Sara Benesh summarizes, the public may be less likely to comply with court rulings, to participate on juries, and to turn to the courts for conflict resolution "without some reservoir of good will or some level of support for and confidence in the justice system" (Benesh 2006, 697). Has the reservoir of goodwill historically enjoyed by the courts been deep enough to withstand the rising political and partisan polarization in the United States? Or have trust in and support of the judiciary taken a hit?

Public support for the judiciary in the United States is often measured by way of public opinion polling. Polls provide a good gauge of attitudes about the U.S. Supreme Court, which is the common focus of attention. Broadly speaking, polls historically find higher levels of public approval and confidence in the Supreme Court than in the executive and legislative branches of the federal government. However, polling also reveals a period of declining approval of and trust in the federal judiciary, especially running from 2011 to 2017. Though a rebound took place in 2019 and 2020, public approval for the Court dropped to a record low in 2021.

Gallup polling conducted in September 2021—the most recent survey available at the time of this writing—shows a strong hit to public approval of the Supreme Court. A total of only 40 percent of survey respondents voiced approval of the way the Supreme Court is "handling its job," while 53 percent expressed disapproval (Jones 2021). These results reveal a remarkable decline from Gallup polling conducted just a little over a year earlier. In the summer of 2020, 58 percent of survey respondents indicated approval of the Court, compared to 38 percent who disapproved (McCarthy 2020).

Compared to public approval of Congress, though, the Court remains a relatively high performer. In polling conducted in September 2021, only 27 percent of respondents approved of Congress's handling of its job, with 69 percent disapproving (Gallup 2021a). The level of approval for the Supreme Court in September looked similar to the ratings for President Joe Biden. At that time, Biden's approval came in at 43 percent, with his disapproval rating at 53 percent (Brenan 2021).

Approval of the Supreme Court has proven vulnerable in the first two decades of the 21st century. In fact, as measured by Gallup, the reservoir of support dipped below 50 percent multiple times. In the 37 polls conducted by Gallup between August 2000 and September 2021, levels of approval ranged between 40 and 49 percent a total of 16 times. In the first decade of the 21st century, the dips below the 50 percent mark occurred once in 2005 and once in 2008. But a notable decline took place between 2011 and 2017, when approval did not get above 49 percent (McCarthy 2020). And though a rebound occurred from 2019 to 2020, the drop to 40 percent in September 2021 marked a historic low in public approval of the Court (Gallup 2021c).

Gallup polling gauges public attitudes about the Supreme Court not only in terms of job approval but also by asking the following question: "How much trust and confidence do you have at this time in the judicial branch headed by the U.S. Supreme Court—a great deal, a fair amount, not very much, or none at all?" (Gallup 2021c). In September 2021, a total of 54 percent of respondents reported either a great deal or fair amount of trust in the federal judiciary—a drop of 13 percent from the previous year (Jones 2021). Though only 10 percent of this total noted a great deal of trust in the federal judiciary, compared to 44 percent expressing a fair amount of trust (Gallup 2021c), this level of public confidence was still substantially higher than trust in the legislative and executive branches. Just 5 percent of poll respondents reported a great deal of trust in Congress, with another 32 percent expressing a fair amount of trust (Gallup 2021a). The "executive branch headed by the president" fared better than Congress, but not as well as the judiciary, with a total of 44 percent indicating either a great deal (17 percent) or a fair amount (27 percent) of trust (Gallup 2021b).

The flip side of this coin is also telling of the relative trust in the judiciary. A majority of respondents in the 2021 Gallup poll expressed "not very much" trust or "none at all" in the legislative and executive branches, but only a minority expressed a similar lack of confidence in the judiciary. Still, 32 percent of respondents expressed "not very much" trust in the Court, while another 14 percent answered "none at all" when asked how much trust they had in the institution (Gallup 2021c).

In a related gauge of confidence, Gallup has for many years provided respondents with a list of institutions and asked "how much confidence you, yourself, have in each one—a great deal, quite a lot, some, or very little?" On this metric, for the 41 years running from 1980 through 2021, the percentage of respondents reporting either a great deal or quite a lot of confidence in the Supreme Court has ranged from a low of 30 to a high of 56. Over the same years, those with very little or no confidence ranged from 8 to 26 percent. Notably, the data indicate a decline in confidence that roughly parallels the recent dips in Court approval. Between 1981 and 2006, the percentage of those with little or no confidence never reached 20; however, between 2007 and 2021, that percentage ranged from 17 to 26 (see Gallup 2021c).

Other polling and research reinforce the Gallup findings. For example, a September 2021 Quinnipiac University poll reported that public approval for the Court was at 37 percent, the lowest rating since 2004 when Quinnipiac first started polling on this question. Approval dropped from the previous year's level of 52 percent. The Quinnipiac poll also reported a 49 percent disapproval rating for the Court (Malloy and Schwartz 2021).

A study of public opinion by research analyst Sofi Sinozich using polls from several sources, including Gallup, found "an unprecedented drop in support for the Court" from 2005 to 2015 (Sinozich 2017, 173). Sinozich cited PEW polling showing that in 2001, "as high as 72 percent of Americans had a 'very/mostly favorable' opinion of the Court, but by the summer of 2012 the percentage had fallen to 51 and remained in that range" (Sinozich 2017, 176). Moreover, citing the General Social Science Survey (GSS)—a nationally representative survey tracking U.S. public opinion and behavior—Sinozich noted that confidence in "the people running" the Supreme Court remained fairly stable for many years but trended downward between 2006 and 2012.

> Since the 1970s, about 30 percent of the public reports having a "great deal" of confidence, 50 percent having "only some," and between 10 and 20 percent "very little" under this formulation. Based on the GSS, the percentage of those with a "great deal" of confidence declined slowly from 33 to 29 percent between 2006 and 2012, with a sharp drop to 23 percent in 2014. This is the longest measured period of sustained decline, wrapping up with the lowest recorded level of confidence since 1973. The previous lowest point was 25 percent in 1980, but ratings rose back to their former levels by the mid-1980s. (Sinozich 2017, 177)

The polling just summarized here focuses on the federal judiciary and, in particular, on the Supreme Court. What do we know about public perceptions of state courts? Historically, considerably less focus has been trained on state courts by pollsters. As political scientists Kenneth E. Fernandez and Jason A. Husser summarized, "prior literature reviews have shown that state courts are often neglected by researchers examining the judicial system in the United States. Furthermore, the study of public attitudes toward state courts is especially thin" (Fernandez and Husser, 2020).

Calls for more attention to studying public attitudes about state courts have generated some results. Political scientists over the past 20 years have used national surveys and state-focused surveys to study not just whether the public has confidence in state courts but also what factors explain these levels of confidence. For example, a national poll conducted in 1999 provided a snapshot of confidence in state courts at that time, though not a measure of change over time. The poll was conducted by the National Center for State Courts (NCSC), an independent, nonprofit organization founded in 1971 as "as a clearinghouse for research information and comparative data to support improvement in judicial administration in state courts" and after Warren E. Burger, then Chief Justice of the U.S. Supreme Court, pushed for its establishment (Cleveland Municipal Court 2022). The NCSC survey found that 23 percent of respondents had trust or confidence in the courts in their community. Another 52 percent had some trust, and a total of 25 percent had only a little or no confidence in the courts in their community (NCSC 1999, 12).

The poll also asked how respondents felt the courts in their communities handled cases. "Overall, only 10% of respondents felt the courts in their community handled cases in an 'Excellent' manner. Twenty percent said criminal cases were handled poorly and 21% said that family relations cases were handled in a 'Poor' manner, while nearly 30% said that juvenile delinquency cases were handled in a 'Poor' manner. It appears that Americans are not especially satisfied with the way cases are handled by the courts. Indeed, more people felt, across all case types examined, that cases are handled in a 'Poor' manner than felt cases are handled in an 'Excellent' manner" (NCSC 1999, 14). Relying on this national survey, political scientist Sara Benesh found that levels of confidence in state courts are affected by the respondents' personal experiences with the courts, perceptions of procedural fairness, and whether or not judges secured their seats on the bench through partisan elections and are thus closely associated with one political party (Benesh 2006).

Other research has delved into attitudes about courts in specific states. For example, a study published in 2004 by a group of political science and criminal justice scholars, based on a 1995 survey of Mississippi residents, found a "lukewarm" assessment of the performance of state courts. Survey respondents were asked to register their overall approval or disapproval of the local court and state supreme court. The results showed that the majority did not express approval of either the local courts or the Mississippi Supreme Court. Seeking to examine the role race plays in public attitudes about the courts, the research found that with respect to approval, only 41 percent of whites and 37 percent of African Americans approved of the state supreme court. In addition, only 45 percent of whites and 41 percent of African Americans approved of local courts (Overby et al. 2004, 169).

In another, more recent study conducted in 2015, political scientists Kenneth E. Fernandez and Jason A. Husser gauged public attitudes about courts in North Carolina and found greater approval than was found in the study of Mississippi. For the purposes of comparison, the survey conducted by Fernandez and Husser asked residents not only about the state courts but about other political institutions as well. In their findings, "[n]early 66 percent of respondents stated they were somewhat or very confident in the North Carolina state courts. This was followed closely by local public schools, with 65.8 percent, followed by the US Supreme Court, with 65 percent. Confidence in the federal government and the media was the lowest among the six institutions, with 37 percent and 36 percent, respectively" (Fernandez and Husser 2020).

More systematic polling of public attitudes about state courts has emerged in recent years, commissioned by the National Center for State Courts. In 2012, and then annually beginning in 2014 and running through 2019, NCSC sponsored national public opinion surveys to monitor levels of public trust and confidence in courts at the state level (NCSC 2020). The surveys found strong public confidence in state court systems from 2012 through 2019, with strong majorities expressing either a great deal of or some confidence in their state courts.

The NCSC survey's other measures, however, found considerable variations in confidence in state courts by different races. As the findings in 2015 state, "there is a massive racial gap on most measures, with African Americans much more distrustful of the courts and the broader justice system" (NCSC 2015, 1). Still, if we take the NCSC annual surveys as a guide, there has not been clear decline in public trust of state courts in recent years.

FURTHER READING

Benesh, Sara C. 2006. "Understanding Public Confidence in American Courts." *Journal of Politics*, 68, no. 3: 697–707.

Brenan, Megan. 2021. "Biden's Approval Rating Hits New Low of 43%; Harris' Is 49%." *Gallup*, September 22, 2021.

Caldeira, Gregory A. 1991. "Courts and Public Opinion." In *The American Courts: A Critical Assessment*, ed. John B. Gates and Charles A. Johnson, 303–334. Washington, DC: CQ Press.

Cann, Damon M., and Jeff Yates. 2008. "Homegrown Institutional Legitimacy Assessing Citizens' Diffuse Support for State Courts." *American Politics Research*, 36, no. 2: 297–329.

Cleveland Municipal Court. 2022. "The Who, What, When, Where and How of State Courts." http://clevelandmunicipalcourt.org/judicial-services/administrative-services/national-center-for-state-courts-video---the-who-what-when-where-and-how-of-state-courts

Fernandez, Kenneth E., and Jason A. Husser. 2020. "Public Attitudes Toward State Courts." In *Open Judicial Politics*. 1st Edition, ed. Rorie Spill Solberg, Jennifer Segal Diascro, and Eric Waltenburgby. Oregon State University, Ecampus. https://open.oregonstate.education/open-judicial-politics/chapter/fernandez

Gallup. 2021a. "Congress and the Public: Historical Trends." https://news.gallup.com/poll/1600/congress-public.aspx

Gallup. 2021b. "Gallup Poll Social Series: Governance." https://news.gallup.com/file/poll/355136/211003TrustinGovt.pdf

Gallup. 2021c. "Supreme Court: Historical Trends." https://news.gallup.com/poll/4732/supreme-court.aspx

Gibson, James L. 2008. "Challenges to the Impartiality of State Supreme Courts: Legitimacy Theory and 'New-Style' Judicial Campaigns." *American Political Science Review*, 102, no. 1: 59–75.

Jones, Jeffrey M. 2021. "Approval of U.S. Supreme Court Down to 40%, a New Low." *Gallup*, September 23, 2021.

Malloy, Tim, and Doug Schwartz. 2021. "Nearly 7 in 10 Say Recent Rise in Covid-19 Deaths Was Preventable, Quinnipiac University National Poll Finds; Job Approval for Supreme Court Drops to All-Time Low." *Quinnipiac University Poll*, September 15, 2021.

McCarthy, Justin. 2020. "Approval of the Supreme Court Is Highest Since 2009." *Gallup*, August 5, 2020.

National Center for State Courts. n.d.a. "About Us." https://www.ncsc.org/about-us

National Center for State Courts. n.d.b. "Public Trust and Confidence Resource Guide." https://www.ncsc.org/topics/court-community/public-trust-and-confidence/resource-guide

National Center for State Courts. 1999. "How the Public Views the State Courts: A 1999 National Survey." https://ncsc.contentdm.oclc.org/digital/collection/ctcomm/id/17

National Center for State Courts. 2014. "Analysis of National Survey of Registered Voters." GBA Strategies, December 4, 2014. https://www.ncsc.org/__data/assets/pdf_file/0020/17804/2014-state-of-state-courts-survey-12042014.pdf

National Center for State Courts. 2015. "Analysis of National Survey of Registered Voters." GBA Strategies, November 17, 2015. https://www.ncsc.org/__data/assets/pdf_file/0018/16164/sosc_2015_survey-analysis.pdf

National Center for State Courts. 2016. "National Survey." GBA Strategies, December 12, 2016. https://www.ncsc.org/__data/assets/pdf_file/0018/16128/sosc_2016_survey_analysis.pdf

National Center for State Courts. 2017. "2017 State of the State Courts—
    Survey Analysis." GBA Strategies, November 15, 2017. https://www
    .ncsc.org/__data/assets/pdf_file/0012/16131/sosc-2017-survey-analysis.pdf
National Center for State Courts. 2018. "2018 State of the State Courts—
    Survey Analysis." GBA Strategies, December 3, 2018. https://www.ncsc
    .org/__data/assets/pdf_file/0020/16157/sosc_2018_survey_analysis.pdf
National Center for State Courts. 2020. "2019 State of the State Courts—
    Survey Analysis." GBAO Strategies, January 3, 2020. https://www.ncsc
    .org/__data/assets/pdf_file/0018/16731/sosc_2019_survey_analysis_2019
    .pdf
Overby, L. Marvin, Robert D. Brown, John M. Bruce, Charles E. Smith
    Jr., and John W. Winkle III. 2004. "Justice in Black and White: Race,
    Perceptions of Fairness, and Diffuse Support for the Judicial System in a
    Southern State." *Justice System Journal*, 25, no. 2: 159–182.
Saad, Linda. 2020. "Trust in Federal Government's Competence Remains
    Low." *Gallup*, September 29, 2020.
Sinozich, Sofi. 2017. "The Polls—Trends: Public Opinion on the US
    Supreme Court, 1973–2015." *Public Opinion Quarterly*, 81, no 1: 173–195.

Q25. DOES THE PUBLIC BELIEVE THE COURTS ARE POLITICAL AND PARTISAN?

Answer: Research and polling have shown that substantial portions of the public see court decisions as influenced by political factors, especially the ideology and personal values of the judges. In addition, while evidence suggests that the public often sees the courts as *influenced* by politics, that does not mean the public views the courts as partisan in character. Evidence of whether the public sees the courts as partisan is mixed.

The Facts: Trust in the rule of law is often premised on the principle that law rather than politics influences judicial decisions. According to this principle, judges should act impartially, guided by legal factors and not their personal or political preferences. In addition, judicial institutions should be distinct from political arms of governance and independent from direct partisan control. Of course, the notion that judiciaries can be fully shielded from any political influence is unrealistic. In many ways, complete insulation is contrary to checks and balances built into the U.S. systems, which include mechanisms for the political branches to shape the courts through such things as judicial appointments. Moreover, according to historian Rachel Shelden, the Supreme Court was openly political for a good portion of this country's history. In the 19th century, for example, the public fully expected the Supreme Court to behave in a partisan fashion. "Public trust in the court did not rely on justices claiming to be apolitical; Americans were far more concerned about limiting judicial power, period" (Shelden 2020).

Still, when it comes to judicial decision making, a sufficient degree of political and partisan insulation is commonly thought to be a centerpiece of the rule of law and the legitimacy of the justice system. It is, for example, the view commonly espoused by nominees to the Supreme Court during their confirmation hearings when they seek to persuade senators and the public to support them by emphasizing their alleged judicial independence.

Does the public view the courts as insulated from political and partisan influence, and as guided by law over political factors when it comes to rendering decisions? With respect to the U.S. Supreme Court, several studies by political scientists and legal scholars have found "that a large share of the American public views the Court in political and ideological terms" (Bartels and Johnston 2012, 106). Some public opinion polling in recent years has corroborated this, showing a growing perception that the Supreme Court is influenced by politics and partisanship. However, other polls suggest that the majority of the public sees the Supreme Court as guided largely by law.

In one political science study published in 2000, researchers surveyed 658 respondents to evaluate whether the public views Supreme Court decisions as influenced primarily by legal principles or political factors. The results show that while respondents identified both legal and political influences on the Court, "they generally regard the justices' ideologies as the most influential element affecting the Court's decisions" (Scheb and Lyons 2000, 933). On the legal side, respondents reported that prior precedent and the intentions of the Framers of the Constitution both had a large impact on the justices' decision: 39 percent and 34 percent, respectively. But on the political side, 42 percent of respondents said ideology has a large impact on judicial decisions. Direct partisan influence, however, was viewed as less influential. Only 29 percent of respondents said that whether the judges are Democrats or Republicans has a large impact on their decisions (Scheb and Lyons 2000, 932).

Another study by political scientists published in 2011 used a nationally representative sample to gauge public attitudes about the factors influencing Supreme Court decisions. Like the 2000 study, this research suggests that a sizeable portion of the public sees decisions as influenced by political views and, to a lesser extent, by partisanship. In particular,

> [m]ost Americans (57.3 percent) agree that judges actually base their decisions on their own personal beliefs, even while a smaller plurality (48.4 percent) recognizes that values and political views influence how decisions are made. On the question of partisan influences on decisionmaking, the balance of opinion changes, with a slim plurality believing that party affiliations have little to do with judges' decisions (43.9 versus 39.2 percent). (Gibson and Caldeira 2011, 207)

A third study, published in 2012, found not only that the public perceives the Supreme Court in political terms, but also that the public *prefers* justices to be selected based on political factors. Relying on a 2005 national public opinion poll, the study reports "a substantial majority of the public perceives of the Court in politicized terms. Roughly 70 percent of the mass public either agrees or strongly agrees that the Supreme Court is 'too mixed up in politics' and 'favors some groups more than others.' Moreover, 64 percent of the public believes the Court is 'sometimes politically motivated in its rulings'" (Bartels and Johnston 2012, 110). Interestingly, the study also found that the public reaction to this politicization is not to find ways to make the Court less political. Instead, "much of the mass public actually *prefers* that justices be chosen on the basis of political factors" and "perceptions of Court politicization enhance preferences for a political appointment process" (Bartels and Johnston 2012, 112).

Some more recent public opinion polling has found that even when the Supreme Court receives strong approval ratings, Americans think political factors influence its decision making. In 2019, for example, polling by the Annenberg Public Policy Center revealed high levels of trust in the Court but at the same time "identified troubling signs in how the Supreme Court and the justices are perceived by the public, suggesting that the distinction between judges and elected politicians is becoming blurred. More than half of Americans (57%) agree with the statement that the court 'gets too mixed up in politics.' And just half of the respondents (49%) hold the view that Supreme Court justices set aside their personal and political views and make rulings based on the Constitution, the law, and the facts of the case" (Annenberg Public Policy Center 2019).

Polling by Marquette Law School conducted in 2020 found that most voters said U.S. Supreme Court decisions are based on law and not politics, with 62 percent of respondents agreeing that Supreme Court justices' decisions are motivated mainly by the law and 37 percent asserting they are motivated mainly by politics (Marquette University 2020). In addition, the

Marquette poll shows that these views were relatively consistent regardless of the party identification and ideology of the respondent. Similarly, along the ideological spectrum from very liberal to very conservative, "all groups share very similar views, with 35–40 percent of each group pointing to politics, while 60–65 percent say the law is the main motivation for decisions" (Marquette University 2020).

However, a November 2021 Quinnipiac poll reported that a strong majority of the public views the Court as political. In that poll, only 32 percent described the Supreme Court as mainly motivated by law, whereas 61 percent indicated that the Court was mainly motivated by politics. Though essentially the reverse of the findings of the 2020 Marquette poll, the Quinnipiac study also shows bipartisanship in views about the political character of the Court. According to survey, 65% of Democrats, 56% of Republicans, and 62% of independents shared the view that the Court is motivated primarily by politics (Malloy and Schwartz 2021). What accounts for the growing perception that the Court is political? Contributing factors likely include recent controversies over Supreme Court nominations (see Q5), several Court decisions seen by legal critics as shamelessly partisan in supporting a conservative political and cultural agenda, the Court's September 2021 decision to let stand a Texas law banning almost all abortions after six weeks of pregnancy, and the expectation the Court will—because of conservative appointments to the bench—overturn the almost 50-year-old precedent declaring abortion a fundamental right.

The findings discussed so far focus on the Supreme Court. With respect to state courts, polls suggest that the public often views their judicial decisions as unduly influenced by politics. Surveys commissioned by the National Center for State Courts (NCSC), for example, indicate that the public holds a strong degree of confidence in state judiciaries yet expresses concern over political influence and bias. As summarized in the analysis of the findings of the 2014 poll, "doubts about partisanship and political bias represent [the] greatest threat to public confidence. The one negative attribute that garnered majority agreement in our survey was *political*, with 53 percent saying it describes the courts in their state and 56 percent saying the same about judges in their state" (NCSC 2014, 2).

Contributing to this view was a close divide between the 48 percent of respondents who said that judges "make decisions based on an objective review of facts and the law" and the 46 percent who said judges "make decisions based more on their own beliefs and political pressure" (NCSC 2014, 3).

It is also noteworthy that the NCSC polling indicates that attitudes about the influence of politics and bias vary based on race. The organization's 2018 survey, for example, found that whereas 66 percent of white respondents agreed that the system was fair and impartial, only 36 percent of African

American respondents felt the same way. Similarly, 56 percent of whites polled agreed the justice system provided "equal justice for all," while only 29 percent of African Americans agreed (NCSC 2018, 3).

Overall, the evidence from multiple sources makes clear that the public does not view the state and federal judiciaries as invulnerable to political factors or pressure. That said, the perception that the courts are *political* is not synonymous with the perception that the courts are *partisan*. Although notable portions of the public see judicial decisions as influenced by judges' political and ideological views, that does not mean the public necessarily sees judges as acting directly in line with their party identification or, in the case of the federal courts, with the party affiliation of the appointing president. In fact, as noted earlier, at least some of the existing research suggests that while substantial portions of the public view court decisions as influenced by politics, a smaller percentage see decisions as influenced by partisanship. Judges influenced by their own political values and ideologies might still be seen by the public as capable and acting in line with sincerely held ideological beliefs. However, when the public comes to view judges as partisans—aligned and consistently voting with the party of their nominating president—they are more likely to see court rulings as being rendered based not on principle but on the goal of advancing the interests of a particular political party (see, e.g., Epstein and Posner 2018).

Whether public perceptions of the courts as political or partisan (or both) decreases perceived legitimacy of the judiciary is another important issue, one taken up in this book's final question.

FURTHER READING

Annenberg Public Policy Center. 2019. "Most Americans Trust the Supreme Court, But Think It Is 'Too Mixed Up in Politics.'" *Annenberg Public Policy Center*, October 16, 2019. https://www.annenbergpublicpolicycenter .org/most-americans-trust-the-supreme-court-but-think-it-is-too-mixed -up-in-politics

Bartels, Brandon L., and Christopher D. Johnston. 2012. "Political Justice? Perceptions of Politicization and Public Preferences Toward the Supreme Court Appointment Process." *Public Opinion Quarterly*, 76, no. 1: pp. 105–116.

Epstein, Lee, and Eric Posner. 2018. "If the Supreme Court Is Nakedly Political, Can It Be Just?" *New York Times*, July 9, 2018.

Gibson, James L., and Gregory A. Caldeira. 2011. "Has Legal Realism Damaged the Legitimacy of the U.S. Supreme Court?" *Law & Society Review*, 45, no. 1: 195–219.

Malloy, Tim, and Doug Schwartz. 2021. "Majority Say Supreme Court Motivated by Politics, Not the Law, Quinnipiac University National Poll Finds; Support for Stricter Gun Laws Falls." *Quinnipiac University Poll*, November 19, 2021.

Marquette University. 2020. "New National Marquette Law School Poll Finds That, Even Amid Partisan Differences on Judicial Philosophy, Most Voters say U.S. Supreme Court Decisions Are Based on Law and Not Politics." Marquette University News Release, September 25, 2020. https://www.marquette.edu/news-center/2020/new-national-marquette -law-poll-finds-that-most-voters-say-supreme-court-decisions-are-based -on-law.php

National Center for State Courts. 2014. "Analysis of National Survey of Registered Voters." GBA Strategies, December 4, 2014. https://www .ncsc.org/__data/assets/pdf_file/0020/17804/2014-state-of-state-courts -survey-12042014.pdf

National Center for State Courts. 2017. "2017 State of the State Courts— Survey Analysis." GBA Strategies, November 15, 2017. https://www .ncsc.org/__data/assets/pdf_file/0012/16131/sosc-2017-survey-analysis.pdf

National Center for State Courts. 2018. "2018 State of the State Courts— Survey Analysis." GBA Strategies, December 3, 2018. https://www.ncsc .org/__data/assets/pdf_file/0020/16157/sosc_2018_survey_analysis.pdf

Scheb, John M., and William Lyons. 2000. "The Myth of Legality and Popular Support for the Supreme Court." *Social Science Quarterly*, 81: 928–940.

Shelden, Rachel. 2020. "The Supreme Court Used to Be Openly Political. It Traded Partisanship for Power." *Washington Post*, September 25, 2020.

Q26. DOES THE PUBLIC'S PERCEPTION OF THE JUDICIARY VARY BY PARTY AFFILIATION?

Answer: Attitudes about the U.S. Supreme Court differ by party identi-fication on many key dimensions, though not all. However, there is less evidence of such variation with respect to perceptions of state courts.

The Facts: As discussed in Q24 and Q25, approval of and confidence in the nation's judicial branch are historically higher than for the other branches of the federal government, though favorable public attitudes toward the Supreme Court have recently taken a hit. However, public atti-tudes about the courts are not monolithic. Available evidence indicates, perhaps not surprisingly, that Democrats and Republicans frequently hold different views about the Supreme Court's performance. Public attitudes concerning trust in the federal judiciary also diverge by party affiliation and ideology of respondents. When asked whether the structure of the Supreme Court should be reformed, responses sometimes, though not always, vary by party affiliation.

Approval of the Supreme Court shows variance by party identification in several different polls. Gallup's polling, which asks respondents whether they approve of the overall job performance of the U.S. Supreme Court, is especially illustrative. It not only shows distinctions by party identification, but also that approval versus disapproval of the Court shifts over time in a way that appears related to which party controls the White House.

Since the beginning of the 21st century, Republicans and Democrats have often diverged on whether the Supreme Court is doing a good job, with independents typically falling in between and close to the national average. At times the divergence between parties is stark. In 2016, for example, Gallup polling found that only 26 percent of Republican survey respondents said they approved of the way the Supreme Court "is handling its job," compared to 67 percent of Democratic respondents (Smith and Newport 2016). That 41-percentage point difference narrowed to a 25-percentage point difference in 2017, after the 2016 presidential election and the switch from a Democratic president to a Republican one. But this narrowing also came with a flip in approval. In 2017, it was Republicans who approved of the Court, with only 40 percent of Democratic survey respondents expressing approval compared to 65 percent of Republican respondents (McCarthy 2017). The margin widened in 2018, and in 2019 only 38 percent of Democrats as compared to 73 percent of Republicans expressed approval (Saad 2019).

Just prior to the 2020 election, approval of the Court converged, with 56 percent of Democrats, 60 percent of Republicans, and 57 percent of independents approving. This marked the first time since 2000 that Gallup's poll showed "all party groups' ratings fall within the margin of error of the national average" (McCarthy 2020). That convergence continued into 2021, with 51 percent of Democrats and Republicans expressing approval, along with 46 percent of independents. When combined, the overall approval of the Court was at 49 percent (Jones 2021).

With respect to confidence in the Supreme Court, Gallup also often shows divergence along party lines, though the gap tends to be less dramatic than the gap in approval ratings. Still, Gallup reported in 2018 that "[c]onfidence in the court has become more politically polarized over the past two decades" (Brenan 2018). From 1982 to 2000, the party gap in confidence in the Supreme Court only once reached as wide as 10 percentage points. By contrast, between 2001 and 2018, the gap fairly routinely exceeded 10 percentage points, including an 18-percentage-point difference in 2001 (Brenan 2018).

Polling by Marquette Law School also shows divergence in levels of confidence in the Supreme Court by party affiliation. In polling conducted in 2019, Marquette found Republicans having higher confidence in the Court than Democrats, and independents expressing lower confidence than either Republicans or Democrats.

This 2019 survey—which was conducted at a time when conservatives composed a majority of the Supreme Court—also revealed differences in confidence depending on the respondent's ideology. Respondents who identified as "very conservative" reported higher levels of confidence in the Court than those respondents who identified as "very liberal." In particular, 52 percent of "very conservative" respondents indicated high confidence; by contrast, only 31 percent of "very liberal" respondents shared the same degree of confidence in the Court. According to the survey analysis, "[a]mong those who perceive the Court as either very conservative or conservative, there is a sharp relationship between the respondent's degree of conservatism and confidence in the Court" (Franklin 2019, 20).

One area where public attitudes do not appear to differ greatly by party affiliation is on the question of whether the Court makes its legal decisions based on politics. Marquette's 2020 survey asked whether justices' decisions are motivated mainly by law or mainly by politics. The findings showed that "[w]hile views of the Court often correspond to political identifications, the view of judicial motivations is quite uniform across partisanship and ideology. . . . Across the parties, between 35 and 39 percent say politics is a primary motivation and 60 to 65 percent say the law is mainly the motivation" (Marquette 2020). Indeed, according to the survey results, Republican and Democratic respondents had almost identical reactions, with 39 percent of each pointing to politics as the main motivation, and 60 and 61, respectively, pointing to law. It was independents who held slightly divergent views, with 35 percent pointing to politics as the main factor influencing decisions and 65 percent identifying law.

Marquette's 2019 poll questioned respondents about their views on two proposals to alter the structure of the Supreme Court. One question asked how much respondents favor increasing the number of justices on the Supreme Court and found that 43 percent either favor or strongly favor such a proposal, while 57 percent opposed or strongly opposed it. A second question asked about having judges served a fixed term on the Court rather than a life term. An overwhelming majority of 72 percent favored or strongly favored such a change, compared to 28 percent who opposed or strongly opposed it (Franklin 2019, 21).

Support for and opposition to the fixed-term proposal did not vary much by party. Democrats and Democratic-leaning respondents were only slightly more in favor of the proposal than Republicans and independents leaning Republican. By contrast, responses to the proposal to increase the number of justices on the Court varied substantially by party. A total of 69 percent of Republican respondents opposed or strongly opposed such a plan, whereas only 50 percent of Democrats and 47 percent of independents expressed such levels of opposition. Likewise, only 31 percent of Republicans favored or strongly favored the proposal, compared to 50 percent of Democrats and 54 percent of independents (Franklin 2019, 22–23).

With respect to attitudes about state courts, research and polling data are not as extensive. As a result, less data exists for use in examining whether public opinion about state-level courts varies by party affiliation. Polls commissioned by the National Center for State Courts (NCSC) provided some insight concerning attitudes about trust in the state courts. The 2018 NCSC survey reported that "[v]oter confidence in the state court system has reached a new high since tracking began in 2012. Three-quarters (76%) now say they have a great deal or some confidence, while les [sic] than a quarter (22%) say they have not much or no confidence at all in the state court system. This confidence holds across party lines" (NCSC 2018, 2).

In particular, the survey data showed that in 2017, 72 percent of Democrats, 75 percent of Republicans, and 67 percent of independents expressed confidence in the state court system. In 2018, the numbers were even closer, with 74 percent of Democrats, 77 percent of Republicans, and 77 percent of independents indicating confidence (NCSC 2018, 2).

There are many other areas where partisan variation in public attitudes on the judiciary is evident. For example, research and opinion polling often seeks to gauge public attitudes about specific Supreme Court rulings, particular Supreme Court justices, or particular Supreme Court nominees. Another area explores public attitudes about how the Supreme Court should interpret the Constitution and whether the Court should adopt an "originalist" or a "living constitution" approach. This last area is addressed in Q27.

FURTHER READING

Barnes, Robert. 2019. "Polls Show Trust in Supreme Court, But There Is Growing Interest in Fixed Terms and Other Changes." *Washington Post*, October 24, 2019.

Brenan, Megan. 2018. "Confidence in Supreme Court Modest, But Steady." *Gallup*, July 2, 2018.

Franklin, Charles H. 2019. "Public Views of the Supreme Court." Marquette Law School Poll: Complete Report. https://law.marquette.edu/poll/wp-content/uploads/2019/10/MULawPollSupremeCourtReportOct2019.pdf

Jones, Jeffrey M. 2021. "Supreme Court Job Approval Dips Below 50%." *Gallup*, July 28, 2021.

Marquette University. 2020. "New National Marquette Law School Poll Finds That, Even Amid Partisan Differences on Judicial Philosophy, Most Voters Say U.S. Supreme Court Decisions Are Based on Law and Not Politics." Marquette University News Release, September 25, 2020. https://www.marquette.edu/news-center/2020/new-national-marquette-law-poll-finds-that-most-voters-say-supreme-court-decisions-are-based-on-law.php

McCarthy, Justin. 2017. "GOP Approval of the Supreme Court Surges, Democrats' Slides." *Gallup*, September 28, 2017.

McCarthy, Justin. 2020. "Approval of the Supreme Court Is Highest Since 2009." *Gallup*, August 5, 2020.

National Center for State Courts. 2018. "2018 State of the State Courts—Survey Analysis." GBA Strategies, December 3, 2018. https://www.ncsc.org/__data/assets/pdf_file/0020/16157/sosc_2018_survey_analysis.pdf

Nicholson, Stephen P., and Thomas G. Hansford. 2014. "Partisans in Robes: Party Cues and Public Acceptance of Supreme Court Decisions." *American Journal of Political Science*, 58, no. 3: 620–636.

Saad, Lydia. 2019. "Supreme Court Enjoys Majority Approval at Start of New Term." *Gallup*, October 2, 2019.

Smith, Michael, and Frank Newport. 2016. "Most Republicans Continue to Disapprove of the Supreme Court." *Gallup*, September 29, 2016.

Q27. HAS THE JUDICIAL PHILOSOPHY KNOWN AS "ORIGINALISM" BECOME DOMINANT IN AMERICAN JURISPRUDENCE AND ACCEPTED BY THE PUBLIC?

Answer: Originalism has gained substantial currency as a form of constitutional interpretation since the 1980s. More and more jurists—including those on the Supreme Court—are self-described originalists, and originalism has become embedded in public discourse and debate over constitutional meaning. But there is no judicial consensus on originalism. Moreover, the public has been closely divided on originalism for much of the past two decades. That close division in public opinion, however, reflects a wide split related to party and ideological identification. Other factors, such as age, are also related to an individual's support for originalism.

The Facts: Originalism is a theory of constitutional interpretation. Though under its broad heading sit multiple variants (see, e.g., Fleming 2013; Whittington 2004), in its most common current form it holds that judicial interpretation of the Constitution should be bound to what its provisions meant at the time the document or its later amendments were ratified. As defined by political scientist Eric Segall, "an originalist judge or scholar is someone who believes the following three propositions: (1) the meaning of the constitutional text is fixed at the time of ratification; (2) judges should give that meaning a primary role in constitutional interpretation; and (3) pragmatic modern concerns and consequences are not allowed to trump discoverable original meaning (although adhering to precedent might)" (Segall 2018, 8–9). This contrasts with "living constitutionalism," the view that judges should interpret the Constitution in light of modern, evolving, and improved understandings of constitutional guarantees such as civil rights. Originalists typically reject this view, arguing that the Constitution should not be seen as a document with an evolving meaning.

Although originalism is not new, it has gained prominence since the 1980s and has become an increasingly common mode of constitutional interpretation among judges on the federal bench and on the Supreme Court. Justice Antonin Scalia played a pivotal role in elevating originalist jurisprudence, as has the Federalist Society, which supports originalism and judges who espouse an originalist approach. Republican presidents George W. Bush and Donald Trump have shaped the federal judiciary by appointing conservative judges inclined toward originalism (see Q3 and Q8).

Identifying which judges are originalists is itself subject to debate. For example, while Justice Samuel Alito described himself as a "practical originalist" (Siegel 2016, 166), according to the account of one legal scholar offered prior to the confirmation of Justice Amy Coney Barrett to the Supreme Court in October 2020, only three justices—Clarence Thomas, Neil Gorsuch, and Brett Kavanaugh—"are self-avowed originalists. Justice Samuel Alito and Chief Justice John Roberts both take a more pragmatic approach, giving more weight to precedents and consequences. Justices Stephen Breyer, Elena Kagan and Sonia Sotomayor believe the Constitution can and should evolve over time" (Wurman 2020). Debate also persists about whether self-proclaimed originalist justices sometimes stray from that path when it conflicts with the decision they wish to support (see, e.g., Segall 2020). These debates notwithstanding, there is no doubt that the mantle of originalism has expanded, along with the number of self-avowed originalist judges on the bench.

Originalism has also gained prominence in public discourse, having "gone mainstream." Discussion of originalism in the media plays out in multiple contexts. In coverage and analysis of oral arguments, court rulings, nominations, confirmation hearings, and electoral campaigns, debates between the originalist approach and living constitutionalism often provide framing (Greene, Persily, and Ansolabehere 2011, 356–358).

Even jurists who take a living approach to constitutionalism use the discourse of originalism, albeit in a formulation at odds with its conventional definition. For example, during her 2010 Supreme Court confirmation hearing, Elena Kagan spoke of how judges take the Framers and the original meaning of the Constitution into consideration. The Framers, Kagan said, sometimes "laid down very specific rules. Sometimes they laid down broad principles. Either way we apply what they say, what they meant to do. So in that sense, we are all originalists" (Kagan 2010).

Kagan's remarks suggested that "we"—that is, jurists—are all some brand of originalist. However, her brand, like that of several other justices past and present, emphasizes a kind of living originalism: the idea that the Framers meant for broad provisions of the Constitution "to be interpreted over time, to be applied to new situations and new factual contexts" (Kagan 2010). This type of originalism—sometimes referred to as "living originalism"—is a far cry from the prevailing form of originalism that cements the meaning of the Constitution to the moment of ratification.

If originalism is understood as fixing constitutional meaning to ratification, it is quite clear that not all jurists and legal scholars are originalists. But what about the public? With the number of self-described originalists occupying the federal judiciary growing, where does public opinion on originalism land? Does the public favor the common understanding of originalism?

Public opinion polling shows a split in public attitudes toward originalist modes of constitutional interpretation. In a survey of Americans conducted in the summer of 2020 by the PEW Research Center, a minority of respondents (43 percent) said the Court should base its rulings on what the Constitution "meant as originally written" (Hartig 2020). By contrast, a clear majority (55 percent) said rulings should be based on the Court's understanding of what the Constitution "means in current times" (Hartig 2020). Majority sentiment against originalism, according to PEW, was also evident in its 2018 polling on the same question, with only 41 percent favoring originalism and 55 percent favoring interpretation based on current meaning. That polling showed some shifting from earlier surveys (Bialik 2018). In 2016, for example, the public was evenly divided, with 46 percent on each side of the question (Bialik 2018).

While the public has been closely divided on these two approaches to constitutional interpretation, the PEW surveys have found wide partisan differences on originalism. In the 2020 survey, 67 percent of Republican (or Republican-leaning) respondents supported originalism compared to only 23 percent of Democrats (or Democratic-leaning respondents) (Hartig 2020). "Democrats were considerably more likely than Republicans to say the Supreme Court should base its rulings on what the Constitution means in current times (76% vs. 32%, respectively)" (Hartig 2020).

Party affiliation alone does not appear to account for varying public views about originalism. For one thing, the data also shows a divide within parties. According to PEW's 2020 survey, "50% of moderate or liberal Republicans said the high court should base rulings on the Constitution in context of current times, while fewer than half as many conservative Republicans said the same (21%). Among Democrats, liberals (88%) were more likely than conservatives and moderates to say the court should base rulings more on current context" (Hartig 2020).

Divergent views about originalism also appear related to race, ethnicity, age, and education. "White adults were more likely than Black and Hispanic adults to say the Supreme Court should base its rulings on its understanding of what the Constitution means as originally written; about half of White adults said this (48%) compared with smaller shares of Black (33%) and Hispanic (35%) adults" (Hartig 2020). In addition, only about one-third of those under the age of 50 and one-third of those who had earned at least a college degree favored interpreting the Constitution based on what it meant as originally written.

Splits in public opinion between those who advocate originalism and nonoriginalism may also be attributable to factors that go deeper than party affiliation and demographics. According to a study conducted by legal scholars Jamal Greene, Nathaniel Persily, and Stephen Ansolabehere, "[i]t should come as little surprise that originalists share the characteristics traditionally associated with political conservatives. Originalism is part of a bundle of ostensibly methodological commitments that opinion leaders and the media associate with the Republican Party, and so it is hardly surprising that originalists seem to support conservative outcomes" (Greene, Persily, and Ansolabehere 2011, 360). But this is not all. The authors used surveys to examine whether certain types of political and cultural issue positions predicted whether individuals advocate originalism. They did so by examining whether "attitudes on issues such as abortion, same-sex mar-riage, and gun rights show additional predictive power not captured by generic labels, such as conservative, or by demographic predictors, such as religiosity," and how much of a role "values of moral traditionalism, lib-ertarianism, and egalitarianism play in predicting whether someone is an originalist" (Greene, Persily, and Ansolabehere 2011, 360).

Their findings suggest stark differences between originalist and non-originalist survey respondents. "For example, on most of the measures of egalitarianism, originalists differ from nonoriginalists by an average of approximately 30 percentage points in their level of agreement. Whereas 83% of originalists agree with the statement '[w]e have gone too far in pushing equal rights in this country,' only 41% of nonoriginalists agree. In contrast, 67% of nonoriginalists agree that '[i]f people were treated more equally in this country we would have many fewer problems,' whereas only 34% of originalists agree" (Greene, Persily, and Ansolabehere 2011, 375). Thus, not only are originalists more hierarchical, morally traditional, and libertarian than their counterparts, the distance between the views held by originalists and nonoriginalists on these points is wide indeed.

FURTHER READING

Bialik, Kristen. 2018. "Growing Share of Americans Say Supreme Court Should Base Its Rulings on What Constitution Means Today." *Pew Research Center*, May 11, 2018.

Emmert, Steve. 2020. "Are We All Originalists Now?" *Appellate Issues*, February 18, 2020.

Fleming, James. 2013. "Are We All Originalists Now? I Hope Not!" *Texas Law Review*, 91: 1785–1813.

Greene, Jamal, Nathaniel Persily, and Stephen Ansolabehere. 2011. "Pro-filing Originalism." *Columbia Law Review*, 111: 356–418.

Hartig, Hannah. 2020. "Before Ginsburg's Death, A Majority of Ameri-cans Viewed the Supreme Court as 'Middle of the Road.'" *PEW Research Center*, September 25, 2020.

Kagan, Elena. 2010. Transcripts from Senate Judiciary Committee confirma-tion hearing. https://www.govinfo.gov/content/pkg/CHRG-111shrg67622 /pdf/CHRG-111shrg67622.pdf

Root, Damon. 2011. "Are We All Originalists Now? The Debate Over Obamacare Highlights a Growing Division on the Legal Left." *Reason*, February 11, 2011.

Segall, Eric J. 2018. *Originalism as Faith*. New York: Cambridge University Press.

Segall, Eric J. 2020. "The Roberts Court: We are All Living Constitution-
    alists Now." *Dorf on Law*, July 8, 2020.

Siegel, Neil S. 2016. "The Distinctive Role of Justice Samuel Alito: From a
    Politics of Restoration to a Politics of Dissent." *Yale Law Journal Forum*,
    126: 164–177.

Whittington, Keith. 2004. "The New Originalism." *Georgetown Journal of
    Law & Public Policy*, 2: 599–613.

Wurman, Ilan. 2020. "What Is Originalism? Debunking the Myths." *The
    Conversation*, October 24, 2020.

6

❖

Politicization, Partisanship, and Legitimacy

Since the turn of the 21st century, Americans from all walks of life, from lawmakers to legal scholars to members of the public, have voiced growing apprehension over politicization and partisanship in the judiciary. Previous questions covered in this book speak to such apprehension: in the nomination and confirmation of federal judges, in changes to judicial elections at the state level, in efforts to reform the number and term lengths of Supreme Court justices, in public perceptions of the courts, and more. This final chapter addresses how politicization and partisanship bear on the legitimacy of the federal judiciary and especially the Supreme Court.

Q28. WERE PRESIDENT TRUMP'S CRITICISMS OF THE JUDICIARY UNUSUAL?

Answer: Yes. There is, without doubt, an extensive history of presidents and courts colliding. Previous presidents, including Donald Trump, have objected to specific court decisions, accused courts of stepping beyond their appropriate authority, and complained about individual judges. But Trump did much more than that. Unlike his predecessors, Trump engaged in a repeated pattern of public and personalized attacks, using contemptuous rhetoric against individual judges and the federal judiciary in general.

The Facts: Criticisms leveled by presidents against the federal courts have a lineage dating back to the founding era. In the early 1800s, the Supreme Court handed down several decisions that elevated the power of the federal government and generated conflicts with presidents who favored states' rights. *Marbury v. Madison* (1803) established the Court's power to invalidate congressional laws deemed by the Court to be inconsistent with the Constitution. That power of "judicial review" was extended to state laws in *Fletcher v. Peck* (1810), with the Court declaring that federal courts, not state courts, have final authority to determine the constitutionality of state legislation. And *McCulloch v. Maryland* (1819) declared constitutional Congress's decision to charter a national bank.

These rulings distressed President Thomas Jefferson, an anti-federalist and fervent supporter of states' rights who worried about the federal government usurping state power. Jefferson also "detested his distant cousin and archrival" Chief Justice John Marshall, the architect of those decisions (Rosen 2017). A critic of the Court both during and following his term as president, Jefferson complained that "[t]he judiciary of the United States is the subtle corps of sappers and miners constantly working under ground to undermine the foundations of our confederated fabric" (Jefferson 1820). Notably, though, this harsh criticism was issued in a private letter, not broadcast to the public at large. In general, according to legal scholar James F. Simon, "Jefferson spoke privately about what he called Marshall's 'twistifications' of the law, but he didn't do it publicly" (Totenberg 2017).

President Andrew Jackson, who also clashed with Chief Justice Marshall, took particular umbrage to the Court's decision in *Worcester v. Georgia* (1832), in which the Court ruled against Georgia's seizure of Cherokee Nation lands. Jackson bitterly protested the ruling in private correspondence, reportedly saying, "John Marshall has made his decision, now let him enforce it" (Rosen 2017).

At other times, however, Jackson went public with his complaints, taking special exception to *McCulloch v. Maryland* (1819). Jackson's veto of an 1832 effort to renew the bank's charter marked the first presidential veto in American history ever handed down on constitutional grounds. In doing so, Jackson issued a broadside against the Court in his speech vetoing the legislation to recharter the bank. Asserting that the Court does not own sole authority to interpret the Constitution, Jackson argued that that duty is also shared with Congress and the president. Still, "Jackson's fight with Marshall over the bank . . . was fought entirely on constitutional, rather than personal, terms. Jackson didn't question Marshall's motives or call him a politician in robes" (Rosen 2017).

Expressions of presidential dissatisfaction with the judiciary became increasingly public in the 20th century. Among the most vocal presidential critics of the federal courts, Franklin Delano Roosevelt was outspoken about his displeasure with rulings that overturned several early pieces of his New Deal legislation to lift America out of the Great Depression. According to political scientists Paul M. Collins and Matthew Eshbaugh-Soha, Roosevelt "changed everything" by choosing to "openly criticize the court" (Collins and Eshbaugh-Soha 2020). Indeed, in a 1937 "fireside chat," Roosevelt aggressively proclaimed that the nation had "reached the point . . . where we must take action to save the Constitution from the Court and the Court from itself" (Roosevelt 1937). The action Roosevelt undertook was his well-known, controversial, and ultimately failed court-packing plan that sought to increase the number of justices on the Court (see Q14 and Q21).

Other presidents in the modern era have followed suit, "going public" in communicating disagreement with court rulings (Collins and Eshbaugh-Soha 2019). However, by and large, these presidential quarrels with the judiciary focused on the substance of court decisions rather than on the judges themselves, and presidents "largely refrained from personal attacks on judges" (Totenberg 2017).

Moreover, presidential criticisms have often been presented with expressions of respect for the courts or an acknowledgment of the judiciary's legitimate role in the governing system. According to Collins and Eshbaugh-Soha, presidents from Franklin Roosevelt to Barack Obama "followed a similar pattern in their public criticisms of the court and its decisions. Typically, a presidential condemnation acknowledged the court's role in the separation of powers system, explained the disagreement and proposed a remedy" (Collins and Eshbaugh-Soha 2020).

As one illustration, Collins and Eshbaugh-Soha cite President George H. W. Bush's response to the Court's 1989 decision in *Texas v. Johnson* that the First Amendment protects the right to burn the American flag: "I have the greatest respect for the Supreme Court and, indeed, for the justices who interpreted the Constitution, as they saw fit," said Bush. "But I believe the importance of this issue compels me to call for a constitutional amendment. Support for the First Amendment need not extend to desecration of the American flag" (Collins and Eshbaugh-Soha 2020).

President Obama criticized the Supreme Court's ruling in *Citizens United v. Federal Election Commission* (2010) during his 2010 State of the Union address, an unusual venue for public criticism of a Court decision. A *New York Times* headline described Obama's comments as a "Rare Rebuke, in Front of a Nation" (Liptak 2010). Still, though plainly and strongly critical of the Court ruling and its implications, Obama aimed his ire at the decision itself. "With all due deference to separation of powers," Obama said, "last week the Supreme Court reversed a century of law that I believe will open the floodgates for special interests—including foreign corporations—to spend without limit in our elections" (Silverleib 2010).

A more recent instance of the pattern of criticism described by Collins and Eshbaugh-Soha is evident in President Joe Biden's reaction to a Court ruling that stopped a federal COVID-19 vaccine and testing mandate for large employers from taking effect (*National Federation of Independent Businesses v. Department of Labor* 2022). In a statement issued by the White House, Biden said,

> I am disappointed that the Supreme Court has chosen to block common-sense life-saving requirements for employees at large businesses that were grounded squarely in both science and the law. This emergency standard allowed employers to require vaccinations or to permit workers to refuse to be vaccinated, so long as they were tested once a week and wore a mask at work: a very modest burden. . . . The Court has ruled that my administration cannot use the authority granted to it by Congress to require this measure, but that does not stop me from using my voice as President to advocate for employers to do the right thing to protect Americans' health and economy. (White House Statement 2022)

During and before his presidency, Donald Trump joined the company of his predecessors in criticizing courts and court rulings—but his criticisms of the judicial branch were distinct and unprecedented in multiple ways. Among other things, they often targeted the race, character, and motivations of individual judges or courts, rather than their decisions; and instead of focusing on policy disagreements, they "personalized" disputes, with Trump often complaining "that courts are treating him unfairly" (Collins and Eshbaugh-Soha 2020).

Numerous examples show Trump aiming his criticisms at individual judges and courts. Consider this sampling of personal attacks from Trump, compiled by political scientists Michael J. Nelson and James L. Gibson:

> Trump's list of judicial targets has been lengthy, including United States District Judge Gonzalo P. Curiel (a "hater" and "a very hostile judge" whose actions are "a total disgrace"), District Court Judge James Robart (a "so-called judge" whose "ridiculous" ruling "put our country in such peril. If something happens blame him and court

system"), the Ninth Circuit (a court that "has a terrible record of being overturned" and issuing "ridiculous rulings"), Ruth Bader Ginsburg (a "disgrace to the court"), and the judiciary in general ("The courts are making the job very difficult!" because they are "so political," showing "unprecedented judicial overreach" by blocking his immigration policy). (Nelson and Gibson 2018, 32–33)

Trump also focused his targeting of individual judges by focusing on their gender or ethnic/racial background rather than the substance of their rulings. Trump's attacks on Gonzalo Curiel, the U.S. District Court judge who presided over several cases claiming fraud by Trump University, are illustrative. Trump University, a for-profit company established in 2005 by the Trump Organization, offered real estate seminars and classes, but shut down in 2011 following student complaints that generated multiple state-level investigations and lawsuits claiming that the company used illegal business practices. The lawsuits came to a close in 2017 when Judge Curiel approved a $25 million settlement, including payments to more than 6,000 former students. But while the litigation was ongoing, Trump attacked Curiel. During his presidential campaign in 2016, Trump called on Curiel to recuse himself, claiming that the American-born judge's Mexican roots made him biased. On June 2, 2016, for example, "Trump told the *Wall Street Journal* that Curiel had 'an absolute conflict' in presiding over the litigation given that he is 'of Mexican heritage' and a member of a Latino lawyers' association. . . . Trump told the journal the judge's background was relevant because of his campaign stance against illegal immigration and his pledge to seal the southern U.S. border" (Kertscher 2016).

Trump also went on the offensive against U.S. District Judge Amy Berman Jackson. Jackson presided over the trial of Roger Stone, an ardent Trump ally convicted of lying to Congress, witness tampering, and obstructing the congressional investigation into alleged Russian meddling in the 2016 election. After his conviction by a jury—but before Jackson issued Stone's sentence—Trump took to Twitter to attack her character and abilities. According to retired federal judge Nancy Gertner, Trump's attacks on Jackson reflected the president's penchant for "trying to delegitimize anyone appointed by someone other than him and say that the only people who can be trusted are Trump judges" (Marimow 2020).

Targets of previous presidents in the judicial system—to the limited extent that there were individual targets—have tended to be Supreme Court justices. Attacking lower court judges, as Trump did with Judges Curiel and Jackson, was itself unusual. But Trump also issued frequent and combative complaints about individual Supreme Court justices. Following the Court's 5–4 support of a Trump administration emergency relief application in an immigration case that provoked a stinging dissenting opinion from Justice Sonia Sotomayor, Trump lashed out at both Sotomayor and Justice Ruth Bader Ginsburg, who also voted in dissent. "Both should recuse themselves on all Trump, or Trump related matters!" Trump tweeted (Flynn and Shammas 2020).

Trump's tone and rhetoric against the U.S. judicial system was frequently filled with ridicule and vilification. For example, reacting a day after a 2017 terror attack in Manhattan that killed eight and injured a dozen more, Trump "denounced the American criminal justice system as 'a laughingstock' and 'a joke' that is too weak to deter terrorism and too slow to mete out punishment" (Qiu 2017). In a similarly harsh tone, he went after the Ninth Circuit Court of Appeals on multiple occasions, calling it "a complete & total disaster" (Brennan Center 2020) and a "disgrace" (Liptak 2018).

There are numerous additional examples of Trump's rhetorical derision. Nina Totenberg, legal analyst for National Public Radio, detailed Trump's "fighting words" in an analysis of his responses to federal judges who issued temporary blocks on his "travel ban," a controversial policy that sought to block entry into the United States of people from seven mostly Muslim countries. "In the space of one week, President Trump. . . . belittled all four judges who have ruled against him so far in the travel ban case," calling one "a 'so-called judge' whose decision was 'ridiculous'"(Totenberg 2017).

According to Totenberg, Trump's "rhetoric left many lawyers and historians on both the right and left aghast, or at least scratching their heads" (Totenberg 2017). Among the people unhappy with Trump's behavior was Jeffrey Rosen, President and CEO of the National Constitution Center. In Rosen's estimation, Trump's responses in the travel ban cases amounted to an "unprecedented personal assault on the motives of judges evaluating the constitutionality of his executive orders" (Rosen 2017).

To be clear, previous presidents have expressed disgruntlement and displeasure with individual judges using harsh language. President Dwight D. Eisenhower, for instance, is known to have complained about individual justices, most especially Chief Justice Earl Warren. And those complaints were in personal terms: "Eisenhower famously said that his biggest mistake had been selecting 'that dumb son of a bitch Earl Warren.' Or so one of his early biographers claims; the remark has come into question. Warren himself wrote that the president was known to have described his appointment as 'the biggest damn fool thing I ever did.' Another version has it that when asked whether he had ever made any mistakes, Eisenhower replied, 'Yes: two. And they are both sitting on the Supreme Court'" (O'Donnell

2018). Though press reports had, at one point, "picked up his bad-mouthing," Eisenhower "sheepishly" apologized to Warren (O'Donnell 2018). Notably, though, Eisenhower did not make a habit of publicly deriding the courts or particular judges. Nor has any other president.

Trump was not unique, however, in *commenting* on cases making their way through the judiciary or pending before the Supreme Court. In fact, Obama frequently commented about pending cases. When the Court was considering the constitutionality of Obama's signature Affordable Care Act (ACA), he publicly remarked that overturning the law would be "unprecedented" and would return the Court to the *Lochner* era of judicial activism on economic issues. In the lead-up to another Court ruling concerning the ACA, Obama commented that he did not have plans for what the administration would do if the Court ruled against him, saying, "I'm not going to anticipate bad law." He further observed that the case, *King v. Burwell* (2015), "shouldn't even have been taken up." According to law professor Josh Blackman, that comment publicly faulted "the Court—or at least four justices—for voting to grant certiorari" (Blackman 2017).

Nevertheless, Trump's brand of criticism stands out as unique. He routinely disregarded longstanding political norms in which it was widely understood that "while presidents are free to criticize court decisions, they should avoid personal attacks on judges" (Totenberg 2017).

FURTHER READING

Blackman, Josh. 2017. "When Presidents Criticize the Courts, Before and After November 8." Josh Blackman Blog, February 4, 2017. https://joshblackman.com/blog/2017/02/04/when-presidents-criticize-the-courts-before-and-after-november-8

Brennan Center. 2020. "In His Own Words: The President's Attacks on the Courts." *Brennan Center for Justice*, February 14, 2020. https://www.brennancenter.org/our-work/research-reports/his-own-words-presidents-attacks-courts

Citizens United v. Federal Election Commission, 558 U.S. 310 (2010).

Collins, Paul M., and Matthew Eshbaugh-Soha. 2019. *The President and the Supreme Court: Going Public on Judicial Decisions from Washington to Trump*. New York: Cambridge University Press.

Collins, Paul M., and Matthew Eshbaugh-Soha. 2020. "Trump Attacked the Supreme Court Again. Here Are 4 Things to Know." *Washington Post*, February 17, 2020.

Fletcher v. Peck, 10 U.S. 87 (1810).

Flynn, Meagan, and Brittany Shammas. 2020. "Trump Slams Sotomayor and Ginsburg, Says They Should Recuse Themselves from 'Trump-related' Cases." *Washington Post*, February 25, 2020.

Jackson, Andrew. 1832. "Presidential Speeches, July 10, 1832: Bank Veto." *Miller Center.* https://millercenter.org/the-presidency/presidential-speeches/july-10-1832-bank-veto

Jefferson, Thomas. 1820. "From Thomas Jefferson to Thomas Ritchie, 25 December 1820." *National Archives, Founders Online.* https://founders.archives.gov/documents/Jefferson/03-16-02-0394

Kertscher, Tom. 2016. "Donald Trump's Racial Comments about Hispanic Judge in Trump University Case." *Politifact*, June 8, 2016. https://www.politifact.com/article/2016/jun/08/donald-trumps-racial-comments-about-judge-trump-un

King v. Burwell, 576 U.S. 473 (2015).

Liptak, Adam. 2010. "Supreme Court Gets a Rare Rebuke, in Front of a Nation." *New York Times*, January 28, 2010.

Liptak, Adam. 2018. "Trump Takes Aim at Appeals Court, Calling It a 'Disgrace.'" *New York Times*, November 20, 2018.

Marbury v. Madison, 5 U.S. 137 (1803).

Marimow, Ann E. 2020. "Trump Takes on Judge Amy Berman Jackson Ahead of Roger Stone's Sentencing." *Washington Post*, February 12, 2020.

McCulloch v. Maryland, 17 U.S. 316 (1819).

National Federation of Independent Business v. Sebelius, 567 U.S. 519 (2012).

National Federation of Independent Business v. Department of Labor, No. 21A244, 595 U.S. ___ (2022).

Nelson, Michael J., and James L. Gibson. 2018. "Has Trump Trumped the Courts?" *New York University Law Review Online*, 93: 32–40.

O'Donnell, Michael. 2018. "Commander v. Chief: The Lessons of Eisenhower's Civil-Rights Struggle with His Chief Justice Earl Warren." *The Atlantic*, April, 2018.

Qiu, Linda. 2017. "Trump Calls Terrorism Trial Process 'a Joke,' Despite Hundreds of Convictions." *New York Times*, November 2, 2017.

Roosevelt, Franklin Delano. 1937. "Court-Packing." March 9, 1937: Fireside Chat 9, "On 'Court-Packing.'" https://millercenter.org/the-presidency/presidential-speeches/march-9-1937-fireside-chat-9-court-packing

Rosen, Jeffrey. 2017. "Not Even Andrew Jackson Went as Far as Trump in Attacking the Courts." *The Atlantic*, February 9, 2017.

Silverleib, Alan. 2010. "Gloves Come Off After Obama Rips Supreme Court Ruling." *CNN*, January 28, 2010.

Texas v. Johnson, 491 U.S. 397 (1989).

Totenberg, Nina. 2017. "Trump's Criticism of Judges Out of Line with Past Presidents." *National Public Radio*, February 11, 2017.

White House Statement. 2022. "Statement by President Joe Biden on the U.S. Supreme Court's Decision on Vaccine Requirements." *White House Statements and Releases*, January 13, 2022. https://www.whitehouse.gov /briefing-room/statements-releases/2022/01/13/statement-by-president -joe-biden-on-the-u-s-supreme-courts-decision-on-vaccine-requirements

Worcester v. Georgia, 31 U.S. 515 (1832).

Q29. HAS THE SUPREME COURT BECOME MORE PARTISAN?

Answer: The consensus among legal scholars is a clear yes, despite Supreme Court justices frequently insisting otherwise.

The Facts: In September 2021, U.S. Supreme Court Justice Stephen Breyer asserted that "judges are not junior league politicians" (Washington Post Live 2021). In the same week and a month shy of her first anniversary on the Court, Justice Amy Coney Barrett gave a speech arguing that jurisprudence—not politics—guides judicial decision making at the Supreme Court. Presenting her remarks at the 30th anniversary celebration of the University of Louisville's McConnell Center—named for and housing the archives of Republican Senator Mitch McConnell, who orchestrated the partisan refusal to consider Merrick Garland's nomination to the Supreme Court—Barrett said, "[m]y goal today is to convince you that this court is not comprised of a bunch of partisan hacks" (Barnes 2021). Breyer's and Barrett's protestations came in the same week and shortly after a divided Court let stand a Texas law banning almost all abortions after around six weeks of pregnancy (see Q23). That highly controversial decision about a highly controversial law generated substantial outcry, including complaints that the decision was emblematic of the conservative-majority Court's increasingly partisan character (see, e.g., Reich 2021; Sarat and Aftergut 2021).

Criticism of the Court is, of course, perennial. But growing expressions of concern focus not merely on claims that ideological leanings or political preferences influence judicial decisions. Instead, the rising critical chorus includes claims of an "alarming" and "extreme" trend in which the Court has "entered a new era of partisan division" (Epstein and Posner 2018).

Partisan influence on the Court is not a new phenomenon. As noted in Q25, historian Rachel Shelden explains that "[n]ineteenth-century

Americans were deeply partisan, and they understood that the Supreme Court would be, too" (Shelden 2020). Similarly, Richard Hasen, professor of law and political science, says that "[c]onsideration of political party in federal judicial selection is not new. Even in the nineteenth century, presidents used the appointment of judges to advance their partisan agendas" (Hasen 2019, 263). Political scientist Howard Gillman provides a detailed case study demonstrating how partisan considerations shaped the expansion of federal judicial power in the late 1800s. In particular, he argues that the expansion "is best understood as the sort of familiar partisan or programmatic entrenchment that we frequently associate with legislative delegations to executive or quasi-executive agencies. In this case, however, the institutional beneficiaries of this entrenchment were courts rather than agencies or commissions" (Gillman 2002, 512).

While partisan influence on the Court is not without precedent, the present context is different. First, as Shelden argues, in the early 19th century the powers of the federal judiciary were much more limited. A partisan Supreme Court that wields limited power does not pose the same threat as a partisan Court that wields extensive power. Thus, though the present-day discussion about partisanship on the Court would be recognizable to our 19th-century counterparts, "they would have been shocked to discover how much power we have given the judiciary over our democracy" (Shelden 2020).

Second, expectations about partisanship on the Court changed in the 20th century. Unlike early 19th-century appointees to the Court, who were often drawn from political and partisan positions, nominees since the mid-20th century have typically been selected from judicial appointments on the lower federal courts (Shelden 2020). Moreover, the narrative of an independent and apolitical judiciary has become more prevalent, as has the linkage between the Court's legitimacy and partisan insulation. "Over the past 75 years, the court's insistence that it operates 'outside politics' has increased," Shelden explains, and while this "new apolitical posture did not create an end to justices' political activity, . . . it did change the relationship between politics, public trust and judicial authority" (Shelden 2020).

The third and most important difference in the present context is the substantial evidence showing that the Court today is "divided ideologically along partisan lines for the first time in history" (Caplan 2018). Court watchers have long identified the presence of ideological blocs on the Court, as well as the link between ideology and politics. Legal analysts have also long emphasized the key influencing factor of judicial selection, a frequently politicized and partisan process. As such, the relevance of party identity to judicial appointments and decision making is an acknowledged component of the Court's history (Devins and Baum 2017, 313). However, the Court becomes *partisan*—not merely ideological, political, or shaped by party—when justices reliably vote in alignment with the political party of their appointing president. "Before 2010, the Court never had clear ideological blocs that coincided with party lines" (Devins and Baum 2017, 301). Law and history professor John Fabian Witt puts it this way: "For 230 years, the Supreme Court of the United States has been a political institution, but only rarely a partisan one. . . . Today, by contrast, coalitions on the court are arranged almost exclusively along party lines" (Witt 2020).

The consensus among legal scholars around this point is robust and well documented. Consider a study by legal scholars Neal Devins and Lawrence Baum comparing the Court from 2010 to 2015 with previous eras. From 1801 to 1937, Devins and Baum noted little evidence of partisan divide on the Court itself. This was, in part, because dissent among the justices was uncommon. But even when the Court divided, it did not usually do so along party lines. "Of the seventy-five most important decisions between 1790 and 1937 in which there were at least two dissenting votes, in only one were all of the Justices on one side appointed by presidents of one party and all of the Justices on the other side appointed by presidents of the other party." From 1938 to 2010, among 322 important cases with at least two dissents, "only one case divided all the Court's Republican-appointed Justices from all of their Democratic-appointed colleagues." By contrast, in high-visibility cases in the 2010 through 2015 terms, at least eight cases divided along partisan lines (Devins and Baum 2017, 311, 316–317).

Consider, as well, evidence presented by legal scholars Lee Epstein and Eric Posner, who argued in 2018 that the United States was in the grip of an unprecedented era of partisan division on the Court. According to their research, prior historical eras showed some strong ideological divisions but not clear partisan gaps. The ideologically liberal Warren Court was not partisan, according to Epstein and Posner, as it was led by two justices, including a chief justice, appointed by a Republican president. The ideologically conservative *Lochner*-era Court was not partisan either, despite its famous clashes with Democratic President Franklin D. Roosevelt. As Epstein and Posner explained, two justices on the *Lochner*-era Court who voted in favor of New Deal legislation were Republican appointees, and among those who voted against it were a Democrat and a Democratic appointee. By contrast, from 2008 to 2018, "justices have hardly ever voted against the ideology of the president who appointed them. Only Justice Kennedy, named to the court by Ronald Reagan, did so with any regularity" (Epstein and Posner 2018).

Relatedly, as *New York Times* legal analyst Adam Liptak observed in 2014, "just as there is no Democratic senator who is more conservative than the most liberal Republican, there is no Democratic appointee on the Supreme Court who is more conservative than any Republican appointee" (Liptak 2014). This is supported by Martin-Quinn scores—developed by political scientists Andrew D. Martin and Kevin M. Quinn—which use a model based on justices' voting records to estimate where justices fall on the ideological spectrum (Martin and Quinn 2022). This now-common measure of judicial ideology "confirm[s] the rise of a court divided on partisan lines" (Liptak 2014).

The research by Devins and Baum and the analysis offered by Epstein and Posner both emphasize the growing ideological homogeneity within the two blocs of recent justices and the growing divide between those blocs. As Epstein and Posner explained, in the 1950s and 1960s, "the ideological biases of Republican appointees and Democratic appointees were relatively modest. The gap between them has steadily grown, but even as late as the early 1990s, it was possible for justices to vote in ideologically unpredictable ways" (Epstein and Posner 2018). Similarly, discussing the Court during the 2010 to 2015 terms, Devins and Baum explain that "the groups of Justices appointed by Republican presidents and by Democratic presidents have each become more ideologically homogeneous. Moreover, each of the distinct groups of Justices lacks centrists, with the partial exception of Justice Kennedy. Instead, there is ideological conformity within each group, even as the groups have diverged over time" (Devins and Baum 2017, 317).

Many legal experts express deep concern that this recent and growing partisan split on the Supreme Court is likely to be enduring. The conservative but swing Justice Anthony Kennedy retired in 2018. Justice Ruth Bader Ginsburg—a Bill Clinton appointee and liberal stalwart—died in 2021. Donald Trump filled both of those vacated seats with far more conservative justices. With Brett Kavanaugh (who replaced Kennedy) and Amy Coney Barrett (who replaced Ginsburg) on the Supreme Court bench, the alignment of party and ideology on the Court only became further entrenched. Meanwhile, response to Joe Biden's nomination of Ketanji Brown Jackson to the Court in April 2022—replacing the retiring Stephen Breyer—split along almost entirely partisan lines. Only three Republican senators joined all 50 Democrats in supporting the nominee, who was generally expected to fill Breyer's place in the Court's small liberal bloc. "Gone are justices appointed by Democratic presidents who sometimes voted conservatively (Kennedy-appointed Justice Byron White voted against abortion rights) and justices appointed by Republican presidents who sometimes voted liberally (Ford-appointed Justice John Paul Stevens voted in favor of abortion rights)" (Hasen 2019, 267).

Notwithstanding protestations of justices about their allegiance to law, their apolitical disposition, and their avowed dedication to impartially "calling balls and strikes" when considering legal issues (Roberts 2005), it is hard to refute the clear evidence that the Court as currently composed is marked by ideological blocs that closely reflect the positions and perspectives of the nation's two major political parties. "We are now at least one decade into a nearly unprecedented experiment in partisan judging at the highest court in the land" (Witt 2020). What this bodes, if anything, for the legitimacy of the Court is addressed in Q30.

FURTHER READING

Barnes, Robert. 2021. "Justices Say Supreme Court Split by Philosophical—Not Partisan—Differences, But Timing Works Against Them." *Washington Post*, September 13, 2021.

Caplan, Lincoln. 2018. "The Political Solicitor General: The 'Tenth Justice' and the Polarization of the Supreme Court." *Harvard Magazine*, September-October 2018.

Devins, Neal, and Laurence Baum. 2017. "Split Definitive: How Party Polarization Turned the Supreme Court into a Partisan Court." *Supreme Court Review*, 2016, no. 1: 301–365.

Epstein, Lee, and Eric Posner. 2018. "If the Supreme Court Is Nakedly Political, Can It Be Just?" *New York Times*, July 9, 2018.

Gillman, Howard. 2002. "How Political Parties Can Use the Courts to Advance Their Agendas: Federal Courts in the United States, 1875–1891." *American Political Science Review*, 96, no. 3: 511–524.

Hasen, Richard L. 2019. "Polarization and the Judiciary." *Annual Review of Political Science*, 22, no. 1: 261–276.

Hasen, Richard L. 2020. "The Supreme Court's Pro-Partisanship Turn." *Georgetown Law Journal*, 109, no. 20: 50–80.

Liptak, Adam. 2014. "The Polarized Court." *New York Times*, May 10, 2014.

Martin, Andrew D., and Kevin M. Quinn. 2022. Martin-Quinn Scores. http://mqscores.lsa.umich.edu

Reich, Robert. 2021. "The US Supreme Court Is Now Cruel, Partisan—and Squandering Its Moral Authority." *The Guardian*, September 2, 2021.

Roberts, John. 2005. "Transcript: Opening Statement before Senate Panel." *New York Times*, September 12, 2005.

Sarat, Austin, and Dennis Aftergut. 2021. "Supreme Court Trashed Its Own Authority in a Rush to Gut Roe v Wade." *The Hill*, September 6, 2021.

Shelden, Rachel. 2020. "The Supreme Court Used to Be Openly Political. It Traded Partisanship for Power." *Washington Post*, September 25, 2020.

Washington Post Live. 2021. "'The Authority of the Court and the Perils of Politics' with Justice Stephen G. Breyer." *Washington Post*, September 13, 2021.

Witt, John Fabian. 2020. "How the Republican Party Took Over the Supreme Court." *The Atlantic*, April 7, 2020.

Q30. IS THE SUPREME COURT FACING A LEGITIMACY CRISIS?

Answer: Signs point to yes. Not all agree that a legitimacy crisis is underway or in the offing, and the Court has weathered past waves of declining legitimacy. Still, the current climate suggests that the "reservoir of goodwill" that the American people have historically extended to the Court is running low.

The Facts: As defined by political scientist David Easton, legitimacy is "a reservoir of favorable attitudes or good will that helps members to accept or tolerate outputs to which they are opposed or the effect of which they see as damaging to their wants" (Easton 1965, 273). Defined in this way, legitimacy—or "diffuse support" for an institution—is distinct from and does not always require "specific support" for particular decisions issued by the institution (Nelson and Gibson 2018, 37). What legitimacy affords is acceptance of and willingness to abide by institutional decisions—even when the particular decisions are unpopular or seen as unfavorable. Simply put, "[w]hen institutions are considered legitimate, citizens more easily accept decisions they dislike" (Nelson 2021).

In considering the authority of the Supreme Court, some offer an alternative definition of legitimacy. This alternative rests on evaluating whether the Court successfully functions as an apolitical institution rather than serving as a political or partisan one. "In particular, people who believe that the Court is functionally a 'political' or even partisan body might say that the Court is (or has become) illegitimate. That claim might be made irrespective of whether the Court has lost popular support or its ability to command obedience to its decisions" (Presidential Commission on the Supreme Court of the United States 2021, 22).

Either way, judicial legitimacy is thought to be a centerpiece of the rule of law and the authority of the Supreme Court, which sits at the apex of the U.S. judicial system. As Justice Elena Kagan explains, "[t]he court's strength as an institution of American governance depends on people believing it has a certain kind of legitimacy—on people believing it's not simply just an extension of politics, that its decision-making has a kind of integrity to it. If people don't believe that, they have no reason to accept what the court does" (Barnes and Leonnig 2018).

Kagan's comments echo those of many others who have observed how critical legitimacy is to the Court and to achieving compliance with its rulings. And there is little question that institutional legitimacy matters to the Supreme Court. There is also relatively broad agreement that, at least in the modern era, the Court's legitimacy has, by and large, been resilient even in times of partisanship and polarization. According to political scientists Michael Nelson and James L. Gibson, two leading scholars who study legitimacy in the judicial system, the bulk of research has suggested that the Court's legitimacy

> is high, stable, and relatively unencumbered by the incredible partisanship that grips American politics today. Indeed, because the public holds courts in such high esteem, research shows, even mere exposure to symbols of judicial authority can mitigate disappointment with institutional performance. While some scholars argue that disagreement with a court's decision affects judgments of its legitimacy, the most recent evidence suggests that ideological disagreement with a court's rulings plays only a minor role in one's support for a court and affects evaluations of institutional performance only among a minority of Americans. Moreover, repeated interviews with the same random sample of Americans over the second half of the Obama administration revealed no meaningful aggregate-level or individual-level change in support for the U.S. Supreme Court. (Nelson and Gibson 2018, 34–35).

Despite this assessment of the Court's resilience in the face of partisanship and polarization, however, Nelson and Gibson caution that "the Court's support is not unflappable. Rather, a growing body of research suggests that perceptions that the Court's decisions are politicized—that is, that the Justices are no more than politicians in robes—are associated with sharply lower levels of support for courts" (Nelson and Gibson 2018, 35). It is also noteworthy that while "earlier research on the legitimacy of the Supreme Court has generally found that the institution enjoys a fairly substantial 'reservoir of goodwill' among the American people," much of that research was conducted during a period predating the more recent era of heightened partisanship and polarization (Gibson and Caldeira 2009, 38–42).

Within this more recent era, expressions of concern about public perceptions of the Supreme Court's legitimacy have increased dramatically from researchers, lawyers, journalists, politicians, and political pundits. Even some members of the Supreme Court have acknowledged the concern—and the very fact that some justices have felt the need to go out and stump for the Court is seen as a sign of an institution on the defensive (Liptak 2021).

Does all of this mean that a legitimacy crisis confronts the Court? One key indicator comes from polling. As discussed in Q24, public approval of and confidence in the Court have both declined in recent years. In September 2021, in fact, public approval for the Supreme Court hit a record low in Gallup polling: "Americans' opinions of the U.S. Supreme Court have worsened, with 40%, down from 49% in July, saying they approve of the job the high court is doing. This represents, by two percentage points, a new low in Gallup's trend, which dates back to 2000" (Jones 2021). Similarly, a September 2021 Quinnipiac University poll reported a 37 percent approval rating, down from 52 percent the previous year and the lowest rating of public approval for the Court since it first began polling on this question in 2004 (Malloy and Schwartz 2021a).

Polling speaks as well to public confidence in the Court and public perceptions about the institution's political character. The September 2021 Gallup poll "reveals a steep decline over the past year in the percentage of Americans who express 'a great deal' or 'fair amount' of trust in the judicial branch of the federal government, from 67% in 2020 to 54% today. The current reading is only the second sub-60% trust score for the judicial branch in Gallup's trend, along with a 53% reading from 2015" (Jones 2021). Results of a November 2021 Quinnipiac poll, meanwhile, found 61 percent of respondents saying that the Supreme Court is mainly motivated by politics, while only 32 percent view the Court as mainly motivated by law. Demonstrating bipartisan convergence, the Quinnipiac poll found that a majority of Democrats (67 percent), Republicans (56 percent), and independents (62 percent) all share the view that the Court is motivated primarily by politics (Malloy and Schwartz 2021b).

The link between partisanship and the Court offers a second indicator of a legitimacy crisis. If such a crisis turns on whether the Court functions as a political or partisan institution, then evidence of a link to partisanship would be telling. On this count, as detailed in Q29, multiple researchers are sounding the alarm. According to legal scholar Jonathan S. Gould, "the Supreme Court has witnessed steadily growing polarization. For the first time in U.S. history, every Justice nominated by a Republican president is ideologically to the right of every Justice nominated by a

Democratic president" (Gould 2021, 137). Legal scholars conclude, in sum, that the evidence shows "a new era of partisan division" (Epstein and Posner 2018), with coalitions on the court "arranged almost exclusively along party lines" (Witt 2020), and the Court today "divided ideologically along partisan lines for the first time in history" (Caplan 2018).

It does not help the Court's reputation that partisan dynamics in the appointment and confirmation process to fill open Court seats have become increasingly transparent and divisive. As explored in Q5, the February 2016 refusal by a Republican-controlled Senate to even consider the nomination by a sitting Democratic president to fill a vacancy on the Supreme Court put partisanship into sharp relief. This aggressively partisan move by Republicans to refuse to act on a nomination made more than eight months ahead of the next election paid off for the GOP, at least in the short term, when President Trump was able to fill the vacancy with Neil Gorsuch, a conservative jurist. That move was followed in 2020 by the Republican-controlled Senate's decision to push forward the confirmation of Amy Coney Barrett, nominated by a Republican president just over one month ahead of that year's presidential election. In Barrett's case, Republican Senate Majority Leader Mitch McConnell ignored his stated justification for refusing to act on Garland's nomination—that "[t]he American people should have a voice in the selection of their next Supreme Court Justice" (Condon 2016).

Nor does it bode well for perceptions of the Court's legitimacy that while some justices insist the institution is governed only by law, other justices publicly admonish the Court for handing down decisions that are transparently political. In 2021, for example, liberal Justice Elena Kagan wrote a scathing dissent in response to the decision by the Court's conservative majority to let a contentious Texas abortion ban take effect: "the majority's decision is emblematic of too much of this court's shadow-docket decisionmaking—which every day becomes more unreasoned, inconsistent, and impossible to defend" (*Whole Woman's Health v. Jackson* 2021, 2500 Kagan dissenting).

Kagan was more explicit in another abortion case, *Dobbs v. Jackson Woman's Health* (2021). The case bears on the Court's legitimacy because it is widely expected to bring about either the reversal or substantial curtailment of the constitutional right to abortion established in *Roe v. Wade* (1973). That right, according to almost 50 years of legal precedent, prohibits states from banning abortion prior to fetal viability. Mississippi nevertheless banned abortion after 15 weeks of pregnancy, well before viability. Longstanding precedent notwithstanding, the Supreme Court agreed to hear the case and reconsider whether all pre-viability bans on elective abortions are unconstitutional. In the face of this straightforward challenge to existing precedent, Kagan explained that one of the most important aspects of upholding prior rulings is to "prevent people from thinking that this court is a political institution that will go back and forth depending on what part of the public yells loudest and preventing people from thinking that the court will go back and forth depending on changes to court's membership" (Wagner et al., 2021). Justice Sonia Sotomayor, meanwhile, noted that the sponsors of the Mississippi law, by their own admission, introduced the legislation because new justices had arrived on the Supreme Court. Sotomayor followed that observation with this ominous and striking warning: "Will this institution survive the stench that this creates in the public perception that the Constitution and its reading are just political acts? I don't see how it is possible" (Gregorian 2021).

The threat seen by liberal justices in *Dobbs* is "that dismissing nearly 50 years of precedent would reek of partisan politics" (Farias 2021). But the threat is not limited to abortion. The Court's 2021 term is a "blockbuster" one (Williams 2021), including explosive cases about abortion, religious freedom, gun rights, affirmative action, and Covid-19 regulations. Not only is the docket brimming with controversial issues, but also—if legal scholars are correct—we are likely to see greater polarization on the Court, a more substantial turn to the right, and more and more modifications to and reversals of legal precedents that have stood for decades.

Part of the reason for an increasingly polarized Court —and relevant to the institution's legitimacy—is the loss of a "swing voter" at the center of the bench (Gould 2021). The presence of a swing voter can stem the perception of partisan alignment on the Court and stem the tide of sweeping decisions for one side of the partisan spectrum. As Justice Kagan observed, "[i]n the last, really 30 years, starting with Justice O'Connor and continuing with Justice Kennedy, there has been a person who found the center or people couldn't predict in that sort of way. That enabled the court to look as though it was not owned by one side or another and was indeed impartial and neutral and fair" (Tatum 2018). However, with the departures of O'Connor and Kennedy, and the success of political parties in selecting "only Justices who will vote in accordance with the party line in most if not all high-profile cases" (Gould 2021, 138), we have seen heightened polarization that compromises the Court's legitimacy.

We have, in sum, a highly charged docket in the 2021 term; a Court presently composed of a firm six-member conservative majority constructed through partisan confirmation hardball; all justices aligned almost exclusively in terms of party politics; and no clear swing justice at the center. It is no wonder that alarm bells are increasingly sounding. "We are," in the view of law professor Steve Vladeck, "within sight of a full-blown legitimacy crisis" (Vladeck 2021). Political scientists Amanda Hollis-Brusky and Joshua C. Wilson explain the "Supreme Court's current legitimacy crisis" this way: "Americans have begun to lose confidence in its decisions because of a long-term conservative strategy that has intentionally and effectively targeted the judiciary as a way to carry out its political agenda" (Hollis-Brusky and Wilson 2021). As for the blockbuster 2021 term, Tom Goldstein, lawyer and publisher of SCOTUSBlog, says, "I think we are going to look back at this as the year in which the conservatives really did fully take over the Supreme Court and American constitutional law, where they got what they were really looking for on the big, hot-button issues that affect all of Americans' lives" (Williams 2021).

If this prediction holds true, the toll on public perceptions of the Court's legitimacy could prove substantial. According to Irv Gornstein, Executive Director of the Supreme Court Institute and a Professor of Practice at Georgetown University Law Center, "[n]ot since Bush against Gore has the public perception of the court's legitimacy seemed so seriously threatened . . . I think we may have come to a turning point. If, within the span of two to three terms, we see sweeping right-side decisions over left-side dissents on every one of the most politically divisive issues of our times—voting, guns, abortion, religion, affirmative action—the perception of the court may be permanently altered" (Gornstein 2021).

Gornstein also offered a sobering rejoinder to those justices who deny allegations of partisanship: "It is all well and good for justices to tell the public that their decisions reflect their judicial philosophies, not their partisan affiliation, but if right-side judicial philosophies always produce results favored by Republicans and left-side judicial philosophies always produce results favored by Democrats, there is little chance of persuading the public there is a difference between the two" (Gornstein 2021).

FURTHER READING

Barnes, Robert, and Carol D. Leonnig. 2018. "Partisan Politics and Kavanaugh's Defiant Words Put Supreme Court in Unwelcome Spotlight." *Washington Post*, September 29, 2018.

Caplan, Lincoln. 2018. "The Political Solicitor General: The 'Tenth Justice' and the Polarization of the Supreme Court." *Harvard Magazine*, September-October 2018.

Condon, Stephanie. 2016. "Mitch McConnell: Senate Should Wait for Next President to Replace Antonin Scalia." *CBS News*, February 13, 2016.

Dobbs v. Jackson Women's Health Organization, Docket Number 19-1392 (2021).

Easton, David. 1965. *A Systems Analysis of Political Life*. New York: John Wiley & Sons.

Epstein, Lee, and Eric Posner. 2018. "If the Supreme Court Is Nakedly Political, Can It Be Just?" *New York Times*, July 9, 2018.

Farias, Cristian. 2021. "'Will This Institution Survive the Stench?': Gutting Abortion Rights Could Damage the Supreme Court's Own Legitimacy." *Vanity Fair*, December 1, 2021.

Gallup. 2019a. "Congress and the Public: Historical Trends." October 2019. https://news.gallup.com/poll/1600/congress-public.aspx

Gallup. 2019b. "The Presidency: Historical Trends." October 2019. https://news.gallup.com/poll/4729/presidency.aspx

Gibson, James L., and Gregory A. Caldeira. 2009. *Citizens, Courts, and Confirmations: Positivity Theory and the Judgments of the American People*. Princeton, NJ: Princeton University Press.

Gornstein, Irving. 2021. "Supreme Court Press Preview: Anticipating the Supreme Court's October Term 2021" [video]. *Georgetown Law*, September 21, 2021. https://www.youtube.com/watch?v=TyoQpra_gqI

Gould, Jonathan S. 2021. "Rethinking Swing Voters." *Vanderbilt Law Review*, 70, no. 1: 85–142.

Gregorian, Dareh. 2021. "Sotomayor Suggests Supreme Court Won't 'Survive the Stench' of Overturning Roe v. Wade." *NBC News*, December 1, 2021.

Hollis-Brusky, Amanda, and Joshua C. Wilson. 2021. "The Supreme Court Might Overturn Roe. It Took Decades of Scorched Earth Conservative Politics to Get Here." *Washington Post*, December 2, 2021.

Jones, Jeffrey M. 2021. "Approval of U.S. Supreme Court Down to 40%, a New Low." *Gallup*, September 23, 2021.

Liptak, Adam. 2021. "Back on the Bench, the Supreme Court Faces a Blockbuster Term." *New York Times*, October 3, 2021.

Malloy, Tim, and Doug Schwartz. 2021a. "Nearly 7 in 10 Say Recent Rise in Covid-19 Deaths Was Preventable, Quinnipiac University National Poll Finds; Job Approval for Supreme Court Drops to All-Time Low." *Quinnipiac University Poll*, September 15, 2021.

Malloy, Tim, and Doug Schwartz. 2021b. "Majority Say Supreme Court Motivated by Politics, Not the Law, Quinnipiac University National Poll Finds; Support for Stricter Gun Laws Falls." *Quinnipiac University Poll*, November 19, 2021.

Nelson, Michael J. 2021. "Biden's Court Commission Is Worried about Supreme Court 'Legitimacy.' So What Is 'Legitimacy,' Exactly?" *Washington Post*, October 22, 2021.

Nelson, Michael J., and James L. Gibson. 2018. "Has Trump Trumped the Courts?" *New York University Law Review Online*, 93: 32–40.

Presidential Commission on the Supreme Court of the United States. 2021. "Draft Final Report." https://www.whitehouse.gov/wp-content/uploads /2021/12/SCOTUS-Report-Final-12.8.21-1.pdf

Roe v. Wade, 410 U.S. 113 (1973).

Tatum, Sophie. 2018. "Justice Kagan Worries About the 'Legitimacy' of a Politically Divided Supreme Court." *CNN*, October 5, 2018.

Vladeck, Steve. 2021. "Why Many of the Supreme Court's Critics Are Trying to Save the Court From Itself." *Slate*, October 4, 2021.

Wagner, John, Ann E. Marimow, Amy B. Wang, Mariana Alfaro, and Robert Barnes. 2021. "Fate of Roe v. Wade in the Hands of the Supreme Court After Spirited Arguments." *Washington Post*, December 1, 2021.

Whole Woman's Health v. Jackson, 141 S. Ct. 2494 (2021).

Williams, Pete. 2021. "Abortion, Guns Top Agenda for New Supreme Court Term." *NBC News*, October 4, 2021.

Witt, John Fabian. 2020. "How the Republican Party Took Over the Supreme Court." *The Atlantic*, April 7, 2020.

Index

About the Author

Helena Silverstein, PhD, is the Thomas Roy and Lura Forrest Jones Professor of Government and Law at Lafayette College, where she also serves as government and law department head. She is author of *The Supreme Court* (2021); *Girls on the Stand: How Courts Fail Pregnant Minors* (2007); and *Unleashing Rights: Law, Meaning, and the Animal Rights Movement* (1996). Silverstein has published research in *Law & Social Inquiry*, *Law & Policy*, *Cornell Journal of Law and Public Policy*, and *Law and Inequality*. From 2014 to 2016, she served as director of the law and social sciences program at the National Science Foundation. She received her PhD and MA in political science from the University of Washington.